It's Your Wedding

A Complete Wedding Guide
for Making the Most Important Day of Your Life
the Most Beautiful and Memorable

FLORA F. T. and KENDALL S. BRYANT

COWLES BOOK COMPANY, INC.
NEW YORK

SBN 402-12481-2

LIBRARY OF CONGRESS CATALOG CARD NUMBER 70-102824

COWLES BOOK COMPANY, INC.
A SUBSIDIARY OF COWLES COMMUNICATIONS, INC.

PUBLISHED SIMULTANEOUSLY IN CANADA BY
GENERAL PUBLISHING COMPANY, LTD.
30 LESMILL ROAD, DON MILLS, TORONTO, ONTARIO

PRINTED IN THE UNITED STATES OF AMERICA

First Printing, May 1970
Second Printing, September 1970

THIS BOOK IS DEDICATED TO OUR CLIENTS,
THOSE WONDERFUL FRIENDS, WHO HAVE
ALLOWED US TO SHARE IN THE STRESS, THE STRAIN,
THE HILARITY, THE HAPPINESS, AND
THE PURE JOY OF SPECIAL DAYS
IN THEIR LIVES.

FLORA and KENDALL BRYANT
November 28, 1969

Contents

Preface

FOR MANY YEARS, WE HAVE BEEN ABSORBED IN THE work of arranging, coordinating, and supervising the details of various types of weddings, receptions, and parties. We are known as social secretaries, as distinct from bridal consultants or social directors, and our activities include the functions of the latter as well as the broader demands of topflight executive secretaries. The term social consultant, or entertainment consultant, is more nearly accurate than the commonly used one of social secretary.

During the course of our years of experience in running The Bryant Bureau, many universal problems have been brought to our attention, questions common to any host or hostess planning a wedding and reception, or party, as well as problems unique to weddings. While there is considerable printed material about weddings available today, it is usually directed toward definite religious, economic, or other groups throughout our country. Much of it is widely scattered within the pages of numerous—and quite expensive—etiquette books, many of which offer somewhat contradictory advice; and also in magazines and pamphlets given out free by some bridal salons, men's clothing rental firms, and so on.

But brides and their parents have told us that they are more confused than assisted by all this printed matter. The amount of it, and the time needed for them to try to absorb it all, stuns them.

This book came into being due, in large measure, to the remarks of a client. About a week after her daughter's elaborate and complicated wedding, we were sitting with her and she said, "You know, you two really should write a book. Not one about your experiences as social secretaries, but a 'how to' one. Had I written down, just in note form, everything you've told me during these last five months, I could have had it ghostwritten and sold for at least what the wedding has cost me."

Therefore we are trying to present one comprehensive book that we hope will succeed in answering specifically the many basic questions we know, from our daily working experience, will inevitably confront anyone planning a wedding. IT'S YOUR WEDDING is meant to delineate in detail all the steps necessary from the moment a girl becomes engaged to the end of her wedding reception.

In order to find answers to questions, and to some pressing problems, there is a detailed index in the back of the book. After the chapter titles in the contents there is a chronological outline of the contents within each chapter. Thus, by scanning, you will be able to pick out at once what you need most.

Here we would like to point out that *you* may mean the bride, or her mother or father, or any collective entity who winds up making the preparations for a wedding.

If the reader detects in the following pages a certain air of provincialism, he or she is right. Our experience lies along the Bost-Wash axis and its extremities, north and south. While these axial inhabitants feel that the "last word" is their right, we are well aware that when it comes to being provincial, they yield to no man, woman, or child.

We know, although not by actual professional experience,

that local customs, procedures, and traditions are as varied as the parts of our country in which they are found. A reporter can cover both the New York and San Francisco waterfronts, but not at the same time. It would take us several lifetimes to cover in full detail the subject matter in this book. So we can give you only a framework that you may utilize to suit your own special life-style. We lay no claim to being social arbiters.

It's Your Wedding

Chapter 1

Background

SINCE THIS BOOK IS MEANT TO BE ONE COMPREHENSIVE source of information for brides-to-be and their parents, or parents without partners, who want to "run their own show" without professional help, it has been written so that anyone following it can do for herself what, for the most part, a topflight social secretary could do.

Successful social secretaries are paid for their wide knowledge in solving individual problems, and for evolving special and seemingly effortless techniques to make any social occasion "go."

The social secretary does all the up-to-the-minute comparative shopping for you, and the firms he or she recommends usually offer the best for the money.

The people who employ this type of professional assistance are, in effect, paying an expert to do this work for them so that they can be free to attend to their daily routines without the interruption of taking on these chores personally.

Almost every father has asked us directly, or has had his wife ask, "How much is this wedding going to cost me? Can you give us a per head breakdown?"

How does one arrive at a per capita cost of a trousseau, or lodging for distant relatives, bridesmaids, ushers, or the cost of that "practical convertible sofa bed" your daughter saw on special sale and just *had* to have for her new home? We have never been able to give any figure more precise than a general range, even in our own bailiwick, New York City. Every parent and bride is very much an individual when it comes to so personal an event as a wedding. Each has a special-interest area she wants to emphasize. Mother may opt for flowers and other decorations, father for certain brands of whiskey, and daughter may be thinking mainly of her wedding gown and trousseau. If a balance is to be achieved, compromise is called for.

There is no such thing as an "average" wedding, so, if we can't give a firm set of figures for a wedding and reception in our own backyard and have it stand up, we can't possibly postulate cost guidelines throughout the fifty states. Price structures vary so widely, both as to area and local customs, that any per capita figures we were to give here would be only wild "guesstimates."

However, we can offer a few general suggestions about costs that should apply nationwide. These suggestions work for us and our clients.

First, set an absolute ceiling on the amount you can, and are willing to, spend. If you wish to enjoy your daughter's wedding, this is essential.

Next, get prices and written estimates on everything from trousseau items to the "getaway car" if one is needed. In Appendix B, on budgets, every single thing that costs money is spelled out. And every item must fit under your ceiling. In keeping them within your budget, you will discover some items are more flexible than others. The number of guests you expect to invite to the reception can often be the determining factor. This number governs the space needed, cost of food, of champagne and liquor—if you are going to serve them—decorations, and music, either background or for dancing. Within each of the firms and services required for a reception lie as many variations in emphasis, and consequent cost, as there are weddings. This is where compromise is of the essence. Father says, "Cut that blasted florist down. After all, you can't eat the things." Mother insists on lots and lots of flowers so it will be "a memorable, beautiful setting," while the bride may have dancing feet.

We well recall a delicate-looking little bride with a whim of platinum who wanted, and got, a wedding reception in a big barn on the home grounds. Two trestle tables were piled high with ham, turkey, and beef sandwiches made on the hefty side. Great old pewter pitchers of milk and soft drinks were available. Outside under a marquee there was an adequately stocked bar "for the older people." Inside the barn that bride had one of the most expensive ten-piece orchestras play continuously for four solid, swinging hours. Her mother just barely speaks to us for not helping her veto her daughter's wishes, which were shared by the groom, but this bride had been promised by her parents that she could have "her day" as she wanted it, and so she did—with our help.

In chapter 3 you will find our suggestions on how to set up the entire list of guests on file cards, together with all necessary information, and forms of wedding invitations, announcements—if any—and other stationery. The rest of this chapter is directed to you on the assumption that your guest list is on file cards.

Whenever a parent wails that he or she is about to go "overboard," the guest list should be scrutinized carefully once more and this question answered honestly by the family members:

"Do we really have to invite this person, or couple?"

Finally, it is going to boil down to whether the person or couple in question means enough to any of you to spend

X number of dollars on him. This may seem a cold and cynical way of looking at things, but it does help to maintain that ceiling you established at the start. Remember: Weddings, like children, grow larger, not smaller.

A second suggestion is the advisability of doing comparative shopping early. Allow yourself a minimum of six months to plan and organize a large wedding (450 or more guests) and a minimum of three months to plan a smaller one (150 guests plus). At The Bryant Bureau we have arranged weddings of both these sizes in six weeks flat, but we have at our fingertips the knowledge of exactly which firms and services to call upon—whereas you do not, unless you are accustomed to entertaining frequently on a large scale.

If you have enough time, ask for competitive bids, especially on catering, canvas, and music. Some firms and services resent "shoppers" (news travels fast in small, specialized circles), since prospective customers who engage in this practice often tend to cut the fat out of their estimates. However, several itemized estimates from reputable firms will enable you to find those most likely to give you the best value for your dollar. There is one caveat here: While you may find bargains offered at certain times of the year, remember that you generally end up getting what you pay for, especially if you use a firm of good repute. Beware of "package deals." We have found them to be a curious grab bag of second bests or worse. In the catering world, there are few, if any, bargains in food and service.

The rest of chapters 1 through 10 is predicated on your having decided upon the service and facility best suited to your various requirements. These chapters are devoted to *how,* not *who* or *why*. If you are wondering whether to have the reception at home or away from home, you should read chapter 7 before proceeding to follow the steps in chapter 2.

Please bear in mind that matters presented throughout this book are merely generally accepted dicta for the greater majority. There are wide divergences among the three leading religious faiths, and even among the adherents to each faith. Social customs vary as widely among these three as they do throughout our fifty states. Consequently you will undoubtedly modify our formulas to fit your own situation. It's *your* wedding.

The word "traditional" is applied to far too many forms that have lingered on after their functions have ceased to be. We consider doing something merely because it is the accepted thing, yet it serves no useful purpose, to be a waste of time and energy. Of course there must be rules and forms to follow, but chances are that almost 100 percent of the ones we keep have been evolved as the easiest and still the best procedures to follow. Doing so is considered to be "good form," but this is a kind of phrase that—like a doorman's large umbrella—covers many things and defines few.

What we mean by good form may be summed up as one's instinctive and unselfconscious ability to do the natural, the comfortable thing on social occasions. Its base is common sense expressed in gentleness of speech and conduct that are the outgrowth of self-respect, human decency and ethical behavior, and a very fine consideration of the rights and feelings of our fellow humans. Life without good form would be miserable indeed for us all, since order is its twin. Lack of both at any of the ceremonial occasions of our lives produces confusion and chaos. Unless there is visible, smoothly flowing, and accustomed order that people can understand and follow, they become uneasy and uncomfortable. So, in following your good form, do it within the accepted procedural customs of your part of the country. Don't be afraid to reject some of those old, dead and dying "traditions" well-wishing friends may try to palm off on you—not if the traditions interfere with "doing your own thing."

Chapter 2

First Things First

WHEN YOUR DAUGHTER COMES HOME AND MUMBLES to you, "Jeff and I are going to get married—he's just outside and thinks maybe he ought to talk to Father. All right if he comes in now?" don't panic.

Try to remain calm, especially if the thought of Jeff as a future son-in-law seems to be more than you can bear. You may be caught up in a situation that is all too frequent today. It is one in which you will need all the empathy, patience, tact, and compassion you are capable of, not alone for your daughter's sake, but for your husband's. He may be faced with the immediate crossing of a bridge he's been sure was located in some distant area of his future. You in any case should be more concerned about him than about your daughter, who's probably going to do what she thinks she wants to do. But your husband, poor soul, may be in a state of emotional shock that's far deeper than even you know, especially if your daughter says she wants to be married right away. And she may say this, not because she's pregnant, but quite simply because so few of the young have any notion of the time necessary to arrange the details of even "a simple little wedding."

Tell her that if she wants a wedding, you and she will have to allow a minimum of three months to put it together—unless she's willing to settle for a ceremony with only the immediate families and a handful of intimate friends present, followed by a luncheon or a sandwiches and champagne reception for thirty-five to forty people in your living room or at a restaurant. Be firm, unless there's some urgent reason for a shorter time span. If there isn't, and she persists, offer her a check and see what happens. You may find out quickly what kind of wedding she does want, and whether or not you have to plan a reception at all.

Many girls yearn for a large wedding followed by a formal reception to which everyone who has attended the ceremony is invited. Others would be happier with a small, intimate group at the ceremony and afterward a meal at home, in a club, hotel, or restaurant, or in the assembly rooms of their church or temple. Often these preferences have little or nothing to do with the question of expense. We have had brides who were married in the little chapel of a school they had attended, followed by a large reception of over five hundred guests. Generally speaking, we have found that a girl's mother is the one who wants a big wedding—often because she herself was married during World War II and had to give up her dream of a wedding.

This is the moment to find out what your daughter really wants. Try to cooperate with her on everything possible except on an unreasonable date that will allow neither of you sufficient time to plan and organize intelligently. The fact that she wants a wedding must mean she has some definite ideas of her own as to what it will be like. Also, in this age we are living in, give her and that young man credit for wanting to enter the honorable estate of matrimony. It may be a vast improvement over their present living arrangements as well as an indication of maturity and stability on both sides. You may have to remind your husband of this fact several times during the planning stages; his burden may be not only emotional but financial.

Your first consideration as parents may be the question of racial and religious differences. Will there be conflicts? Some of the most serious problems are those involved in mixed marriages. We cannot stress too strongly the importance of working out satisfactory adjustments to problems, differences, and conflicts at the very outset. Whether you know the young man's parents or whether they are total strangers to you, it is essential to try to find solutions to any problems regarding religion.

Usually the young people have discussed such differences themselves and may have arrived at their own solutions. However, it is important that the parents understand and accept whatever compromises have been arrived at before the girl's parents announce the engagement. In these areas of religious conflict, look to your minister, priest, or rabbi for guidance and advice. He is quite accustomed to dealing with such problems, and he has the training and experience to assist young people and their parents. Often the parents need more assistance than their sons or daughters.

We have seen some almost incredible solutions worked out as the result of meetings between the young couple and their minister, priest, or rabbi. Recently, we have been involved in several mixed marriages between Protestants and Roman Catholics in Episcopal (and Presbyterian) churches. The bride took her vows from her minister and the groom took his vows from his priest as the two representatives of both faiths officiated at the marriage ceremony. These are days in which to keep open minds.

If you and your family are not affiliated with a church or religious organization, remember that, with the exception of Christian Science churches, all their doors are open to you. (Christian Science readers are not ordained ministers of the church. They are merely elected officers and may not perform the marriage service.) Usually there is a secretary in the church or synagogue who will be happy to try to answer your questions.

If you should find yourself in a situation where there is an irreconcilable religious conflict between your daughter and the man of her choice, there are nonsectarian community churches in many areas, both urban and suburban, whose ministers are ordained in a Protestant faith and are willing to perform marriage ceremonies in their churches or in private homes.

Lastly, there is always the civil ceremony, which can be performed by a justice of the peace, or a judge in his chambers, in a home, or at some other place.

When a couple becomes engaged, it is customary for the parents of the prospective groom to write or telephone to the girl's family and arrange for a convenient time to visit them. If the parents already know one another or are close friends, this meeting is a most informal one. Usually, the girl's parents will invite the other couple for dinner at home or in a club. The four parents may dine alone or ask the young people to join them.

The parents of the girl return this visit as soon as possible and are usually entertained by the man's parents, but the exchange of calls is the important thing, not the manner of entertaining.

If either set of parents is divorced, these calls can well become sticky wickets, especially if the divorces have been recent and either partner, or both, has remarried. The young people can be of enormous assistance to both sides—perhaps all four sides—in these sensitive areas where relationships are difficult.

When the mother of the groom-elect is divorced from his father, she should have the privilege of making the first call on the girl's parents. If she has recently remarried, she may elect to make this call without her present husband, but if the girl's parents invite her to dinner, their invitation must include her new husband.

Then the young man's father calls on the girl's parents, with or without his present wife, if any, and the same procedure is followed.

A simple rule of thumb to remember is that the mother takes precedence over the stepmother unless there is some extreme, obvious circumstance that would give the stepmother priority. For example, the stepparent may have raised the young person or legally adopted him or her.

The manner in which these initial calls are made is worth all the tact the parents can put into them, particularly if none of them were acquainted previously, for the calls can go far toward making the wedding ceremony and reception joyous, beautiful, and free of unnecessary emotional strains and tension. No matter how the calls are arranged, they must be made, and in person if possible.

When this is impossible for reasons of health or distance, then the parents of the groom-to-be should write to the parents of the girl as soon as they are told of the engagement. Usually his mother writes for herself and her husband, expressing their happiness over the match and, if she knows the girl, mentioning her sweetness, attractiveness, and good qualities. This is a fine opportunity to get the new relationship with a prospective daughter-in-law off on a harmonious basis.

The girl's mother should reply promptly and in kind for herself and her husband and offer words of welcome for the young man and his parents as members of the family circle.

Fortunate indeed is the newly engaged couple these days whose parents have remained married to their respective partners. If the parents happen to be old friends as well, how can the wedding day be less than a happy one for all concerned.

Should the man your daughter plans to marry be divorced (with or without offspring of his previous marriage), you may have serious objections on religious grounds, and the same may be true if the positions are reversed. In many faiths, obtaining a religious annulment or divorce may be either out of the question or, at best, a long-drawn-out, embarrassing, and time-consuming affair that neither party wishes to undertake. As we mentioned earlier, matters of this nature are so personal and involved that only your minister, priest, or rabbi can assist with the solution. All we can say is to get such problems ironed out *before* you even think of announcing your daughter's engagement.

If you are fortunate enough not to have such a problem, the following steps are immediately ahead of you in planning a wedding of any size. We are listing these steps in the order of importance, and will treat each one in greater detail later in the book. They are:

One: The wedding, and some approximate "guesstimate" of size of the ceremony and the reception. The date must be reserved at your church or synagogue at the earliest moment possible. If the date your daughter wants is not available, ask that two possible alternate ones be held open until the young couple can make a decision and coordinate their plans around the one they choose. This will buy you a little time in which to turn around—possibly as long as ten days or two weeks, depending upon the time of year. (The dead of winter in northern climes is the most flexible.) If another bride-to-be requests one of the two dates that are being held for you, the church or synagogue will let you know immediately, but you still have first choice. This kind of choice must be exercised promptly, of course, but at least you have it.

Two: Follow this same procedure with your club, hotel, community house, or restaurant. (Please see chapter 7.)

Three: If you plan to have the reception at home, reserve the date or take options on the other two dates being held for you by the church or synagogue with two leading caterers. Make an appointment with each caterer to come to your home to see the facilities and discuss the menu and prices. Give the caterer you select a prompt answer and thank the other one for his time in a note saying you have made other arrangements.

Four: If you are having a home reception and need canvas, follow the same procedure as above with two tent and equipment rental companies. Or, if you have decided on a caterer, ask him to recommend a firm he is used to working with. It would be well, if you live in snow country, to arrange to have your grounds measured when they are bare; a snow-covered lawn tells a canvas man almost nothing by which he can give you an accurate estimate. If you live in an area of heavy rainfall, have the estimates taken at the wettest time so that the man can see what his gutter and drainage problems might be on the wedding day. By the time the estimates are submitted, you may have read again the contents of chapter 6, which should give you all the information you need to have about a canvas firm.

Five: Locate a good florist or professional flower arranger and reserve the wedding date with one or both of them, pending a meeting to discuss color scheme and prices. If at all possible, follow the "options" procedure. Many people in the flower business are not only highly competent professionals but regard their work as an art form. The outstanding ones limit their engagements for any given date, whether they be florists with shops or flower arrangers without shops. A word here about the latter: they are usually very talented women who have developed their gift of working with flowers into a profession. They work from their homes, where they have installed reefers in the basement in order to condition and keep flowers at the correct temperatures. These women go personally to the wholesale flower markets in the cities nearest them and have accounts there just like florists. (Going personally to shop is part of the secret of their success.) No customers come to them; they go to your home, church, or synagogue and to your club or wherever the reception is being given. They take only one wedding or party on any given date, depending upon size, time of year, and other factors. There is nothing "made at home with loving hands" about these professionals. Their flower business is recognized as a "home industry" by the IRS. They are sufficiently well considered that some brides-to-be must set their wedding dates to meet the schedules of the flower arrangers. These women offer a highly individual type of personal service that many of the commercial florists who depend mainly on funeral work cannot afford to give. The results these women achieve, and the unusual flowers they use in specially selected containers, can be far more interesting and beautiful than the products of commercial florists. Surprisingly enough, their prices are often the same or lower. The Bryant Bureau is blessed in having first call on the services of two wonderful flower arrangers. Incidentally, this is such an interesting profession for women, it's a wonder more of them do not take it up. (Please read chapter 8.)

Six: When it comes to music, you have a little latitude unless your daughter must have a name bandleader and his first musicians. If the wedding date is set for the off-season, you're "in," but if it falls on one of the crowded Fridays, Saturdays, or Sundays that are considered prime dates, you should line up your music the same day you follow steps one through five. Don't delay! (In Appendix C you will find a checklist of "what to do when." Please bear in mind that prime dates differ regionally. If you are not familiar with those in your area, ask a caterer, florist, or club manager; they have them engraved on their minds.) Prices among the leading orchestras do not vary greatly because they are based on union scales. Telephone the office of two or more leaders and ask them about price per man, continuous basis, and overtime. They will send you written estimates. The number of musicians should be based on the number of guests and other factors. (Please read chapter 9.) For a reception in your club or another place where there is a regular four- or five-piece orchestra working seasonally, you can save this step by employing them.

Seven: If you have a favorite photographer, particularly one whose candid work you have seen and admired, the sooner you establish your date with him, the better. As we point out in chapter 10, good candid photographers are rare. Most of them are well known and in demand. Few can cover two large weddings in one day unless the photographer works in tandem with an assistant who can be left at the first wedding while he goes on to the next one, which has a late afternoon ceremony. Most of the real pros contend that it's easier to get candids of horses and dogs than it is to get outstanding wedding coverage.

Let us suppose you are now at the point where you have made all the necessary reservations, or have taken the options mentioned, and are still considering where to have the reception. This "where" depends upon your daughter's preference, and on whether it can be supported. To a lesser degree, it depends upon your basic preference. In any case, the question boils down to having a home reception or one away from home. Convenience, both personal and logistic, possible weather factors—we always plan any wedding or party on the theory that it will fall on the worst possible day of the year and make provisions accordingly for weather conditions—adequacy of facilities, esthetics, family traditions, the all-important matter of expense are all considerations.

Another primary consideration is size. Is the area selected large enough to accommodate the total number of guests you want to invite so that they, the music, food, and liquor are all together, rather than separated into different rooms? If this is not possible, look elsewhere or cut your guest list. No party will ever get off the ground if you have the bar in one room, the food in another, and the dancing in a third. Never, that is, unless the rooms can be opened up in such a manner as to give the feeling of one area. This is particularly true under canvas. If possible have one big marquee. If not, make certain that all marquees are set up so that the space covered appears to be one area.

Should the decision be made for a home reception, don't feel you have to redecorate your home, unless it has attained a degree of fustiness you had planned to rectify before that word wedding was mentioned. And having a chair re-covered or those new slipcovers made won't do the trick; this course generally points up the need for a complete job. We advise our clients: "Don't paint the living room unless you have to!" If you must have something painted, do over the bathrooms your guests will use and the room where the gifts will be displayed. When there is to be a marquee on the lawn, use a connecting canopy from it to the driveway and don't route your guests through the house. We have found that most people at weddings or parties notice only things that are at eye level or above—especially decorations. Besides, with a marquee you and your guests will be under it and not in the house at all except to use the bathrooms and see the gifts. So don't call in the interior designer or the decorating crew; call the best available caterer you know.

Right now you may be in limbo, but it won't last. Very soon your daughter will have to set a definite date—and it will have to be coordinated with each of the firms and services you decide to use. After you have completed those basic seven steps, your real footwork begins, for we urge an early search for a bridal gown and the bridesmaids' dresses.

Unless you have a favorite shop that has a good bridal department, this search can be a real ordeal. We have found it better to purchase the bridal gown, the veil—if there isn't one in the family—the bridesmaids' dresses, and whatever they are going to wear on their heads (circlets of ivy and fresh flowers are attractive) in the same place. This gives the shop more incentive to work on an order and later cuts down on the confusion of having various items coming from different sources. No matter what the people in the bridal salon may tell you, allow a full eight weeks for delivery of the gown and bridesmaids' dresses. There are always delays, and they seem to get longer each season.

We urge you to refrain from announcing the engagement in the newspaper until most of your plans have been completed. In fact, the ideal time to announce it publicly is just before you leave for a trip around the world! We always advise our clients to "announce the engagement in the press and leave town." You may think this is a joke. Far from it. Until your first time around, you can't imagine the deluge of calls, both local and long-distance, and mail that can follow the announcement in a newspaper. The most unbelievable variety of businesses and commercial enterprises are out there just panting to help you, and they have highly skilled and highly paid solicitors who call you at all hours to tell you so. The only halfway satisfactory answer you can make, short of hanging up the telephone on these persistent pests, is to thank them for their interest and tell them very firmly that each and every conceivable detail connected with the wedding has been taken care of. If you tell them no date has been set and that this may be a long engagement, they will keep on calling you at regular intervals. If necessary, be rude, but get rid of them.

This is the age of short engagements. Few are longer than four to seven months, although there are exceptions now due to the draft. Often a young couple will want to have their engagement announced prior to the young man's induction into the service or, as many girls say, "because I want to wear my ring."

Other girls have an idea that accepting a ring and wearing it make the engagement official. This is not accurate. A young girl's engagement becomes official only when her parent or parents, if living, or an older member of her family, a godparent, or guardian, announces it formally by writing notes to personal friends or by sending a formal announcement to the newspapers. This denotes parental consent, if not approval, and is the modern equivalent of publishing the banns. In many religious denominations, engagements are published in the parish bulletin or notices.

Incidentally, an engagement ring may have little or nothing to do with the announcement of a betrothal. The giving of an engagement ring is a personal matter between the couple, and depends very much on the state of the man's finances. Many girls prefer to have a wedding band set with diamonds or other precious stones rather than an engagement ring with a diamond so infinitesimal that it can best be viewed through a microscope. In a marriage it is the wedding ring given and received that is important, but this is often overlooked because we are deluged by publicity that "a diamond is forever." There probably isn't a girl alive who hasn't dreamed of receiving one, but other considerations can be more important than a precious gem.

If a couple decide to have an important wedding band and "wait until later on to purchase the engagement ring" (and "later on" may well be the twenty-fifth wedding anniversary), the young man should go alone to the best jeweler he can find and have him set aside several of the finest wedding bands he can afford. He should then return with his fiancée and have her choose the one she wants. She will not see this ring again until he places it on her finger during the marriage ceremony. Under no circumstances may she wear the wedding band until her marriage. Frequently, in cases like this, the young girl will wear her fiancé's class ring, or a family ring of gold, in lieu of the more usual engagement ring.

The engagement announcement should be typed on a sheet of standard-size typing paper. Use double spacing. If you are going to have an engagement party, it is customary for the announcement to appear in the papers on the date of the party, so that your guests may read it before they arrive. If not, you may decide to mark the announcement "FOR IMMEDIATE RELEASE." This means that you are leaving it up to the society editor or the editor of the women's page, as the case may be, to print the story when it—and the photograph you have sent with it—can best be run. This suggests that you want it to be printed immediately if space is available.

When you wish to specify a release date, send in the copy, marked with that date, at least one full week in advance. In the case of large metropolitan newspapers, it is advisable to send your release a full two weeks in advance. You may be sure that the date you specify will be respected by the editors. Here is sample format:

ANYWHERE, ILLINOIS
APRIL 25, 1970

FOR RELEASE SUNDAY, MAY 3, 1970

Mr. and Mrs. John Jones Brown of Anywhere, Illinois, and Summertime, Michigan, announce the engagement of their daughter, Miss Alice Mary Brown, to Mr. George Willing Mason II. Mr. Mason's parents are Mr. and Mrs. August Willing Mason of Wilmette, Illinois, and Land O'Lakes, Wisconsin.

Miss Brown graduated from Anywhere High School in 1966 and from Northwestern University in 1969 with a degree in education. [If she was presented at a private party or at one of the mass presentations, state this here, and the year.] She is the granddaughter of Mrs. Cyrus Brown of San Mateo, California, and the late Mr. Brown, and of Mr. and Mrs. [or the late Mr. and Mrs., as the case may be] Conreid Haffenreffer of Marshfield, Wisconsin. Miss Brown is on the teaching staff of the Anywhere Elementary School. Her father is the owner of Brown's Hardware Company, which was established in Anywhere in 1869 by his grandfather, Amos Brown, a leading merchant of this community.

Mr. Mason graduated from Wilmette High School in 1963 and from Northwestern University in 1967, where he was made a member of Sigma Chi. He served in the U.S. Army for two years between 1967 and 1969. He is the grandson of the late Mr. and Mrs. George Willing Mason of Milwaukee, Wisconsin, and of Mrs. Luther Acheson of Naples, Florida, and the late Mr. Acheson. His father is retired from the Mason-Ford Agency in Milwaukee. Mr. Mason is employed by Brown's Hardware Company.

Plans have been made for the wedding on September 5.

Mr. and Mrs. John Jones Brown
1970 Cyrus McCormick Lane
Anywhere, Illinois [add zip code for the convenience of out-of-town newspapers to which you may also be sending releases and glossy prints]

Area code: ________
Residence telephone number: ________

This is the format The Bryant Bureau has used for years for the *New York Times* and other leading newspapers throughout the country and abroad. It gives the editor the pertinent information and may be printed as submitted, or changed to suit the individual editor. Many of the smaller newspapers do not have large staffs and therefore welcome receiving a press release that can be run as is. Correct information about grandparents and forebears whose achievements your family or the groom's family takes pride in should be mentioned in the copy. An editor may be given the choice of using this information in connection with the wedding. You may also call or write to the newspapers involved and request that they send you blanks to be filled out, and then let them write the copy from the information you supply.

As to the wedding press release itself, here is how it might be written for the same young couple whose names were used for the engagement announcement:

ANYWHERE, ILLINOIS
SATURDAY, SEPTEMBER 5, 1970
FOR RELEASE SUNDAY, SEPTEMBER 6, 1970

If your home paper has no Sunday edition, use this:
FOR RELEASE AFTER SEPTEMBER 5, 1970

The marriage of Miss Alice Mary Brown and Mr. George Willing Mason II took place here this afternoon (Saturday, September 5) in St. John's Lutheran Church. The bride is the daughter of Mr. and Mrs. John Jones Brown of Anywhere and Summertime, Michigan. The bridegroom's parents are Mr. and Mrs. August Willing Mason of Wilmette, Illinois, and Land O'Lakes, Wisconsin. The pastor, the Rev. Adolph Diemer, officiated. [Be sure to give full title and name of the officiating clergyman, and the same for another clergyman who may be assisting him, as well as the name and location of his church.] A reception followed at the home of the bride's parents on Cyrus McCormick Lane.

Mr. Brown gave his daughter in marriage. She wore a gown of white silk peau de soie with reembroidered Alençon lace at the neckline and bodice. Her veil of French tulle [sometimes called illusion] was attached to a caplet of matching Alençon lace and extended to the end of her chapel-length train. She carried a bouquet of white phalaenopsis orchids and stephanotis with miniature ivy.

The bride's sister, Miss Anita Louise Brown, was maid of honor, and the bridesmaids were the Misses Melanie and Stephanie Jones, cousins of the bride, of Land O'Lakes, Wisconsin, Miss Wendy Mason, sister of the groom, of Wilmette, and Miss Joann Meeker of Chicago. The groom's little sister, Miss Overjoyed Mason, was flower girl. The bride's attendants were dressed alike in floor-length gowns of apricot saki with jewel necklines and front trim of Venice lace. They wore matching bows in their hair and carried natural straw baskets of Peruvian lilies, white marguerites, and gypsophila with miniature ivy. The flower girl was dressed in white organdy with a sash of apricot saki and carried a basket of miniature white and yellow roses with gypsophila.

The groom's cousin, Luther Acheson, Jr., of Sarasota, Florida, was best man, and the ushers were [list here names of ushers, give relationship to bride or groom, if any, and state where they are from. The editor, if space is short, may not list any attendants but the maid of honor and the best man, but supply the information anyway and let the editor cut your copy if necessary].

Continue by repeating the same information regarding the bride as given in the second paragraph of the engagement press release. Repeat in the next paragraph the same information regarding the groom that you gave in the engagement release.

The conclusion of wedding release: "Following a wedding trip to Bermuda, Mr. and Mrs. Mason will make their home in Anywhere, Illinois." You may not want to say anything about a wedding trip, but will write a concluding sentence as follows: "Mr. and Mrs. Mason will make their home in Anywhere, Illinois, where Mr. Mason is with Brown's Hardware Company."

Be sure to repeat the name of the bride's parents, the address and zip code, and their area code and residence telephone number as shown in the first example.

Glossy prints for the engagement release should be the standard eight-by-ten size. They are called glossy prints because of their shiny finish, which makes it possible for them to be reproduced in a newspaper. The eight-by-ten size is best unless you are dealing with only one newspaper and have called in advance to see whether they can use a five-by-seven size.

The formal wedding picture has to be taken well in advance of the time you will send it to the newspapers—usually it is taken at the final fitting of the bride's wedding gown. She holds a "pretend" bouquet of artificial flowers as nearly like those she will carry on her wedding day as possible. Ordinarily this formal photograph of the bride is taken in the bridal salon, where the bridal consultant or salesperson can drape her gown and veil properly. Brides who are wearing family gowns have their photographs taken at the studio of the photographer or at home. Where the picture is to be taken is a matter for you, your daughter, and the photographer to work out together. Some ace photographers are not happy about taking formal pictures outside of their own studios, where they have enough space for background and perspective—and their strobe and other lights—to insure a successful sitting.

When you receive proofs, make a first and second choice of the ones you like best, take down the numbers on the backs of the proofs, call the studio and have the photographer make up the number of glossy prints you need and send them to you. If you have any serious questions as to choice, ask his advice, for the ones you like the least may be the best for reproduction in a newspaper. Order only those you do like. Don't hesitate to ask a photographer to give you a second sitting for wedding pictures if the results of the first sitting displease you. Another reason for having these formal photographs taken early!

When you receive the glossy prints, be sure to write your daughter's future married name in pencil lightly on the back, and in parentheses write her maiden name as well. Then clip a copy of the press release to each glossy print, put them in photo mailers, and send by special delivery to the newspaper editors. Incidentally, these glossy prints will not be returned to you, whether they are used with the press release or not.

We send in all press releases and glossy prints to society editors a full four weeks in advance of any prime date, and two to three weeks ahead for other dates. Writing the bride's maiden and new married name directly on the back of the glossy prints may well make the difference between her formal wedding photograph's being used and not. Newspaper offices are deluged with releases and glossy prints—usually a great many more of both than the society editor is allowed space for—during their busy times before prime dates. It just could be that *your* daughter's photograph and that wedding press release might become separated and never meet again!

PRIME DATES

March-April: The first Friday, Saturday, and Sunday following Easter. The others are also crowded but not as badly.

May: Every Friday, Saturday, and Sunday.

June: Same as May, but in a month of four Saturdays the second and third are just plain ghastly. In a five-Saturday month, the third and fourth are the overcrowded ones. Reserve far in advance!

July: Weekend of July 4 should be avoided. The rest of the month is not too bad, but it does have all those would-be June brides who were unable to find dates free during that month.

August: Avoid the last Friday, Saturday, and Sunday. The other weekends are gaining in popularity all the time. A great month for evening weddings in the suburban areas of the Greater New York metropolitan complex.

September: The first weekend after Labor Day is especially crowded. Other weekends, too, but not as badly.

October: The real "crunch" has abated, but reserve early. A beautiful wedding month.

November: The weekends before and after Thanksgiving. Dates for these are often reserved a year in advance.

December: Same as November, if not even worse! Again, people reserve the weekends before and after Christmas a full year in advance.

January-February-March: The weekends in these months are the slow ones in the Greater New York metropolitan area but are in much demand in other regions of the U.S. Please check on the prime dates in your area.

We urge our clients to avoid setting wedding dates around any major holiday such as Mother's Day, Memorial or Veterans Day, the Fourth of July, and Labor Day. It is not fair to ask relatives and friends to travel any distance on such dates. It is also poor economy for the bride's parents because catering help, if available, and club help are paid extra for working on holidays.

Chapter 3
Invitations

In this time of rapidly changing social customs, there are some that remain constant, and one is the use of the third-person wording spaced on specific lines in formal invitations and announcements, and in their acceptances or regrets, which are always answered in the same form by hand in black or blue-black ink on one's best personal stationery. These formal invitations are always engraved on the first page of a double sheet of ecru or white stock. Double envelopes are used; the smaller one has no mucilage on its flap, but the outer, or "mailing," one has. The primary function of the outer envelope is to protect the inner one in which the invitation is placed.

We think there is no equivalent for formal wedding invitations and announcements that are engraved. Resorting to the use of less expensive substitutes is not the ideal way to cut corners in a limited wedding budget. If you can't afford to send the best, chances are you can't afford the type of wedding you're planning. Besides, there isn't that much difference in cost today between copperplate engraving and thermography, better known as "raised printing." However, if you are forced to use raised printing, at least have it done on good stock and choose one of the plain and straight-up-and-down typefaces, such as modified or shaded Roman, or the antique or solid Roman. Avoid English script and all of its variations, for any script typeface produced by thermography can be identified easily as imitation engraving by a person with a discerning eye, while other typefaces are more difficult to detect.

There are those who say it's silly to spend money on engraved invitations "because people only look at them briefly and throw them in the wastebasket." We don't agree. The kind of invitation you send out for your daughter's wedding may be your initial introduction to the groom's relatives and friends, so think twice before you settle for second best.

We have had clients say, "Our daughter thinks she wants us to use St. James script, but we would prefer another less formal typeface for the invitations." We find it fascinating to speculate on *how* and *where* the idea of "semiformality" in invitations had its origin. Either invitations and announcements are formal or they are informal. The third-person wording makes them formal, and the choice of typeface, whether the stock is ecru or white, is ordered with a fold or not, is engraved with a raised margin (also called a plate mark or panel), or is embossed with your husband's family coat of arms or the crest only at the top center of the paper (please see the section devoted to heraldry in Appendix A), cannot alter in one iota the degree of formality.

The forms and spacing of the formal wedding invitations we use are very nearly as fixed as the stars in their courses, and they are recognizable to anyone. Sample below:

Doctor and Mrs. Wilhelm Johann Eckhardt
request the honour of your presence
at the marriage of their daughter
Neltje Louise
to

Mr. Peter Griffin Graves III
on Friday, the twelfth of June
at half after four o'clock
Saint Thomas Church
Fifth Avenue and Fifty-third Street
New York, New York

Reception
immediately following the ceremony
The Pierre

R.s.v.p.
653 Fifth Avenue
New York, New York 10022

Or:

The favour of a reply is requested
Four East Fifty-fourth Street
New York, New York 10022

Note *u* in honour. It is always "the honour of your presence" for the ceremony as opposed to "the pleasure of your company" for the reception.

Note spelling of "favour." We suggest spelling out short house numbers. Zip codes are part of a person's address and should be used.

The question of the use of "R.s.v.p." or "R.S.V.P.," "The favour of a reply is requested" or even "Please reply" is raised from time to time, so we may as well digress here to discuss them.

R.s.v.p. and R.S.V.P. are both correct, and conservative people have never given them up. In France, in diplomatic circles, and in world capitals everywhere R.S.V.P. is always engraved in capital letters. An easy way to remember this is to think *capitals for capitals* when using it. Otherwise, the R.s.v.p. is correct.

As to "The favour of a reply is requested" and "Please

reply," both are less popular these days than they were a few years ago when, for some reason, they were considered to be more "friendly." Again, this is one of those ideas with a dim, mysterious origin that is difficult to track down. Both are accepted forms, and using them is a matter of personal taste and has nothing to do with being either friendly or unfriendly.

Below are samples of an acceptance and a regret to the Eckhardt wedding invitation:

Mr. and Mrs. Kendall Stebbins Bryant
accept with pleasure
Doctor and Mrs. Eckhardt's
kind invitation for
Friday, the twelfth of June

Or:

Mr. and Mrs. Kendall Stebbins Bryant
regret that they are unable to accept
Doctor and Mrs. Eckhardt's
kind invitation for
Friday, the twelfth of June

Or the combination acceptance and regret:

Mrs. Kendall Stebbins Bryant
accepts with pleasure
Doctor and Mrs. Eckhardt's
kind invitation for
Friday, the twelfth of June
but regrets that
Mr. Bryant
will be absent at that time

The same wording may be used by a husband who is

accepting an invitation that his wife cannot accept; just transpose Mrs. and Mr. in this instance.

The wedding announcement sample follows. (Announcements are *never* sent to those who have been invited to the wedding. They need no type of acknowledgment other than one that the recipient may care to make out of personal interest, and they of course require no gift unless you have a desire to send one to the bride.)

Doctor and Mrs. Wilhelm Johann Eckhardt
have the honour of
announcing the marriage of their daughter
Neltje Louise
to
Mr. Peter Griffin Graves III
on Friday, the twelfth of June
One thousand nine hundred and seventy
Saint Thomas Church
New York, New York

The following variation of the formal wedding invitation is sometimes used by Roman Catholics, although we see it less frequently today than in former years:

Mr. and Mrs. Timothy Standish O'Grady
request the honour of your presence
at the Marriage in Christ of their daughter
Rita Kathleen
to
Mr. Owen Kildare Callaghan
and your participation in the offering of the Nuptial Mass
Saturday, the twenty-ninth of June
at twelve o'clock noon
Saint Patrick's Cathedral
New York, New York

Or the more usual formal invitation may be used by the O'Gradys with the following card enclosed (it is engraved to match the invitation and in the same typeface):

All who wish are invited
to receive Holy Communion
with the bridal party

Then there is this form that combines the invitation to the church ceremony and the reception:

Mrs. Wellington Weems
requests the honour of your presence
at the marriage of her daughter
Honoria Kip
to
Leffingwell Luddington
Lieutenant, Army of the United States
on Saturday, the twenty-ninth of August
One thousand nine hundred and seventy
Saint Luke's Church
Darien
and afterward at
"Woodlands"
274 Middlesex Road

The favour of a reply is requested
Box 7, Darien, Connecticut 06820

The Weems invitation illustrates a number of points, the first of which is that the bride has a middle name that is a family surname. Since it is part of her name, she has every right to use it even though there may be a degree of confusion on the part of some of the recipients as to whether her last name is Kip or Weems. Disregard this and have her name engraved as shown in sample.

In this case the bridegroom is a Reserve officer on active duty, so his name is engraved on the wedding invitation without "Mr." before it. Were this particular bridegroom to have the rank of Captain in the Army, Air Force, or Marine Corps or Lieutenant (senior grade) in the Coast Guard or Navy, or above, his name would appear this way:

Captain Leffingwell Luddington
Army of the United States

If he were a noncommissioned or enlisted man in the armed forces, this is how his name would appear:

Leffingwell Luddington
(Apprentice Seaman, U.S.N.R.)
or:
Leffingwell Luddington
(Pvt. 1st Class, U.S.A.)

Note that a smaller typeface is used within parentheses.

Reserve officers use their titles on wedding invitations and announcements *only when they are on active duty,* and then the wording of "United States Army" is changed to "Army of the United States."

Retired Regular Army and Navy officers of high rank keep their titles in civilian life, while retired or inactive Reserve officers below the rank of full Colonel do not use their former titles, socially or otherwise.

When the bride's father is in the armed forces and absent on active duty at the time the invitations to her wedding are issued, his name would appear this way:

Major (overseas) and Mrs. John Yeamans
request the honour of your presence

We have assisted with any number of weddings at which the reception, and sometimes the marriage ceremony, was given by the bride's parents in the home of friends. Often there are godparents, childless couples, or close friends of the bride's family who have a large home or apartment and who welcome having it used for a wedding. Let us say that Major and Mrs. Yeamans of the sample above have decided to have both their daughter's ceremony and the reception in the home of a friend. And also let us suppose that they want to use the type of invitation that is rather more personal and old-fashioned than those we are accustomed to seeing, one in which there is a space left open for the name of the guest or guests to be written in by hand in black ink. It would be engraved this way:

Major (overseas) and Mrs. John Yeamans
request the honour of

presence at the marriage of their daughter
Margaret
to
Mr. John St. Aubyn Moore
Saturday, the twenty-fifth of November
at four o'clock
at the residence of Mr. and Mrs. James Rhett
Charleston, South Carolina

R.s.v.p.
Fort Jackson
South Carolina 29207

In the case of a bride whose father or mother is deceased and who has a stepparent, the invitations are as follows:

Mr. and Mrs. Lloyd Hunttington
request the honour of your presence
at the marriage of her daughter
Mary Elizabeth Waters
etc.

If a bride has no relatives and the wedding is being given by friends, this would be the wording of the invitations:

Mr. and Mrs. Thomas Truefriends
request the honour of your presence
at the marriage of
Miss Olivia Orphan
to
Mr. Minus Motherinlaw
etc.

Note the use of "Miss" before the bride's name.

When a bride's parents are deceased but she has brothers, the eldest traditionally sends her wedding invitations and announcements in his name and gives her away at the ceremony. Or, if another relative has taken the place of a parent, his or her name is used. If a bride is the eldest in a family of brothers and sisters whose parents are deceased, she may prefer to send the invitations in her own name, using the following form:

The honour of your presence
is requested
at the marriagc of
Miss Olivia Orphan
to
etc.

Note the use of "Miss" before the bride's name.

Or she and the bridegroom may announce their own marriage this way:

Miss Olivia Orphan
and
Mr. Minus Motherinlaw
announce their marriage
etc.

The "unusual" situation of yesterday is quite often the usual one of today. A case in point is that of the bride coming from abroad to be married in this country without her own family present. It is entirely accepted that the groom's family give the wedding and send out the invitations in their name. If they do this, then "Miss" is used before the bride's name. This is the only case where it is used other than in the sample given previously in which the bride is an orphan. The foreign bride's family may send out announcements from abroad to all their relatives and friends and to a list of those on the groom's side that should be supplied them by his mother. Here is how this type of wedding invitation would be engraved:

Mr. and Mrs. John Murray
request the honour of your presence
at the marriage of
Miss Ann Alice Australia
to their son
Mr. Philip Murray
etc.

There are many international marriages between American girls and foreign men. We thought it might be interesting to our readers if we showed a sample of a wedding invitation we prepared not long ago. It was used as a courtesy to the bridegroom and his family abroad. The extra large size invitation—11½ by 7½—was used with a center fold and inserted into extra large double envelopes. English was engraved on the left side and French on the right. On the French side the names of the groom's grandmother and mother, both widows, appeared.

Such invitations are not difficult to prepare, and in every large city there is at least one stationer who will be happy to set up copy in another language and even in other characters, such as Hebrew. All he requires is that the customer provide a sample from which the engraver can work. And the sample should be typed out in the exact form, spacing, wording, and spelling of the foreign language involved. Both Cartier's and Tiffany's in New York offer this service.

Mr. and Mrs. Lawrence Kip Remington
request the honour of your presence
at the marriage of their daughter
Lily
to
Mr. Edouard Frederic Redon-Vuillard
on Friday the first of August
One thousand nine hundred and sixty-nine
at half after four o'clock
Saint Andrew's Church
and afterwards at the reception
Cascade Road
Stamford, Connecticut

R.S.V.P.
Cascade Road

Madame Guy Mercier Daubigny
Madame Jules Corot Redon-Vuillard
ont l'honneur de vous faire part du mariage de
Monsieur Edouard Frédéric Redon-Vuillard
leur petit-fils et fils

avec Mademoiselle Lily Remington
et vous prient d'Assister à la Bénédiction Nuptiale
qui leur sera donnée le Vendredi premier Août
mille neuf cent soixante-neuf
à quatre heures et demie à L'Eglise de Saint Andrew
Stamford, Connecticut
Etats-Unis
Réception après la cérémonie religieuse
à Cascade Road
Stamford, Connecticut

14 Rue Chaptal, Paris IXe
7 Rue de l'Université, Paris VIIe

When there is to be a ceremony in a chapel or a small church with only the immediate families and intimate friends present, the following forms should be used.

These are actual samples of the wedding stationery of two sisters whose respective weddings we assisted with four years apart. Both girls were married in the same church at the same hour, and their receptions followed in the same club. Also, it happened that both brides chose the identical style of engraving (antique Roman). As we were preparing the order for the second daughter's wedding stationery, we were struck with the thought: no need to order new church or reception cards since they would be identical to the first set. We checked with the stationer to be sure the plates were still on file from the earlier wedding and hadn't been used for a tray or other keepsake. They were there. When we pointed out this fact to the mother, she was pleasantly surprised, for it represented a small saving, but a saving nonetheless, and all such are most welcome to any family planning a large reception.

St. Mary's Church is one of the most beautiful examples of Gothic architecture here in the East, but it is very small. With the help of additional movable pews and some chairs

Mr. and Mrs. Thomas Newman Lawler
request the pleasure of your company
at the wedding reception of their daughter
Ann Reynolds
and
Mr. Thomas Edmund Dewey, Jr.
on Saturday, the twelfth of September
at five o'clock
Sleepy Hollow Country Club
Scarborough, New York

The favour of a reply is requested
54 Hemlock Drive
North Tarrytown, New York

Mr. and Mrs. Thomas Newman Lawler
have the honour of announcing
the marriage of their daughter
Ann Reynolds
to
Mr. Thomas Edmund Dewey, Jr.
on Saturday, the twelfth of September
Nineteen hundred and fifty-nine
North Tarrytown, New York

Mr. and Mrs. Thomas Newman Lawler
request the pleasure of your company
at the wedding reception of their daughter
Martha Elisabeth
and
Mr. David Tevele Schiff
on Saturday, the eleventh of May
at five o'clock
Sleepy Hollow Country Club
Scarborough, New York

The favour of a reply is requested
54 Hemlock Drive
North Tarrytown, New York

Mr. and Mrs. Thomas Newman Lawler
request the honour of your presence
at the marriage ceremony
at half after four o'clock
Saint Mary's Church
Scarborough, New York

in the back, a shoehorn, and special prayers of thanks to dieters, 178 people may be seated in it. This little church is situated on the Albany Post Road between the entrance and the exit of the Sleepy Hollow Country Club, so please note that in both weddings only a half hour was left between the time of the ceremony and the reception, rather than the longer time that is necessary in most cases.

All those who were invited to attend the marriage ceremony received with their invitations the small cards using the wording "request the *pleasure* of your company." The larger number received the invitation to the reception only. We wish to acknowledge our thanks to the Lawlers, the Deweys, and the Schiffs for their kind permission to use these samples here to illustrate the forms to be used under such circumstances.

Every few years we are asked to assist with the double wedding of two sisters, and once, many years ago, we helped with one for two first cousins. As far as the invitations are concerned in the wedding of two sisters, the elder girl's name appears first. In the second case, the invitations must include the surnames of both parents and both brides.

Mr. and Mrs. Thomas Lewis
request the honour of your presence
at the marriage of their daughters
Hannah Ann
to
Mr. Webb Anderson
and
Leila Louise
to
Mr. Freed Judkins
Saturday, the fourth of November
Trinity Church
Hamilton, Ontario

Mr. and Mrs. Amos Now Brown
and
Mr. and Mrs. James Later Jones
request the honour of your presence
at the marriage of their daughters
Wendy Now Brown
to
Mr. First Bridegroom
and
Jennifer Later Jones
to
Mr. Second Bridegroom
etc.

R.s.v.p.
Box 21
Anywhere, Texas

Note that alphabetical order is followed in the above circumstances.

The surnames of both brides are repeated so there cannot be any confusion as to their identities. The Browns and Joneses may give a reception together at a club or at the home of either family depending upon which is larger. In any case, it would be wise for them to take a post office box for the replies—and the gifts. All gifts would then have to be picked up every day by both brides-to-be. Otherwise the poor post office staff would go crazy! The acceptance to this double wedding invitation would be:

Mr. and Mrs. Kendall Stebbins Bryant
accept with pleasure
Mr. and Mrs. Brown's
Mr. and Mrs. Jones'
kind invitation for
etc.

The use of a post office box for replies to invitations to weddings and parties can be a great convenience under many circumstances, and not just for double weddings. Boxes are especially useful for people who are giving December and January weddings because the replies go directly to the post office box number indicated, instead of coming to your home where they can so easily become mixed up with Christmas cards and other mail.

If you are planning a small ceremony in your home, to be followed by a wedding breakfast or buffet lunch to which only members of the immediate families and a few intimate friends are to be asked, we suggest writing personal invitations by hand or inviting by telephone. Either method works very well when there are only some twenty to fifty guests involved. In this case, engraved announcements are definitely indicated. These should be ordered ahead of time, addressed, stamped, and ready to be mailed *after* the ceremony has taken place. Here is a sample of a handwritten invitation to a small, informal wedding:

> Dear Polly,
>
> Susie is being married at home to Ward Burton, Jr., Saturday, March 31st, at twelve-thirty. We hope very much that you and Ed will be with us and will be able to stay on for lunch afterward.
>
> Affectionately,
> Nancy

And the acceptance:

> Dear Nancy,
>
> Ed and I are so happy about Polly's wedding and you are kind to include us. We'll drive up and stay at that new motel near you where I have already made reserva-

tions. Looking forward with so much pleasure to being with all of you on Saturday, March 31st.

Love,
Polly

The regret:

Dear Nancy,

Ed and I are so happy for Susie and Ward Burton, Jr. He is a very lucky young man—and we are very unlucky that March 31st falls on the day when Ed and I are scheduled to be at the Greenbrier in White Sulphur Springs for sales conferences, which will go on into the following week.

Please give Susie our love and congratulate the young man, whom we are looking forward to meeting very soon.

Love,
Polly

Thus far, we have dealt with invitations and announcements mainly to the wedding of a bride who has one or both parents living and has none of the problems connected with being the daughter of divorced parents. We have run into too many situations where divorced parents—one or both of whom have remarried—wait until the wedding of their daughter from their first marriage to start sinking hatchets into each other all over again—and into her as well. Some of these situations could be viewed as hilarious were they not tragic for those immediately concerned.

There are those who insist that it is the worst possible form for the names of divorced parents to appear together on any type of invitation. In the case of wedding invitations and announcements, we do not agree with this at all.

If the bride-to-be lives with her mother, and her father,

who has remarried, wishes to pay for her wedding and give her away at the ceremony, this is his privilege as her father, and his name should appear on the formal wedding invitation as well as the announcement. Unless the divorced parents happen to be on truly comfortable speaking terms, we suggest that the reception be held on neutral ground, *not* at the home of the mother of the bride. Here is a sample invitation:

Mrs. Rogers Alexander
and
Mr. George Jeremy Alexander
request the honour of your presence
at the marriage of their daughter
Alice Anita
to
Mr. Roland Montgomery
etc.

In the above example, we are assuming that the divorced mother's maiden name was Alice Rogers. Hence she would be Mrs. Rogers Alexander, *not* Mrs. Alice Rogers Alexander, on the invitation. In any case, her name should appear first and her former husband's name second. If there is a second Mrs. George Jeremy Alexander and relations are still strained between the parents, the mother of the bride-to-be may not be willing to be under the same roof with her former husband's second wife. The father may pay for the wedding, attend the church ceremony without his present wife, give his daughter away, sit afterward in the second or third left pew facing the altar, and not attend the reception. This is done quite frequently. It is the duty of the father's second wife to offer, and to offer in good faith, not to attend either the church ceremony or the reception. Her offer may be rejected by the former wife, but it should be made as graciously as possible. Then, if she is urged to be present at both, it becomes a different situation entirely.

Again we have a different set of circumstances if the bride makes her home with her mother and stepfather and her own father, who has either remarried or not, wishes to pay for his daughter's wedding, give her away at the ceremony, and attend the reception with his present wife. Still all the more reason to have the reception on neutral ground (neither the club of the father or stepfather, unless they happen to be members of the same club, and not in the home of the stepfather). The invitations would read like this:

Mrs. Thaddeus Ellery Hunt
and
Mr. George Jeremy Alexander
etc.

However, if the bride's parents were divorced when she was very young and she has been raised by her stepfather, whom she has asked (of her own free choice) to give her away, the invitation would be:

Mr. and Mrs. Thaddeus Ellery Hunt
request the honour of your presence
at the marriage of her daughter
etc.

Note the use of "her daughter."

In this case, the bride's own father should be sent an invitation—without the reception card—and it should include his present wife, if any. If he attends—with or without his present wife—the ushers should be alerted to seat him and his wife in the third reserved pew on the left side of the church facing the altar. It is doubtful that a bride's father would attend her wedding under these circumstances, but we have known some to do so.

If the bride lives with her mother and was legally adopted by her stepfather when she was a child, then, and *only* then, may she be called "their daughter." However, whether her own father is living or dead, the press release for her engagement should include a sentence as follows: "Miss Alice Anita Alexander Hunt is the daughter of Mr. George Jeremy Alexander of Lost Area, Mars. Her name was changed legally at the time of her adoption by her stepfather, Mr. Thaddeus Ellery Hunt." And for the press release of her wedding: "The bride, also the daughter of Mr. George Jeremy Alexander (or the late Mr. George Jeremy Alexander of Lost Area, Mars) was adopted by her stepfather." The question of the bride's or groom's true identity should never be clouded over. If half sisters or half brothers are included in the wedding party, they should not be called "sisters of the bride" or the "groom's brothers."

When the bride was adopted as an infant by her parents, there is no need to add this information, for she is, in effect, their child and bears their name because they chose her.

When the bride lives with her father, who may or may not have remarried, and there has been a bitter custody hassle between her parents that has resulted in her not seeing her mother, the phrase "his daughter" may be used on the invitations, which are issued in his name alone. But perhaps in this case there is a stepmother who has raised the bride from infancy. However, the bride is still *not* "their daughter" on wedding invitations issued by them. Again, there is the question of the bride's identity. The bride's own mother should, of course, be sent an invitation to the wedding, without the reception card, and her name should be included in the engagement and wedding press releases. If the bride's mother chooses to attend, she sits in the first left pew, and the bride's father and his present wife would occupy the second pew, or the third, on the left facing the altar.

These are the hairy, tragic situations we at The Bryant Bureau are left to cope with constantly, and our clients tell us they can never find any mention of them in all the etiquette books they have bought, borrowed, or been given by well-wishing friends!

When both parents have remarried and are on cordial terms, it is truly great for the engaged girl and her fiancé—*but* don't overdo the cordiality bit at the ceremony! We have encountered the extreme situation where the bride's mother and stepfather and her father and stepmother all wanted to share the first left pew. We say, "Don't do it." Somehow this seating arrangement is all too, too cozy and only serves as a distraction to the guests, who sit there with thoughts of "Why did they ever part in the first place?" instead of having their full attention on the bride, where it belongs on her wedding day.

The following is a sample of how a formal wedding announcement was engraved for a bride whose professional name was different from her own:

Mr. John William Tobin
has the honour of announcing
the marriage of his daughter
Flora Fairchild Tobin
(Peregrine Pace)
to
Mr. Kendall Stebbins Bryant
on Wednesday, the thirtieth of May
nineteen hundred and fifty-six
Round Hill Community Church
Greenwich, Connecticut

In this case, the professional name was added to the plate after the number of announcements needed without it had been engraved. Then a second run was made. This is the practical way to order either invitations or announcements in such circumstances.

A divorcée, especially one who is an older woman (thirty and over), does not send formal wedding invitations for a second marriage, but she or her family may send announcements.

A very young widow may have engraved wedding invitations issued by her family or by herself. If her family issues them this is an acceptable form:

Mr. and Mrs. Alvin Allstein
request the honour of your presence
at the marriage of their daughter
Muriel Lillith Gordon
to
etc.

Or this young widow may prefer to state her name as Muriel Allstein Gordon.

But please note that she is *not Mrs.* Muriel Lillith Gordon, or *Mrs.* Muriel Allstein Gordon. She is her husband's widow. If she were issuing her wedding invitations they would read:

The honour of your presence
is requested at the marriage of
Mrs. Lawrence Wolff Gordon
to
etc.

If the older widow marries again, she issues her own wedding invitations and uses the full name of her late husband, for that is the name she bears until her remarriage. She is never Mrs. Samantha Brown Smith, but Mrs. Thomas Smith, and if she is being married at a church ceremony, the first line of the invitation is:

The honour of your presence
is requested at the marriage of
Mrs. Thomas Smith
to
etc.

There are certain cards that may be enclosed in formal wedding invitations and announcements (other than reception cards, of course).

Church cards. These are used only at very large weddings in certain churches or synagogues in big cities that are likely to be filled with sightseers, such as St. Patrick's Cathedral, St. Thomas Church, Temple Emanu-El, and the Cathedral of St. John the Divine in New York City. Church cards should be engraved on the same stock and in the same typeface as the invitation. If a coat of arms or a crest is used on the invitation, do not use it on the church card, which would read like this:

Please present this card
at Temple Emanu-El
Thursday, the first of May
Or:
at St. Patrick's Cathedral

Note that "saint" may be abbreviated in this case.

The use of a church card means that the church has been closed to the public just for the period of the wedding ceremony and that only those who have cards are to be admitted.

Train cards and plane cards. These are seen rarely. A train card means that a private car, or cars, has been reserved by the bride's parents to take guests from a central point to and from the wedding. It may be printed (raised printing) on stock to match the invitation and would read:

A special car will be attached to train leaving
Union Station at 2:05 p.m. for Baltimore.
Train returns to Washington at 9:45 p.m.
Please present this card to the Conductor.

A plane card would read:

Transportation is being provided
to Upperville
Guests are requested to be at (name of airport)
on July the thirtieth at twelve noon
Eastern Daylight Saving Time
The return flight will leave Upperville
at ten p.m. Eastern Daylight Saving Time
the same day
Please present this card at
(give name of airline and exact location at airport)

People who are having a country wedding, or one in a suburb, often have maps printed for the convenience of guests coming by car. These maps are also printed on the same stock as the invitation and are enclosed with it. We think there is a more economical way of doing this, and that is to have maps printed or reproduced in any clear and neat manner and have them available at the church. Strangers will often have no difficulty locating a church in the country, unless, of course, it is practically hidden. But they *may* encounter considerable difficulty finding your home or club from the church. Or the church may be in one suburb and the club where you are having the reception in another. Here is one example of an adequate map and directions.

DIRECTIONS FROM CHRIST CHURCH, PELHAM MANOR,TO SHENOROCK COUNTRY CLUB, RYE, NEW YORK

1. Drive north on Pelhamdale Avenue, passing under New England Thruway.
2. Make right turn onto Boston Post Road.
3. After passing two principal intersections, get on New England Thruway, going east, at Exit 7.

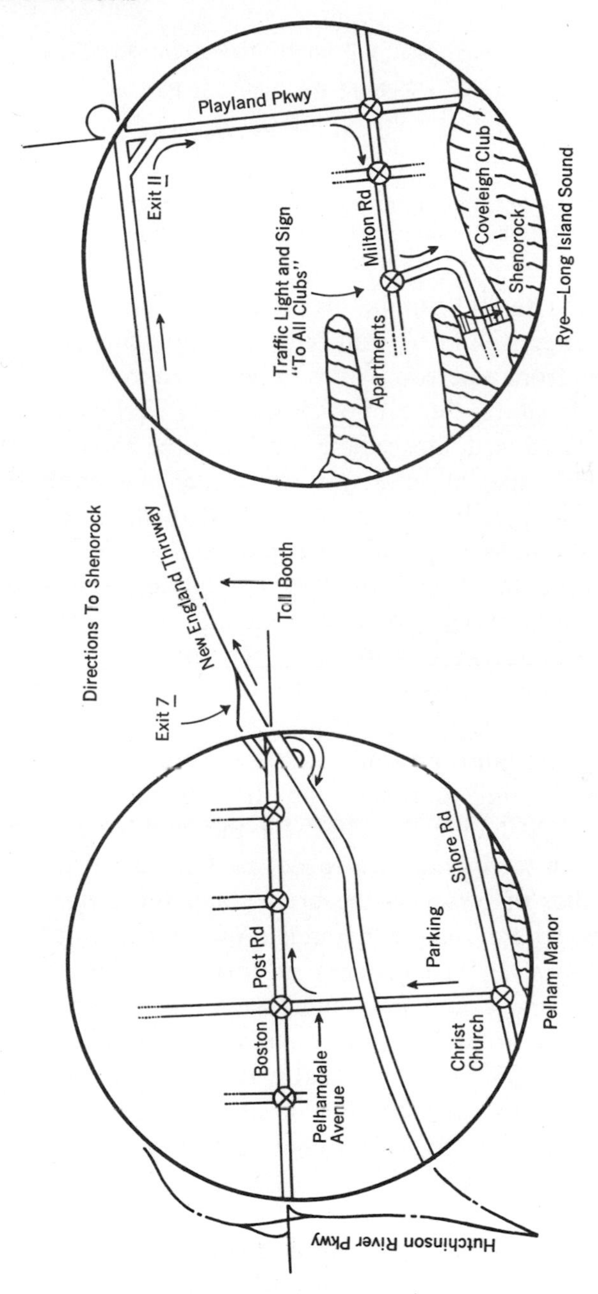
Directions To Shenorock
Playland Pkwy
Exit 11
Traffic Light and Sign
"To All Clubs"
Milton Rd
Apartments
Coveleigh Club
Shenorock
Rye—Long Island Sound
New England Thruway
Toll Booth
Exit 7
Post Rd
Boston
Pelhamdale Avenue
Parking
Shore Rd
Christ Church
Pelham Manor
Hutchinson River Pkwy

4. Travel along Thruway, past toll booth and as far as Exit 11.
5. Turn off the Thruway at Exit 11 for Playland Parkway.
6. Follow the signs for Playland. At the first traffic light turn right on Milton Road.
7. After passing one traffic light, you will reach a fork; turn left at the sign "To All Clubs" and follow Stuyvesant Avenue to Shenorock.

Pew cards should not be enclosed with formal wedding invitations. They should be sent only after an acceptance has been received from a person who is to be seated in the reserved section, "in front of the ribbons," or by a designated pew number. At large weddings where there may be forty or more people seated in special pews, you may order pew cards from the engraver to match the invitations and mail these out to specific guests following their acceptances, or (this is the system we use) the bride's mother may order, if she does not already have a supply on hand, some informals or fold-over cards that are engraved with her own and her husband's name and use these as pew cards. They should have matching envelopes.

The bride's and groom's mothers should discuss the reserved pew seating and agree on the number of pews on the left and right facing the altar, for this number has to be the same if white ribbons are to be used in the aisles. (An uneven number of pews on the bride's and the groom's side of the church would make for confusion when the ushers were seating the guests.) The groom's mother sends her reserved seating list by name and pew number to the bride's mother, who compiles a total list. She then sends out all the pew cards for both lists. This is usually done about two weeks to ten days before the wedding, or at least in time for the guests to have the cards before coming to the wedding ceremony.

If one family has numerous relatives and the other only a few, they should decide between themselves to use up all available space on both the left and right side of the main aisle, without care as to whether it is on the bride's side or the groom's side. Let's say the groom's family needs only the first three right pews, while the bride's family is very large and needs many more pews. The bride's mother might well have a total of six pews on either side reserved, fill all those on the left side, and then have the bride's relatives spill into three more pews on the right side.

The question always arises of who should be seated in these reserved pews beyond the immediate family of the bride and of the groom. Certainly among them should be relatives, on a basis of first cousins only, with the eldest ones seated nearest the parents, as well as godparents, wives and husbands of members of the wedding party, parents of members of the wedding party (whether the bride's mother knows them or not), friends who have given showers or parties for the bride or who have put up houseguests, and old family retainers, nurses, or governesses. The mother of one of our brides recently did a most considerate bit of seating: all her guests who were doctors were seated with their wives in reserved pews, and the head usher knew precisely where to find each one of them in case an emergency call came to the church during the ceremony. She was a very wise woman indeed, for as we observed these doctors' pews we wondered who was left on duty in the town of New Canaan, Connecticut, to take an emergency call!

Or—and this is often the best solution of all in the case of two very large families—have no reserved pews and then *nobody* can be offended. Simply use white ribbons that start at the back of the first left pews (where the bride's parents are seated) and the first right pews (same for the groom's parents) and let the ushers do the seating on a first-come, best-seat basis.

An enclosure that may be used with wedding announcements is the at home card. Sample here:

At Home
after the first of May
(*or* After the First of May)
Fifty Sutton Place South
New York, New York 10022

Or:

Will be at home
after the seventh of December
Twenty-one Longhorn Avenue
Brownsville, Texas 38012

If your daughter already has personal stationery with her initials, have her use it up for thank-you notes prior to the wedding. If not, or if she has only a small quantity of such stationery, simply have her order some plain informals or fold-over cards with matching envelopes, and use these rather than ordering stationery.

There is, as we all know, no substitute for a thank-you note written personally by the bride who has received a wedding gift. However, in the case of a large wedding or one where the bride's or groom's father is an officer of a large corporation or is prominent in legal, political, medical, banking, or other circles, do by all means arm yourself with fifty to one hundred gift acknowledgment cards. They may never be used in lieu of the thank-you note from the bride herself, but they can be used to relieve the great pressure on the bride and her family at the most difficult time of all—those two weeks to ten days immediately before the wedding.

These cards may be printed on good stock as follows:

Miss Ann Reynolds Lawler
acknowledges the receipt of your
wedding gift and will take pleasure
in writing you herself in the near future

People forget or do not know that the wedding invitation, without the reception card enclosed, may be used in lieu of an announcement. Using it this way may solve the problem of what to do about friends who live a great distance away. The bride's parents may have made numerous company moves, either in this country or abroad, that resulted in lasting friendships. When the first wedding in their family is being planned, their thoughts go out to good friends whom they would like to include although they know there is little chance of their attending. If such friends are sent invitations with reception cards enclosed, a reply is required, and there is the vague implication that a gift is expected. On the other hand, the parents are reluctant to send these friends formal announcements because they seem too cold.

The wedding invitation (without the reception card), in lieu of an announcement, requires no reply, and yet says to the recipient, "We wish you could be with us," and it often prompts letters to the bride and her family that add greatly to their happiness before the wedding date. Old friends who intend to send gifts will do so regardless, but this is a more pleasant way to let them know about your daughter's marriage. It also saves the cost of having an additional copperplate made for announcements.

Printed reply cards are, of course, entirely improper and should not be considered in connection with formal wedding invitations. The myth that these self-addressed, stamped reply cards will expedite receiving replies is just that: a myth. What will expedite replies is to send wedding invitations one full month in advance and to put them into the mail so that they will be received on a Friday or a Saturday—even if it means mailing them a few days more than a month ahead. After considerable research on this subject, we have discovered that married women who receive invitations between Monday and Friday put them aside until they can ask their husbands whether to accept or regret.

They are more likely to respond promptly to invitations they receive at the end of the week when their husbands are at home.

The best way to prepare the invitation list is to type, or print clearly, the names of your guests on three-by-five white file cards, the last name first, followed by Mr. and Mrs., or whatever the case may be, and the address in full with zip code. You are better off not to use abbreviations on these file cards, especially if you are going to do the addressing yourself. Have the bride-to-be put her list on cards also.

If the mother of the groom can send you her list on cards —the same size but in a different color of her choice—so much the better. If not, when you receive her list and the groom's list, *you* put them on cards. This will save you time and grief later.

Then put all these file cards, irrespective of color, in strict alphabetical order in a box where they will stand up. (You need not buy some kind of expensive file case for this purpose; a shoebox will do nicely.) Check them through for any duplications, and have your daughter and her fiancé do the same. Then you and your husband should give the list a final check—before you place the order for wedding invitations. Whatever number you arrive at, be sure to overorder by fifty. (It is better to overorder now than to run out.)

If you are going to send out announcements as well, make a separate list for them and mark each card with a large A in the upper right-hand corner. You may discover that there are a number of people on the invitation cards for the church and reception whom you wish to move into the announcement file!

Should you be fortunate enough to be able to devote a room, or a section of one, to these files, by all means do so. Keep the files, the invitations, the announcements, stationery for thank-you notes, the book with duplicate sets of stickers for gifts, and everything you need for addressing all together, where they will not be disturbed until the day before the wedding. This is your control center for the entire operation.

When the invitations are delivered from the engraver, leave the tissues in. Formerly, it was considered bad form not to remove the tissues that the engraver inserts in invitations to protect them until they reach you. With the heavy canceling machines in most post offices, the engraving needs all the protection it can get.

The inner envelope is the one that has no mucilage on the flap. If you are right-handed, take the inner envelope in your left hand with the flap lying open against your fingers. Practice inserting the invitation, with tissue between it and the reception card, which should have a second tissue (smaller) on top. If the invitation is the large size with a fold, insert it complete with its tissue and the reception card and its smaller tissue into the inner envelope with the fold down. Turn the inner envelope over in your hand: now write the last name or names of your guests on this inner envelope.

On the outer, or mailing, envelope abbreviations are to be avoided except for "Dr.," "Mr.," "Mrs.," "Jr.," and "Lt." when combined with "Colonel" as part of a rank. Also avoid using an initial of a name. If you know what the initial stands for, write it out in full. Sometimes this is impossible, so use your common sense. Please write out the names of towns, cities, and states in full, and include the zip codes.

Avoid the use of "and family." If there are several family members and you do not have all their names, you may have to use "and family." If so, use it on the inner envelope only. If children are to be invited, boys over fifteen should receive separate invitations, but daughters may be included in their parents' invitations.

Sample of outer envelope:

Mr. and Mrs. James Jones Brown
The Misses Brown
1970 Cyrus McCormick Avenue
Anywhere, Illinois 12345

The inner envelope:

Mr. and Mrs. Brown
the Misses Brown
Or:
Susan and Kim

If the Browns had two sons who lived at home, they would be addressed as the Messrs. Brown, or as the Messrs. James Jones Brown, Jr., and Samuel Brown on the outer envelope of a separate invitation to them.

We urge the use of return addresses on the outer envelopes of wedding invitations. You may have them embossed by the engraver, or invest in a desk-type embosser and do them yourself. This is less expensive. Avoid using stickers, which look tacky and cheapen the appearance of a formal invitation. So do stamps that are put on crooked. Needless to say, wedding invitations should be mailed by first-class postage.

Should it become necessary to recall wedding invitations, if there is time to have cards engraved they would read:

Doctor and Mrs. Wilhelm Johann Eckhardt
announce that the marriage of their daughter
Neltje Louise
to
Mr. Peter Griffin Graves III
will not take place

If there is not time for cards, and telegrams must be sent, they would read:

> The marriage of our daughter Neltje Louise to Mr. Peter Griffin Graves 3rd will not take place.
> (Signed) Dr. and Mrs. Wilhelm Johann Eckhardt

If a bride decides to call off her marriage, unfortunately or otherwise, she usually does it *after* the invitations are out. She need make no explanation at all for doing so, but the invitations must be recalled and every last gift returned. She returns the engagement ring, of course, to the young man. Her parents should send the following notice to the society editors of the newspapers that received a wedding press release and glossy print (if one had been sent) or press release of the engagement announcement:

> Dr. and Mrs. Wilhelm Johann Eckhardt announce that the marriage of their daughter, Miss Neltje Louise Eckhardt, to Mr. Peter Griffin Graves III will not take place.

If the wedding invitations have not been sent, use the following form:

> Dr. and Mrs. Wilhelm Johann Eckhardt announce that the engagement of their daughter, Miss Neltje Louise Eckhardt, to Mr. Peter Griffin Graves III has been terminated by mutual consent.

Whether mutual consent had anything to do with breaking the engagement or not, the phrase is always used.

A death in a family is such a deeply personal matter that there is no way of knowing how those involved are going to feel about canceling or postponing a wedding. The death of an elderly grandparent or relative (aunt, uncle), especially one with a lingering disease, is seldom the cause of canceling or postponing a wedding these days. However, if a family conference is held and a decision is made to recall the invitations, the guests must be notified by wire, cable, or telephone. If there is time, printed cards in the same typeface as used for the invitations should be sent. Below are samples for a cancellation and for a postponement:

Mrs. Amos Kendall
regrets that the death of
Mr. Kendall
obliges her to recall the invitations
to the wedding of her daughter
Mary
etc.

Mrs. Amos Kendall
announces that the marriage of her daughter
Mary
to
Mr. Lowell Eliott
has been postponed from
Thursday, the fourth of June
until
Friday, the second of October
at half after four o'clock
Church of the Advent
Boston, Massachusetts

We are often asked if wedding invitations should be sent to people in mourning. The answer is, "Yes, even if they are in deep mourning." And they will often accept, too. They may attend the ceremony only, or they may go on to the reception and remain long enough to go through the receiving line and then leave. It is an entirely personal matter.

If a member of the wedding party goes into mourning before the wedding date, he or she still dresses according to the plans made by the bride and takes part in the ceremony and reception. Everyone understands that wedding clothes are uniforms worn in the service of the bride and groom for that one day alone.

The question of whether to send formal invitations to the members of the clergy and their wives—if they are married—is another one we are asked constantly. We suggest that they be spared the time and effort required to respond to written invitations. Ask them by note or, preferably, in person. Any minister, priest, rabbi, or cantor takes part in so many ceremonies during a given year and is invited to so many receptions that it is unfair to him to burden him with a formal invitation. Usually the officiating clergyman and his wife—if he is married—are personal friends of the bride and her family, so it is easy to extend a personal invitation. If you are using a church to which you do not belong (perhaps in the large city nearest your suburban home) and have only met the clergyman, find out if he is married and write him and his wife a note inviting them to the reception following the ceremony.

We are frequently asked how invitations and announcements should be addressed to specific people or people with special titles. Here is a ready checklist:

The President of the United States: (Domestic mail)	The President and Mrs. Nixon The White House Washington, D.C.
(From abroad)	The President of the United States and Mrs. Nixon The White House Washington, D.C. U.S.A.

Also use the above forms for the Vice-President and his wife.

The Speaker of the House of Representatives: (Domestic mail)	The Speaker of the House of Representatives and Mrs. McCormack Home address
(From abroad)	The Speaker of the House of Representatives of the United States and Mrs. McCormack Home address
Members of the Cabinet: (Domestic mail)	The Secretary of Defense and Mrs. Laird Home address
(From abroad)	The Secretary of Defense of the United States and Mrs. Laird Home address

When Cabinet officers are married women:

(Domestic mail; diplomatic invitations)	The Secretary of Labor and Mr. Perkins Home address
(Domestic mail; social invitations)	Mr. and Mrs. (full name) Home address
The Attorney General: (Domestic mail)	The Attorney General and Mrs. Mitchell Home address
(From abroad)	The Attorney General of the United States and Mrs. Mitchell Home address
Assistant Secretaries:	The Honorable and Mrs. (full name) Home address
The Chief Justice: (Domestic mail)	The Chief Justice and Mrs. Burger Home address

(From abroad)	The Chief Justice of the Supreme Court of the United States of America and Mrs. Burger Home address
Associate Justices:	Mr. Justice and Mrs. (full name) Home address
United States Senators, Members of the House of Representatives, State Senators, Representatives, and Assemblymen:	The Honorable and Mrs. (full name) Home address

Governors:

(Massachusetts, New Hampshire, and South Carolina have officially adopted the title "Excellency" for their governors, but this title is in general use in all our states.)

	His Excellency the Governor of New York and Mrs. Rockefeller Executive Mansion Albany, New York
Mayors:	The Honorable and Mrs. John V. Lindsay Gracie Mansion New York, New York
Judges:	The Honorable and Mrs. (full name) Home address
American Ambassadors:	The American Ambassador and Mrs. Annenberg The American Embassy London, England

American Ministers:	The American Minister and Mrs. (full name) The American Legation Bern, Switzerland
American Chargés d'Affaires, Consul Generals, or Vice-Consuls:	Mr. and Mrs. (full name) The American Embassy Rome, Italy

PROTESTANT CLERGY

The Presiding Bishops of the Protestant Episcopal Church in America may not marry if they are members of one of the orders of the church. This is the single exception among the Protestant clergy, and all others may marry if they wish. Address formal invitations to:

	The Presiding Bishop and Mrs. (last name only)
Bishops:	The Bishop of Massachusetts and Mrs. Stokes
Deans:	The Very Reverend and Mrs. (last name only)
Archdeacons:	The Archdeacon and Mrs. (last name only)
Canons:	The Canon and Mrs. (full name)
Clergymen with a Doctor's degree:	The Reverend Dr. Silas Saintly and Mrs. Saintly
Clergymen without a Doctor's degree:	The Reverend and Mrs. Thomas Allgood

THE ROMAN CATHOLIC HIERARCHY

The Pope:	His Holiness, the Pope *or* His Holiness Pope Paul VI Vatican City Rome, Italy

Cardinals:	His Eminence (full name, e.g., Terence Cardinal Cooke) Archbishop of New York
Bishops and Archbishops:	The Most Reverend (full name) Bishop of Austin (Archbishop of Austin)

Abbots:

(If they are members of the order of St. Benedict—O.S.B.—"Dom" should be used following "The Right Reverend.")

	The Right Reverend Dom (full name), O.S.B.
Other Abbots:	The Right Reverend (full name) plus any designated letters
Prothonotaries Apostolic, Domestic Prelates, and Vicars-General:	The Right Reverend Monsignor (full name)
Papal Chamberlains:	The Very Reverend Monsignor (full name)
Priests:	The Reverend Father (full name)
Brothers:	Brother (full name)
Sisters:	Sister (followed by her taken name)

THE RABBINATE

Rabbis with a Doctor's degree:	Doctor (or Rabbi) and Mrs. (full name)
Rabbis without a Doctor's degree:	Rabbi and Mrs. (full name)
Cantors:	Cantor and Mrs. (full name)

CLERGY OF THE EASTERN ORTHODOX COMMUNION

(Priests may marry or remain celibate. However, if they do

marry, they may do so only *before* their ordination. If they are widowed, they may not marry again. Patriarchs, archbishops, and archimandrites are celibates. In the Eastern Orthodox Communion the Ecumenical Patriarch of Constantinople is the supreme head, the equivalent of the Roman Catholic Pope.)

Patriarchs:	His Holiness, the Ecumenical Patriarch of Constantinople Constantinople, Turkey
Archbishops:	The Most Reverend (*first* name only) Archbishop of Pittsburgh
Bishops:	The Right Reverend (full name)
Archimandrites:	The Very Reverend (full name)
Priests:	The Very Reverend and Mrs. (full name)

The word "Esquire" or "Esq." was originally used to denote a lesser English title, usually that of a knight's next to eldest son, or the younger male members of a noble house whose hereditary title had passed to the eldest male heir. "Esq." is used in our country by lawyers in written addresses on all correspondence and by the lay public as a courtesy, although the Correspondence Review Staff of the State Department has been trying to discourage its use within the United States for some time. If "Esq." is used following the name, "Mr.," "The Honorable," or any other title such as "Lord," "Sir," or "Dr." may not be used. Nor may it be used in the written address of a man and his wife. "Esquire" is written out in full only for diplomatic and very formal correspondence.

"The Honorable" or "Hon." and "Mrs." may be used together, but "The Honorable" may never be used before "Mr." The following example will be helpful in this connection and will serve to answer a question we are asked very frequently concerning how to address an invitation to U Thant and his wife to a formal wedding. The invitation should go to U and Mrs. Thant. The "U" in his name stands for "Mr." in his native Burmese and therefore may not be preceded by "The Honorable" in this case. While the Burmese do have given names as we do, these familiar names are not used publicly. U Thant's given name is Maung, which means *young* in Burmese, but it should never be used in addressing him formally because its use is reserved for family and intimate friends only.

Chapter 4
Clothes

THE BRIDE'S CHOICE OF A WEDDING DRESS DEPENDS UPON many things: her age, the size of the place where she is getting married and whether it is a church, chapel, synagogue, temple, the living room at home, the garden, where a marquee may or may not be used, a ballroom of a club or hotel, the rectory, or, if a civil ceremony, the municipal building, town hall, or judge's chambers. It also depends on the hour and the formality of her wedding. There are both formal and informal daytime weddings and formal evening weddings. The latter have the ceremony at six o'clock or after. A bride's veil and her train, if any, may also vary accordingly.

Many families have one or more wedding gowns and, perhaps, a special family heirloom lace veil or veils. Some of these veils are truly priceless examples of eighteenth-century rosepoint or other lace and are kept in bank vaults. There may be a wedding gown that was worn by a bride's mother, grandmother, or great grandmother—but that may not suit the girl at all. No matter what is available, we don't believe that a bride should be put under pressure to wear one of these old gowns unless she chooses *freely* to wear it at her wedding.

Modern brides often wish to start their own traditions, and we think they should be allowed the privilege of doing so.

The court train has been back in favor for several years now. Old ones worn, perhaps, by the bride's mother or grandmother (or the groom's) at a presentation at the Court of St. James or in Imperial Russia or Austria are usually very elaborate, beautiful—and heavy. They should be worn only at the most formal daytime and evening weddings in large churches.

Family heirloom veils are a different matter, and a bride may decide to wear one because it suits her perfectly or can be made becoming to her by a lace expert. Some of these old veils can turn out to be the crowning glory of a simple, well-cut gown of candlelight silk satin, either of heavy or light weight, depending upon the season. If a bride is going to wear one of these antique veils at a formal daytime or evening wedding, she should take it to the best bridal salon she knows and show it to the consultant, who will then be able to assist her intelligently in her choice of a gown to complement it.

A bride-to-be should shop in, or at least take with her, a pair of shoes with heels that are as nearly as possible the height of those she will wear on her wedding day. She should *not* go in sandals or loafers. Most bridal salons have slippers available for her to step into, but her own are preferable. Her undergarments—girdle, body stocking, panty hose, or whatever—should be similar to what she plans to wear under her wedding gown.

And *hair!* Please, no wigs, "falls," ponytails, or "weirdo" cuts—unless she is going to appear with hair that way on The Day. Pity the poor bridal consultant who has to work with a girl dressed for a ride on a Honda when she goes shopping for her wedding gown.

The so-called traditional material for wedding gowns is white or pale ivory, often called candlelight, silk satin, or one of the domestic or imported heavy slipper satins, peau de soie, faille, faille velvet, antique moiré, poult, taffeta, lace, chiffon, silk or rayon organza, mousseline de soie, Swiss organdy, linen, or sometimes even very lightweight wool, to mention a few of the most favored ones. There are many other materials, and the list of them seems to grow longer every season. And then there are the very elegant pants gowns, too. Your best course is to consider what suits you—taking into consideration the advice of an expert bridal consultant.

Some of the pale pink, blue, or aqua tints, a deeper shade of ivory that is nearly ecru, and a deep ivory are more flattering to the older bride—thirty and over. In choosing a gown in January for a June or summer wedding, you should consider whether it will be equally becoming with a suntan. If the gown is to be worn with an old family veil, its color should also be considered in relation to that of the veil. Some antique lace remains very light in color, while other lace becomes quite dark. Much of this variation depends on how the veil has been packed and where it has been stored. Often a lace that has darkened evenly will look better with a white rather than off-white gown, on blondes as well as brunettes, for the contrast in shades of white and ecru or deep ivory may be more interesting.

The bride who is starting on "the pill" should watch her weight very carefully; she may gain anywhere from five to fifteen pounds between her first fitting and the final one.

Slippers should, above all else, be comfortable. The smart bride wears them around the house at least a week before her wedding. If the bride is taller than her groom, the height of the heel is an important factor to be considered before alterations are made in the gown. And there always seem to be "necessary" alterations whether you are a perfect size 6 or 16. Perhaps it's one of the rules of the game.

The choice of wearing a face veil—until that moment when she has been pronounced a married woman—is a very personal one for a young bride at a Protestant or Roman

Catholic ceremony. Orthodox and Conservative Jewish brides always veil their faces unless they are mature women or have been married previously. In Orthodox and Conservative Jewish weddings, there is a custom of the veiling of the bride by the groom before the wedding service. (For further details about it, consult *The Jewish Wedding Book* by Lilly S. Routtenberg and Ruth R. Seldin, Schocken Books, New York. Paperback.)

If a bride decides to wear a face veil during her wedding ceremony, the front veil is made of a short separate piece of tulle, usually about a yard square, shirred into an invisible band and pinned at either side—*after* her regular veil has been arranged. Or it may be attached to her headpiece or caplet in such a manner that it can be folded back off her face. The way it is arranged, and removed, must be thought out very carefully in advance or a face veil can become a real booby trap—as well as an unwanted diversion—at an otherwise beautiful ceremony. Unless you are obliged to wear one, *think* about it.

The face veil is removed, or folded back over the bride's head, by her maid of honor at the *conclusion* of the ceremony and *before* the bride is given her bouquet or prayer book. And the maid of honor should use *both* hands while she is removing the face veil or folding it back. Both girls should rehearse doing this at least once after the bride has dressed for her wedding.

The length of the bride's train depends on the type of veil she wears, and both should depend upon her height, the type of wedding, and the size of the church or other place of worship where she is going to be married. If a small chapel is the scene, it is better for her to wear a chapel-length train and a fingertip-length veil, or a veil arranged mantilla-style, or merely a caplet or headpiece (a very small piece of family lace can be used effectively this way) and a short veil that falls gracefully to her shoulders. The veil may be all tulle without any lace. Incidentally, tulle is called "illusion" in many bridal salons for some mysterious reason.

If the decision is made to wear a long veil, then a cathedral-length train or a court train is appropriate. Whatever else you do, hold out for a train that is detachable. This can make all the difference in your being comfortable or uncomfortable at your wedding reception. Unfortunately, many fine designers think of a bride in a standing position only. Their "creations" make her a vision of beauty walking up the aisle, standing during the ceremony, and walking down the aisle, but then they stop. These designers should be *made* to attend wedding receptions and watch at least a hundred brides move around *before* they make one single sketch of a bridal gown.

Gloves for a bride can be a nuisance during the ceremony. Gloves are not necessary for even the most formal daytime weddings, since a properly made bouquet will cover a bride's hands. She will need a glove for her right hand later when she is standing in the receiving line, for a hot moist palm extended to a guest is undesirable at any season of the year. However, at formal evening weddings where brides usually wear gowns without sleeves, opera-length gloves of white kid are indicated to counteract an otherwise "bare" look in church, synagogue, or temple. In this case, the glove for the left hand may be rolled back and turned under so her hand is free, or she may have the seams slit on the third finger and either fix it under her glove securely or snip it out entirely, whichever is more comfortable for her.

Jewelry suitable for a bride is mainly colorless, such as a pearl necklace worn with unobtrusive earrings of pearls and diamonds, or a pin of pearls and diamonds. However, if the groom's wedding gift to her has colored stones, she wears it. Some brides have worn family lavalieres of colored stones as the "something old." It is best for a bride, especially a young one, to keep the jewelry she wears as simple as possible.

This simplicity applies to her use of cosmetics as well.

Makeup applied with a heavy hand detracts from the fresh look of youth. So do elaborate hairdos. It seems to us rather unnecessary for a young girl to have beauty experts come to her home, or wherever she is dressing before her wedding, to work on her until she emerges from their expensive hands looking like a model ready to walk the ramp at a fashion show. Our advice is "Don't gild the lily."

Her attendants' costumes, including their slippers, stockings, headpieces, hats, gloves—if any—and flowers, should be chosen by the bride and her mother, if their tastes are compatible, without consulting the girls as to their preferences. While the attendants purchase their costumes, except under special circumstances, they are supposed to wear what the bride selects. A wise bride will not even try to seek the agreement of several girls, to say nothing of eight or ten, on their attire for that one day when they are "in the service" of the bride.

It's pretty difficult for any bride to choose a dress in a color that is becoming to a number of bridesmaids, all of whom are dressed alike these days, unless she wishes to use the old rainbow trick. This is coming back into favor again. It works as follows: The first bridesmaid who follows the ushers up the aisle, or the first pair of bridesmaids, might wear the dress the bride has chosen for them in pale yellow, the next in lime green, the next in lavender, while the matron of honor will wear powder blue, and the maid of honor, who stands next to the bride on her left facing the altar, wears a deeper shade of blue or pale pink. All would carry the same flowers. Often, when there are only four bridesmaids and a maid of honor, one color is chosen, but in graduated shades.

An all-white wedding can be beautiful, but it must be done carefully or the bride runs the risk of "disappearing" among her attendants. Colored sashes with wide streamers down the back, panels to relieve the too-white look, and the choice of flowers can help. If you want an all-white wedding, you need the combined skills of a good bridal consultant and a florist working together to make it look right. Brides seem to think of all-white weddings for winter, but they are even more beautiful in summer gardens where the attendants have a frame of green foliage to set off their costumes.

Just about every bride we have ever known says, "Believe me, I'm going to find bridesmaids' dresses for *my* wedding that the girls can wear again." This is a great idea that, alas, generally falls by the wayside. Many popular girls who have been invited often to serve as attendants in weddings have each and every costume they ever bought hanging in garment bags and almost never wear them again. Why this should be so is interesting but sad. It's not because the bride has chosen unwisely, but usually because there are so few bridesmaids' dresses available for a price she considers reasonable to expect her friends to pay. The older the bride, the more she worries about this, for many of her friends will be newly married themselves and cannot afford to buy a dress for over fifty dollars to wear in a wedding party.

And then there are certain years when a streak of models that are decidedly "lemons" hits the market. We speak with feeling since we have only recently emerged from several seasons running in which it was very nearly impossible to find a bridesmaid's dress not cluttered up with bugles, beads, chains, and every kind of jewel-encrusted bodice, neckline, sleeve, and hem. Those seasons were a heyday for anyone who could sew professionally, and lots of brides and their mothers could. They saved themselves a lot of anguish, to say nothing of money.

Whenever we run into a spate of "lemons," we suggest to brides that they bypass them entirely and start looking for simple, well-cut dinner dresses to which sleeves may be added or not, as the case may call for, order them in the same color for all the attendants, and forget about "bridesmaids' dresses."

Dresses of this type are more individual and they *can* be worn again.

The problem of how to dress young girl attendants between the ages of ten and fifteen who are too big to serve as flower girls and are yet too young, or too small of stature, to be bridesmaids is often acute. These junior bridesmaids are frequently the younger sisters of the bride or groom. They should be dressed in *modified* copies of the older attendants' costumes. This, generally speaking, means having their dresses made. Here is another area where a good bridal consultant can assist you greatly. She probably won't be able to find dresses to fit the junior bridesmaids, but, if you give her time, she *can* order sufficient material from the manufacturer for you. If this can be done, you will have a better-looking wedding party because all the dresses will be of the same material and in the same color.

Flower girls are easier to dress than junior bridesmaids. A white dress a little girl would wear to a party is perfect. She might have a sash of the same material and color as the bridesmaids' dresses. Circlets of miniature ivy with tiny flowers for their hair are effective, and so are flower baskets—preferably ones that can be held in both hands—filled with miniature dianthus, ivy, roses, and so on. White socks and white patent leather shoes with a strap can complete the costume of a "little scene-stealer" very nicely.

The ring bearer should wear a white suit, one he could wear to a party where he might expect to meet a magician with real live rabbits in his hat. He may wear white socks and either black or white patent leather shoes with straps and a miniature white carnation boutonniere or a larger one that has been "shattered" down to the right proportions, and he would carry a white satin cushion to which the wedding ring or rings have been attached. We suggest using "pretend" rings that can be sewn on, since ring bearers tend to be between three and a half and seven years old and should not be given the responsibility of carrying the real ring or rings. These are better off on the little finger of the best man and on the thumb of the maid of honor. It is a simple matter for the ring bearer to turn over the cushion, or for the best man to do this for him if he forgets, for the return trip down the aisle following the ceremony. (Please see chapter 13 for directions for ring bearers, or pages, and flower girls.)

Of the two mothers, the bride's mother has the first choice of color of dress and hem length. She should choose her dress as soon as the general color scheme of her daughter's wedding has been decided upon. The groom's mother then chooses her dress in a contrasting shade, but with the same hem length (measured to her individually) as that of the bride's mother. Gloves are necessary for both mothers, especially while they are in the receiving line, and can be removed afterward if they choose. Both mothers should remember not to wear rings on the right hand for that hour or more when they are shaking hands with the guests, otherwise both of them will end up with sore, bruised right hands. Their flowers should be worn with any ribbon or florist's binding *down,* not *up,* or maybe pinned to their purses if they prefer not to wear flowers. Or they may have fresh flowers attached to combs and wear them as headpieces, which can be simple and effective.

This is a tip on shopping for the mother of the bride as well as for the mother of the groom: Unless you frequent a shop where there is a trusted saleslady who knows you, make the rounds of the best shops available, but never, never, mention the fact that you have a daughter or a son getting married. Tell the saleslady you are shopping for a dress you can wear to informal dinners, on a cruise, to the wedding of a favorite niece, one in which you will feel happy and comfortable. In fact, tell her anything, but don't let yourself get trapped into the category of "mother of the bride" or "mother of the groom." If you follow this advice you stand a fair chance of finding something you can wear again. Shop early, take a pair of slippers with you, and wear comfortable shoes. Good luck —you'll need it!

We have been asked if a young woman who is marrying a divorced man may wear a wedding gown and veil if she has not been married previously. Of course she may. She wears any gown and veil that become her and plans her wedding exactly as she would have had her fiancé never been married.

A divorcée, however, whether or not her groom has ever been married before, does not wear the same type of wedding gown and veil that the "first time" bride is entitled to wear. The same applies to widows of all ages.

As for the mature bride—thirty and over—who marries for the first time, she would be well-advised to consider carefully the decision to wear the gown and veil she would have worn at twenty. What she chooses to wear depends very much on how she looks in it. We would suggest she try on bridal gowns and veils, look at herself as objectively as possible, and ask herself this question: "Do I look like mutton dressed as lamb?" If she can answer this one with an honest "no," then she may wear the dress and veil of her dreams, or anything that is becoming to her. If not, she should start shopping for a pretty dress she would wear to cocktail parties or informal dinners, or find herself the best-looking costume with long or short skirt and matching jacket or coat she can afford. This will save her the cost of a traditional gown and veil and the expenses of a big, formal wedding, for what she wears determines the degree of formality or informality of her wedding and reception.

TROUSSEAUX

The many basic and far-reaching changes in the life-styles of young people, particularly during the past decade, have resulted in the loss—perhaps—to them of many fine old customs. One of these is the old-fashioned and elaborate trousseau, those "little trousses" (bundles) that brides traditionally brought with them to their new homes. Gone are the days of hope chests filled with the finest linen hand-embroidered with the bride's initials—and meant to last her a lifetime. And the exquisite lingerie, the beautiful peignoirs, and that extensive wardrobe of new clothes designed to see her into the first years of her marriage.

The bride's scene today is a fast-paced one of rapid changes in attitudes, modes of living, fashions in everything, including wardrobes and furnishings for homes and apartments. So we are going to assume that you have provided your daughter with a "going away" costume and whatever wardrobe you care to send her forth with, and will concentrate on household trousseaux only.

In planning for her new home, a girl and her family should be very practical. Therefore, base the contents of her "little trousses" on her real requirements. The important questions are: What kind of home is she going to live in? How long will she live in it? Where will it be located geographically? And what does she really need? These questions apply to all brides, from the most privileged to the least affluent.

The bride's new requirements may be very different than yours were when you were married, or even those to which she is accustomed. Don't despair if you discover that your daughter's life-style is going to be very different and much simpler than the one you had in mind for her. Besides, there's no more revealing time to find out what she's thinking than when she's planning her new home. Keep an open mind—and keep that chest of fine old family silver if she so much as hesitates about using it. You can give it to her later when she might appreciate it more and be willing to give it the care it needs.

Most of the brides we know have a complete set of heavy forged stainless steel flatware as well as sterling silver five-piece settings for eight, ten, or more, and use the latter for dinner only. In any case, as soon as she chooses her silver pattern—or the old family silver, and some of those patterns are still available today—register it at the bride's gift registry in several of the leading stores in your town or city. All the good firms have them, and they are a great convenience to a bride's relatives and friends when they are buying her wedding gifts, so be sure to make use of this service.

Each store has its own particular manner of running the bride's gift registry, but most of them have forms for brides to fill out listing their silver, fine china, everyday china, crystal, everyday glassware, and stainless steel patterns. Also listed is the bride's preference in holloware, serving pieces in sterling or stainless, and so on. The store keeps a record of what she has received and what remains open on the list of suggestions for other gifts. And people do use these bride's gift registries.

The following is what we consider to be a basic household trousseau. Like a good soup stock, it may be enjoyed as is, watered down, or used as the starting point for a more elaborate dish:

6 sheets for each bed or
 8 sheets for a double bed
 (Percale is best, especially the kind that requires no ironing. We suggest white ones unless the bride has definite color schemes established; three fitted, or four fitted with the others for top sheets.)
1 dozen pillowcases for each bed
1 quilt for each bed
 (eiderdown preferably)
2 pairs of blankets for each bed
Blanket covers for each bed
Bedspreads for each bed
2 quilted mattress covers for each bed, the ones with fitted corners or elastic bands

1 dozen bath towels
(6 of one color, 6 of contrasting shade, or all white ones with colored monograms, unless the bride has a color scheme planned.)
8 matching or contrasting face cloths
1 dozen guest towels and
1 dozen fingertip towels
(Linen guest towels have to be ironed. Think about a year's supply of good paper ones, or get more fingertip towels.)

A bride and her mother would do well to take full advantage of the January and August white sales if these months fall into the shopping time for her trousseau. For anyone who is budget minded, sheets and towels and all such household items can then be purchased at great savings. Don't forget that, if you have enough time, you can have monograms embroidered for a small additional cost. While shops that specialize in trousseaux have beautiful things of quality, they are expensive and very often impractical for today's bride.

1 nylon or plastic shower curtain for each bathroom
1 bath mat and seat cover for each bathroom
1 dozen kitchen towels
1 dozen towels for glasses if there is no dishwasher
1 damask or linen tablecloth, dinner size or banquet size, in white or a pale color, with 1 dozen dinner-size matching napkins
2 everyday luncheon sets with matching napkins
2 good luncheon sets with matching napkins of fine linen and perhaps bordered with lace
3 tray cloths of various sizes
2 tray sets with 2 napkins, 1 for toast or muffins
1 dry mop
1 step-on garbage can
1 kitchen stool and ladder combination
1 four-speed electric mixer-blender

1 meat grinder
1 meat and general kitchen scale
1 rolling pin
1 cookie sheet
1 eggbeater
1 set of wire whisks
Sieves, 1 large, 2 small
1 flour sifter
2 wooden ladles
1 funnel, plus large and small pitchers
1 vegetable parer, which can be used for French-style string beans
Jelly molds and custard cups
1 large grater, 1 small
1 large chopping bowl, 1 small
1 combination wall dispenser for paper towels, wax paper, and aluminum foil
1 griddle
1 covered kettle
1 electric can opener and several magnetic bottle openers
1 spice set
1 wine rack
1 set of canisters
Kitchen carving knife and fork, plus steel for sharpening
4 paring knives of the best stainless steel available, with *good* handles
4 potholders and 1 mitt
Vegetable bin and bread box (if not built in)
1 set of measuring spoons and glasses
1 package of nylon sponges of different sizes
1 nylon wet mop and pail with step-on wringer
1 toaster (usually a shower or wedding gift)
1 nest casserole dishes with tops (Pyrex is best)
Breadboard and bread knife
1 dish drainer (if there is no dishwasher)

1 apple corer
1 colander and set of small strainers
1 coffee maker
1 Dutch oven (large enough *without* the cover to roast a turkey)
1 large, 1 smaller saucepan
1 large, 1 smaller skillet
1 double boiler

As to the electrical items on the above list it would be wise to wait before purchasing them until after the bride sees what she receives as shower gifts.

If the bride is not going to have two sets of china—one fine and the other for everyday—whose patterns are on record at the bride's gift registry, she and her mother should shop for a set of basic utility china in a simple pattern that *is in open stock* for replacements are most important, whether you are buying porcelain, pottery, or even one of the unbreakable compositions. Usually such sets contain many pieces that can be substituted for others with less practical uses. An example of what we mean is that most brides' households do not need a dozen eggcups or a dozen soup cups and saucers, but they could use six more medium-sized plates instead. The advantage of buying sets is, of course, that you save money over buying the same pieces separately. However, before you decide, talk to the buyer in the store and find out if you may make substitutions of any kind. Some stores in larger cities will go along with this, but those in smaller communities are unable to do so. You are still better off with a set from a pattern in open stock, for you can add the additional plates you need when necessary, or you can add them to your list of gifts you prefer from friends or relatives.

The china pattern you choose will, to a large extent, determine the type of glassware you select; if you are using only utility china, naturally you will be thinking not in terms of finely chased or cut glass or crystal, but heavier utility glassware to go with it. But if you are one of the lucky brides who can have two sets of china and glassware, this problem is solved. In any case, it's wise to make a list of the basic pieces of china and glassware you really need and have space for in your new home or apartment.

The bride sets the tone of her new home, and we don't know a single one who doesn't enjoy setting her table for dinner and having it as attractive and nearly as festive as it would be if she and her husband were having guests. Don't go overboard on basic utility china and glassware unless you have no choice because of economics. And another word of caution: Avoid that real bargain lot of china in the *discontinued pattern,* for it will no doubt be of some wild floral design that will never mix with anything later.

Incidentally, you should let the bride's gift registry know if you want any gifts of silver unmarked (most people give it this way in any case), or should tell them how you want it marked. In former times, silver was marked with the bride's maiden initials, and older people still follow this custom, but a triangle of block letters made up of the last initial of her new married name and her two maiden initials seems to be the favorite now. Here's an example of how a bride's silver would be marked if her maiden name was Susan Ann Brown and she was marrying Seth Jones: J

S B

The single initial J might be done in Old English instead of in the block letter.

CLOTHES FOR THE GROOM*

Today, very few young men have both formal afternoon and evening wear. In addition, fathers who still have such

* Now and then we come across a reference to the groom's trousseau in books and magazines. As far as we are concerned, this boils down to clothes for the place he is going on the wedding trip (if he doesn't know what's necessary, any travel agency will tell him) and what he will need that he does not already have. Brand-new everything is fine, but only if he has nothing else to spend his money on.

remnants of a more leisurely age may not now be able to get into them, either because of an increase in girth or the industry of moths.

Unless the wedding is quite informal and will permit the wearing of dark business suits, rental of formal attire by all the adult male members of a wedding party is now almost universal. In every large metropolitan area there are rental concerns that specialize in providing formal clothes for all occasions. Many men's clothing stores also have rental departments. They all have size slips that you can pick up and send to the members of the bridal party who are out of town. All necessary measurements should be taken by a tailor, wherever the individual may be. Then the completed size slips may be mailed back either to you or to the groom. They are then sent in to the rental concern. Below is a sample of a complete order size slip:

NAME ....
ADDRESS ....
WHEN FOR ....
CHEST ....HEIGHT ....
UNDERSLEEVE ....WEIGHT ....
WAIST ....HAT ....
SEAT ....SHIRT ....
(if needed)
INSEAM ....GLOVES ....
(For Suspenders Only)
SHOES ....
(if needed)
GROOM'S NAME ....
REMARKS ....
....
....

Please have a tailor take the measurements.

The suits are packed in individual boxes (it is a good idea to request the firm to put the wearer's name on a card and paste it in the top of his box), which may be picked up by the best man or someone delegated by the groom. If the groom, his best man, and the ushers are from out of town, someone from the bride's family may oblige. Or the rental firm will mail the suits to you or have them delivered to your home or to the place where the groom and other men are to dress.

In most cases, all or part of this clothes rental detail is assigned to the best man. It is he who should collect all suits, ascots or ties, gloves, and other accessories that belong to the rental firm and see that they are paid for and returned. Also, someone has to act as treasurer if the members of the wedding party cannot go in to be fitted and pay the cost of the rental personally. The ideal way of coping with this detail is for the groom to delegate one person to do it for him, possibly his father. The groom's father may or may not elect to dress the same way as the other male members of the wedding party, but it is customary for him to do so.

What should the groom, best man, and ushers wear? This is usually the initial subject of difficulty for the groom. What he wears is by tradition his choice. However, he must be guided in his choice by the type of gown his bride will wear, the hour of the ceremony and the formality of it, and the reception to follow.

He usually wants to dress down, while his bride is apt to want him to dress up—and probably cut his hair to at least collar, rather than shoulder, length. What he is to wear may be the basis for their first real quarrel. She usually wins the round, and she should. If a bride is wearing an expensive gown and an heirloom family veil, the very least the groom can do is to dress accordingly, i.e., the full formal bit.

We like to see groom, best man, ushers, and both fathers all dressed alike, with variations only in ascots or ties for the groom and best man. There is an occasional exception to this dress-alike dictum: It's when the father of the bride dresses more formally than the groom, best man, and ushers for an afternoon wedding. One father of our acquaintance let it be known to the entire countryside that he was wearing the cutaway *he* had been married in to give his only daughter away, complete with ascot and the works, and that as far as he was concerned the groom could wear skivvies and levis.

The groom in this instance was so put down by his future father-in-law's stand that he even cut his hair and wore a cutaway—but no ascot. We found out that the collar and ascot were his real hang-up, not the cutaway. He wore a turndown collar and a pinstriped tie instead.

The chart on page 85 shows what goes with what. Most men's clothing rental firms have similar ones. We give this here as an illustration and for use in settling those prenuptial arguments.

The witching hour for formal evening dress is 6:00 P.M. Before that time, men customarily wear some kind of informal dress, or formal afternoon (cutaway) attire. We have often noticed (not at any wedding with which we have assisted) black or white dinner jackets running around the countryside at high noon. We don't know how or where this practice arose, but we do know of its sectional use. We believe it is as easy to rent a stroller as a dinner jacket. The wearer is more comfortable in a stroller, especially if he is ushering at a wedding, and he certainly looks better in one at that hour of the day, or at any hour before 6:00 P.M.

As we have already said, the bride almost invariably dictates what the groom will wear, even though this decision is supposed to be his alone. Certainly if a bride is wearing a cocktail gown, her groom should wear either a dark business suit or a stroller, and if she is wearing a traditional gown, with or without a chapel-length train and a short veil, her groom should most definitely wear a stroller—or a dinner jacket if the ceremony is at 6:00 P.M. or later. But if a bride is wearing an elaborate veil with a gown that has a cathedral-length or court train, her groom had better get himself, his best man,

	EVENING FORMAL	EVENING SEMIFORMAL	DAYTIME FORMAL	DAYTIME SEMIFORMAL	SUMMER EVENING WEAR
COAT	Black tailcoat, silk-faced or grosgrain lapels.	Dinner jacket, black, S.B., shawl or peaked lapels.	Oxford gray cutway with peaked lapels.	Single-breasted Oxford jacket.	S.B. white evening jacket, tropical weight.
WAISTCOAT	White washable fabric, single-breasted.	Black silk cummerbund or vest.	S.B. of same material. S.B. white. S.B. or D.B. pearl gray.	S.B. of same material. S.B. white. S.B. or D.B. pearl gray.	Black or maroon silk cummerbund.
TROUSERS	Material same as coat, braid down side.	Material same as coat, braid down side.	Black with white or silvertone stripes.	Black with white or silvertone stripes.	Black tropicals, braid down side.
HAT[1]	High silk or opera.	Black homburg.	High silk.	Homburg.	Homburg.
SHIRT	Stiff bosom white pique. Single cuffs.[2]	Pleated bosom.	Plain white or pleated bosom.	Plain white or pleated bosom.	Plain white or pleated bosom.
COLLAR	Bold wing.	Fold.[3]	Bold wing or fold.	Fold.	Fold.
CRAVAT[4]	White, rounded or pointed ends.	Black silk, rounded or pointed ends.	Ascot or four-in-hand in plain color, stripes, or modest design.	Four-in-hand in plain color, stripes, or modest design.	Bow, color to match cummerbund.
GLOVES[5]	White.	Gray.	Gray.	Gray.	NONE.
JEWELRY	White pearl studs, cuff links to match, pocket watch.	Black pearl studs, cuff links to match.	Pearl or jeweled pin, cuff links to match or gold or colored stones.	Pearl or jeweled pin, cuff links to match or gold or colored stones.	Your own preference.
HOSE	Black.	Black.	Dark silk or lisle.	Dark silk or lisle.	To harmonize.
SHOES	Patent leather, low-cut pumps or plain black calfskin oxfords.	Patent leather, low-cut pumps or plain black calfskin oxfords.	Black calfskin oxfords with or without spats.	Black calfskin oxfords with or without spats.	Patent leather or black calfskin oxfords.

[1] Hats are included only because they are required for certain Jewish weddings. They are still worn at many other types of weddings in cities, and at more formal weddings in the suburbs.

[2] Single cuffs for evening formals only. We prefer French cuffs for all others if possible.

[3] "Fold" means a turndown collar as opposed to a wing collar. It is *never* a button-down.

[4] The four-in-hand tie is worn with the fold collar. The trend now is to substitute the four-in-hand tie with pinstripe for the ascot, particularly in the summer in suburban and country weddings.

[5] We recommend no gloves for the groom and best man for either single or double ring ceremonies. Gloves should be worn by all other male members of the wedding party.

and his ushers into cutaways and ascots—or white tie and tails, if the ceremony is at 6:00 P.M. or later—if he wants to be correct. And there should be no arguments about this.

Here we would like to enter a plea for comfort. It is quite acceptable to wear a turndown collar and a pinstripe four-in-hand tie with a cutaway. They are more comfortable in warm weather, and the cutaway should be tropical weight for the groom and all his ushers. Almost all males will agree that a batwing, ascot, and ninety-degree heat for five or six hours are pure murder.

We want to add several *musts* here. If a groom and best man are to kneel during the ceremony, the soles of their shoes must be inspected before the wedding. Unless the soles are already black, they should be dyed black in plenty of time to dry before the ceremony.

If lapel buttonholes are not slit (rental firms usually sew them up before each dry cleaning), they should be slit so that a boutonniere (made of a flower that is also used in the bride's bouquet, or a carnation) may be put into the buttonhole and pinned onto the *inside* of the lapel.

If a wing collar is worn, the ascot may have to be pinned to the top of the waistcoat (vest) strap in back to keep it from riding up the collar.

Black loafers are not considered proper although we have often seen them worn. However, the black loafer with a bow is replacing the old-fashioned pump.

We wish to stress again the value of tropical weight worsted in all formal and informal clothes for weddings. The groom who has his own suit, which may have been his father's —and a pre-World War II model at that—is going to suffer in really hot weather, since those suits were usually cut from heavy serge or alpaca. We haven't heard of tropical worsted frock coats, the old-fashioned morning clothes with which either four-in-hand or, after twelve noon, ascot was worn, although we have seen one or two on grandfathers of the bride during the winter. If the bride's grandfather is bound and determined to wear his "claw-hammer" in midsummer, that's his privilege. About all you can do is be on the alert for signs of apoplexy.

Summer evening wear is customary everywhere. A white dinner jacket is merely substituted for the black, and a cummerbund for the waistcoat. Often midnight blue replaces black trousers. The suit may be either wool or tropical worsted. White double-breasted dinner jackets made of tropical worsted are about the coolest. They eliminate the necessity for wearing a tight cummerbund.

Nonconformity can wreck the effect of an otherwise beautiful ceremony. Informality in dress is one thing, but the sight of a business suit intermingled with strollers and striped trousers, or of a pair of tan shoes, goes far beyond the limit. The only mixture of clothing for members of a wedding party that doesn't jar the senses is that of men in uniform walking in procession with ushers in strollers or cutaways.

Just a thought in closing: Why, if the bride can spend a small fortune on her gown and veil, can't the groom go to one of the talented designers and have his wedding suit made to order? It only seems fair, and, after all, he should look as good as she does.

Chapter 5

Catering and Rentals

REGARDLESS OF THE NATURE OF THE OCCASION, WHENever you find that the number of people who are to be fed exceeds the facilities of your household, or your own capabilities, you call in a caterer.

Throughout this chapter we shall assume that your caterer is a man, although today there are probably as many women as men involved in the field.

"Be a guest at your own party" or some similar sentiment describes succinctly what a caterer can, and will, do for you. A fully staffed and equipped company can provide everything needed, including complete postparty cleanup service. Choose your menu, show the caterer his area facilities, such as kitchen and garage or the size of the cook tent, and the general layout of the reception area. Then, theoretically, you are free to worry about something else. This is the ultimate in catering service. Every large urban area has at least one. At the other end of the spectrum is the man from the delicatessen or the local restaurant who arrives at your back door with your order in containers, and that is it. How this food gets from those containers to your guests' plates is strictly your business. Between these two extremes there are infinite varieties and combinations.

It might help if we discuss the most complete estimate forms used by one of the top and most expensive caterers in the East. This will enable you to check your own service, deleting all unnecessary items, and to determine what he can provide and what you must. The more picky little things, such as nuts, candies, matches, cigarettes, that the caterer will provide, the less it will cost you in time and money. The caterer buys wholesale over the phone; you would have to run all over town to retail stores.

Most estimates are separated into equipment, service, and food. The first includes silverware, chinaware, glasses, tubs for chilling the champagne, bar and bar accessories for all sorts of beverages, serving utensils, ashtrays, salt and pepper shakers, serving trays, bowls, coffee urns, chafing dishes, candelabra, and table containers for decorations. Your caterer may not have all the above, but what he doesn't have he can rent. Included also is all the equipment necessary to complete the preparation of your menu, such as stoves, cooking utensils, and preparation tables. Most of these items are not listed but are implied under accepted concepts of catering. However, many caterers don't supply all these items under the per head price. Quite a few items, such as stoves, candelabra, coffee urns, and chafing dishes, may be listed and charged separately.

Next is service. This is a term that includes waiters, waitresses, and the other attendants in and out of the kitchen or cook tent. It normally includes the bartenders as well. The type and number of help vary widely both as to local usage and menu. Obviously, a seated and served dinner needs the most; a buffet on which canapés and sandwiches are placed, the guests helping themselves, with nothing to be passed, needs the least. As soon as a hostess decides to have trays passed, either food or beverage, the number of help needed increases in direct proportion to the number of guests expected and the number of different types of canapés, hors d'oeuvres, and sandwiches requiring separate trays. She must also remember that a pickup waiter or waitress will be necessary.

The mechanics of serving your guests depend on the menu and the numbers. While some very formal seated and served dinners may have a waiter assigned to each table (we had one prenuptial dinner at which the host ordered one waiter behind each guest), it is customary when the dinner is buffet to have waiters so stationed as to be able to care for several tables. This latter technique is often used also when you have an elaborate afternoon collation, with hot and cold dishes on the buffet in addition to passed hors d'oeuvres and canapés. Here it is necessary that two waiters be on duty at the buffet at all times. We personally prefer this method. It is less stiff. Your guests have freedom to move around and choose what food they want. Besides, today people queue up so often that it is almost second nature to them. A rule of thumb: one large buffet for up to 250 guests; two identical buffets for 250 to 500 guests. The ratio continues in this pattern. As you decrease the variety and amount of your menu, the service requirements also decrease. In other words, the more show you put on, the more dough you will have to put out.

At the outset you should find out the overtime rate. You should also determine the length of service, normally considered to be eight hours. Is it portal-to-portal or eight hours on the premises? You should find out at what time overtime charges begin. This charge is often forgotten when the host decides to have the orchestra play for an extra hour. Everyone is having so good a time. He only thinks of the cost of overtime music, which is relatively small when compared to that of the caterer's staff.

The greater part of your caterer's estimate will, of course, be concerned with food. While the airwaves and printed media are full of party ideas, suggestions, and recipes, the hard facts of economy and mass production in arriving at the cost per head for an afternoon collation eliminate many of these. Also one has to consider the actual eating process. The canapés and hors d'oeuvres should not be greasy, or if greasy they should be served with toothpicks. Tea sandwiches and other "finger food" should be thin, moist, dainty, and bite size, with no tendency to slop over. Personally, one of us is addicted to plump egg salad sandwiches, but to eat one calls for a bib and complete privacy.

There are many, many spreads and combinations produced both from the can and the kitchen. Every caterer has a number of personal specialties he has tried on countless clients and found to be popular and not too fattening. He will recommend those found to be pleasing to most and at the same time easiest to make, serve, and eat. You may have some wonderful ideas for new hors d'oeuvres or canapés, but not only does the caterer have to make them; your guests also will have to eat them. So play it safe. Were you to attend an average of forty afternoon receptions during the year as we do, you would know at once who the caterer was by the specialties and style of service. They are as distinctive as a signature.

Hot and cold dishes for the buffet for an afternoon reception range all the way from crêpes Nicholas to cold cuts and potato or macaroni salads, including Newburgs, casseroles, shrimp bowls, aspics, and assorted cheeses and crackers. Whatever they may be, they must be so prepared and served as to be readily eaten on a small plate with a fork. The addition of a plate and fork immediately adds to your cost per head, for now you have a buffet, rather than just "finger food"—a horrible name for it, but currently in use.

Every homemaking or women's page of every daily and weekly newspaper, and many magazines, carries original or syndicated recipes. Most bookstores have an assortment of cookbooks that go into the whole subject in detail. So look in your papers, consult the books available, talk to those who have gone the reception route before you. Above all, consult your caterer. What we might offer, for example, as a menu for a reception in the Greater New York area could well meet with hoots of derision from another section of the country.

This same advice is equally applicable to the selection of the menu for a complete dinner, either seated and served or buffet style. Ask your caterer about plate service. Cost can be an important limiting factor: usually beef is the most expensive, fowl the least. Here you should consider what the majority can eat. There seem to be more diets abroad in the land nowadays than there are fleas on a yellow hound dog, although many leave their diets at home when they go to a wedding.

You should determine next what your caterer can do best. The chefs at the largest firms can cope with almost anything, but the average firm seldom has specialists, although we have noticed within the last ten years an increasing number of cordon bleu people in catering. Keep in mind that almost all of the menu is prepared in the caterer's kitchen and then brought by truck or station wagon to your house in some form of traveling container. Some dishes can go bad in hot weather. Does your firm use dry ice or have refrigerator trucks? Not only does the expected weather have some bearing on your choice, but so does the season. What food will be in plentiful supply? This affects not only the ingredients of hot dishes, but also fruits and salads. Your caterer will know the answer.

Sudden changes in the weather can cause unexpected trouble. We remember only too well an early September wedding in 1955. There had been five days of high temperatures and higher humidity, the miserable kind of conditions that Westchester County can often experience. We had a large late-afternoon reception with supper to follow, all under canvas. The weather broke in the middle of the reception. No one got wet, but everybody became ravenous. They were all trying to make up for five noneating days at that reception. The caterer's lockers were cleaned out, and she had to call everyone she knew for additional hams and turkeys, but there were pretty slim pickings at the end.

While such conditions cannot be forecast with any degree of accuracy, your caterer should be aware of the possibilities in light of the twenty-four-hour forecast. He might well plan to have additional "fillers" in reserve.

We can't recommend any set menus; we can only offer this suggestion: If you serve the same balanced meal for many that you would normally serve for a handful of dinner guests, you can't go very far wrong.

The last items on your estimate will include mints, salted nuts, petits fours, ice cream and/or fruit cup, and coffee. Ice cream goes with the wedding cake, which is separate, a distinct item with its own size and price listed.

There are two traditional kinds of wedding cake, fruit and white, or "Bride's," cake. The size is predicated on the number of people expected to get a token piece. We say "token" because so few eat cake these days. The cake eaters thus get several "tokens" to equal a standard helping.

If you are having fruit cake, have it made several months in advance. Occasionally a client has asked, in addition, for individual little cake boxes. They are nice as mementos, but the cake, once cut, tends to dry up rapidly despite the brandy and the aluminum foil wrappings. And they are expensive. If you get a white cake, ask to have it baked no sooner, if possible, than the day before the reception. We once knew a cake maker who, to save time, baked cakes in large batches in advance and froze them. Her only problem came when she defrosted a cake before icing it on the morning of the wedding. Her defrosting technique was awful. The frosting was moist and tasty, the cake pure sawdust. She was horrified when she inadvertently tasted one of her own cakes at the reception of a friend's daughter.

Cake making is a special art form. The maker takes genuine pride in his or her work, whether at home or in a shop.

Don't try it unless you are one of these artists. You already have enough to do.

The cake table should be placed where it can be seen easily, but out of the way of traffic. If you have a bride's table, place the cake table in front of it unless this area has dancing. If there is dancing, place the cake table off to one side. Never place the cake table so that the bride is hidden behind it. In any event, you and the bride can find more than one advantageous place to spot a thirty-inch round table. When the cake is to be cut, it is customary to remove the table to a central spot, either in front of the bride's table or in the middle of the dance floor, where everyone can see.

The actual ceremony of cutting the cake is too well known to go into here, but your caterer should have at least one waitress standing by to help the couple. We have seen several cakes attacked in too determined a manner, resulting in a certain amount of mangling. Have the couple take their time. Use your own cake knife if you have one; otherwise, your caterer will supply it. If the bride receives one as a wedding gift, by all means use that. After the ceremony and toasts, if any, are over, we usually have the cake table moved off to one side where the caterer can finish cutting it for serving. The pieces of cake, if it is a buffet, can be left on a coffee table. Or the guests can come up and be served. If you have ice cream and cake, which many do, you should have a separate buffet table on which this combination is placed. Personally, we like to see cake and ice cream served rather than self-served. This latter combination is slippery.

Once in a great while we run into a hostess who says, in effect, "Feed 'em anything—sandwiches, canapés. No one eats at a wedding. I know I never do!" This is a singularly unobservant breed. But what kind of menu to select, and how complete it should be, depends in part on the kind and the time of the ceremony. A nuptial mass is usually followed by either a full buffet or a seated and served breakfast or luncheon. An evening wedding, after six o'clock, also calls for quite a complete menu, as the reception goes through the dinner hour. A ceremony at 3:30 or 4:00 P.M. is usually followed by a reception with a simpler menu. Your guests will normally leave before their dinner hour. The ceremony set between four-thirty and six in the afternoon is harder to determine. We suggest that you start with the hour of the ceremony, calculate how long it will last and how long it will take your guests to get from the church to the reception, and then select your menu and the amounts based on the time the reception should begin. As the average reception seldom exceeds four hours (without music, nearer to two hours), this selection will depend upon local dining habits and how far the majority have traveled to reach the ceremony. The earlier in the afternoon the reception starts, the less food is needed.

You may well have a contingent coming from quite a distance. The easiest way to give them adequate food, short of taking them all to a restaurant or club, is to have your caterer leave a light supper, such as a casserole or ham and turkey, with a complete service for the expected number, in your kitchen. This can be a bit tricky if you have a marquee and plan to use it after the reception. Your closest neighbors will still be there after the majority have gone. You will wonder how you are ever going to be able to feed the hungry out-of-towners without offending the neighbors. This is one time you could have the caterer start taking the tables and chairs away while placing "reserved" signs on the few tables to be used later.

Luncheons given by the bride for her attendants are most informal affairs and strictly up to the bride. The prenuptial or rehearsal dinner is usually given by the groom's family. But they may live too far away or he may have no family. In this case get one of your friends to give it. And whatever you do, keep this affair away from your house, even if it is not being used for the reception. The last forty-eight hours are hectic enough as it is. One exception to this is, in a case where you have more than one tent up, and the arrangement is agreeable to the groom's side, it may be easier and less expensive to use the smaller tent for the rehearsal dinner and have the caterer take care of it. All the canvas and catering equipment have to be in place by the following morning anyhow.

The rehearsal dinner is an excellent occasion to take care of the toasts. While it is "traditional" to give toasts at the cake-cutting ceremony, or between courses of a breakfast or dinner, either a great many people can't hear the speaker or he can't handle a microphone. A toast that makes a great hit when given within the intimate bonds of the immediate wedding party can fall flat before two hundred less well acquainted guests.

Another extraceremonial event you need only worry about is the fading custom of the bachelor dinner. Enough has been said about the lethal combination of gasoline and alcohol, to which we have twice lost prospective members of wedding parties. If the groom must follow this late Edwardian custom, first have him read Emily Post's *Etiquette,* first edition, pages 230, 336–337, and 375. This contains quite a description of the stag or bachelor's dinner. After reading this, maybe he will schedule the event several days ahead of the main event, time enough for you to make certain who will be in the wedding party.

During the discussion of menus, the question of seating is always raised. "How many do I have to provide tables and chairs for?" There are few positive guidelines. It depends upon your local customs. There is an axiom that the more elaborate the meal becomes, the more accommodations you should provide. If people are to enjoy a four-course dinner, they need ample table space. If you have self-serving buffets with only canapés and sandwiches plus the addition of a hot dish and possibly a choice of salad, all of which need only a fork, few of your guests will need more than a perch or a place to set down an empty plate. We have found in serving the so-called afternoon collation, without a hot dish requiring a plate and fork, that only one-third the number of guests expected will need tables and chairs. As hot dishes and other buffet items are added, the ratio rises to two-thirds. These ratios generally hold true not only under canvas, but also in clubs, church parlors, community halls, and in your own house. In addition, you should provide for specially reserved tables for both families and, if there is no bridal table per se, a third for the bridal party to call home base. In this case, the caterer will assign one or more waitresses to take care of these tables. In addition to the formal bridal table, a special one is usually assigned to the "fifth wheels": wives, husbands, and fiancés of members of the wedding party. It should be placed near the bridal table. It is wise to use place cards for the bridal table, the family table or tables, and that "fifth wheel" table if you are having one.

The size of the tables is related directly to the type of menu and the space available. If you are using your home, you may find that the most economical use of space calls for a sixty-inch round table that seats twelve. Under marquees and in community halls that don't have their own seating equipment we prefer round tables to square or long banquet tables of eight feet or more. The round table offers your guests more freedom and looks much better. These come in thirty-six, forty-two, fifty-eight, and sixty-inch diameters, seating respectively six, eight, ten, and twelve people. But keep in mind that the more use of table space your menu requires, the fewer can be seated at any given table.

If you are using banquet-type tables, usually eight feet long, please read the appropriate section in chapter 7. In chapter 11 you will find outlined in detail one method for seating your guests.

Several types of chairs are available. The most expensive and the hardest to find in large quantities, except in the largest metropolitan hotels or in the stock of the largest catering and canvas firms, are ballroom chairs in various colors. However, the majority of canvas or rental equipment firms now have polished wooden folding chairs with various colored seats and backs; gold, blue, green, and dark red are the most common choices. These are more all-purpose, suitable in either a room or under canvas. They have a less affluent brother that is more to be found at country auctions, dog shows, and political meetings. These have wooden slats substituted for the colored seats and backs of cloth or plastic. They are both the least expensive and the least attractive, but they serve the purpose. Just in passing, have someone dust every chair coming out of a bag of six; they never fail to need it. Open trucks and warehouses, we suppose, do it.

The question of tables and chairs leads us to consider the equipment rental firms and allied services available when neither you nor your caterer is able to complete the necessary requirements. The tent (canvas) and equipment company in your area will have most of what you need (see chapter 6). But for more specialized things, the big equipment and rental companies are your best bet. There are at least two of these concerns that operate all over the United States on a local franchise basis. They rent almost anything from wheelchairs to power tools. They have complete lines of tableware, service implements, linen, and glassware. Being a franchise operation, the local outfit is able to keep abreast of what his area wants. They have very complete brochures and fully stocked showrooms. A trip to see what they have to offer is well worth your while.

Unless you are using one of the large catering firms and a well-equipped tent company because your guest list has really soared, it is probable that either your caterer or your tent company is using one of the rental firms. It takes a great deal of capital to fully equip a caterer. The same is true of the small canvas company. We don't know how many persons the average American caterer can handle, but in our area the smaller firms are fully equipped to take care of 250, the largest up to 1,500. Some of our best caterers are very long on food and very short on plate. So the rental companies have to keep them going. When either of these concerns rents specialties for you, neither you nor they are paying capital recovery costs or insurance charges except on a national wholesale basis. Even when equipment rentals are computed, the caterer would still have to charge you more for a special item were he or she to stock it. The same goes for tables and chairs to accommodate over five hundred, at least as far as most of the tent people are concerned.

Those of you who are using the pickup type of caterer, who is providing food in containers, will find an equipment rental company the answer to many problems. The same is also the case for those of you who are using your home and need extra tables, chairs, and other accessories.

Quite recently we held a watching brief for a friend who found herself in the unhappy position of having no money and a large reception to finance. She was a woman with fine organizational abilities and had a large house with capacious verandas. She also had boundless energy. The catering cost was her major problem, as her house could take care of accommodating her guests. This was how she solved her problem: First, she decided on self-service buffet tables. Then, to stock them, she called upon a number of her friends—well in advance—who, in addition to being handy in the kitchen, had large freezers. To each she assigned a different kind of tea sandwich or canapé, with the amount specified. Casserole dishes were parceled out in the same manner. That took care of feeding the hordes.

Once this plan was in the works, she visited the local equipment rental company, where she ordered all the necessary items to serve her guests, including tables, chairs, and eating utensils. To lessen the effect of "made at home with loving hands," she splurged on colored linen and smart containers that would complement her own late spring planting and the flowers she planned to get from a friend's cutting garden. The help included bartenders she recruited locally. So the only store-bought catering necessities were the wedding cake, nuts, mints, petits fours, rose petals, matches, and cigarettes.

Speaking of cigarettes, we have recently been asked if they must be supplied at all in view of the anti-smoking campaign. While we have attended receptions where there were none on the tables, we feel that they should be available. Not all of your guests have as yet joined the unhooked generation, and it looks pretty tacky if they have to go about scrounging cigarettes from those who have them. At least start off with approximately two cartons of mixed brands. These can be put in shot glasses at each table.

Potables—liquors, wines, and champagne—should rate a separate chapter. However, food and wine go together. Of course, you don't have to serve any alcoholic beverages at all. We have attended several receptions where nothing stronger than coffee, tea, and pure fruit punches was provided. No one we saw seemed to miss either champagne or an open bar. But we would like to enter a caveat here: If the majority of your expected guests do not drink anything strong, you are on sure ground, but if a large majority or the majority would like a glass of champagne or something stronger, the dictates of hospitality should prevail. If only a few of your guests are inclined to drink alcohol, forget it. Four hours of abstinence won't kill them; it might even do them good.

Still, the completely "dry" reception is an exception. Most families today serve some form of alcohol in the home. In serving alcohol at receptions, however, let whatever you have be recognizable. Those of you who have tried a spiked punch can remember some unexpected results. "Fish house" or "artillery" punch, along with their less deadly cousins, is not recommended. The average drinker knows his limitations and his tolerance level in ounces consumed. But he has little idea of what he can handle when he comes up against dynamite disguised as velvet.

As recently as ten years ago, if a client had wanted an all-champagne wedding reception, we would have complied after cautioning her that her guests would be unhappy with champagne only. Now, thanks to mass European tourism and the educational public relations work of the Wine Advisory Board in our own country, Americans have begun to like and understand champagnes and wines. But there are still many, especially among the male of the species, who may take a token sip of the grape, then look around for something more to their taste: gin, vodka, bourbon, or Scotch.

If you have an all-champagne wedding reception, buy a good dry (brut or sec) brand, be it imported or domestic California or New York. We find California dry champagne to be as good now as many of the imported French champagnes, and the cost is less. Drinking an inferior sweet champagne on a hot afternoon may be pleasant at the time for some, but the aftermath may be both painful and embarrassing. Champagne has been taken up in recent years by the young set, who seem capable of handling it in substantial amounts. If your guest list is heavily weighted on the young side, keep this in mind when ordering.

Serving beer is strictly a matter of preference and local custom. If serving it is your normal custom, have it. And if your reception is of such size as to include parking attendants and area guards, you should have beer rather than hard liquor available for them in the kitchen or cook tent.

Hard liquor is a term generally used to describe Scotch, bourbon, rye, gin, vodka, and rum. Both the season and the actual outside temperature have an important bearing on the choice and the rate of consumption. The first three are in greater demand in cold weather, while the last three are in demand when it is warm.

Whenever we order liquor for a client, we always ask, "What are your guests most likely to drink?" The client never knows. When you reach this point, consult your local liquor dealer. Not only does he know what the favorites are, but he also can tell you the number of people per case or bottle, the brands to use (usually a middle choice between bar liquor and the boss's tipple), and the ratio among the types mentioned above, e.g., in our area Scotch runs two to one over all the other whiskeys. Your liquor dealer will usually take back any unchilled champagne and bottles with unbroken seals. So don't be afraid to overorder. It's far better than running out.

The ratios usually run as follows: Seven units of hard liquor to four units of champagne; if all champagne, one case per forty people; Scotch is two to one over other whiskeys; gin and vodka run two and one-half to the other whiskeys. These ratios vary widely according to customs and locale. For instance, at Jewish receptions a great deal of wine is consumed, including champagne, but little hard liquor. The contrary holds true for the five o'clock WASP reception. It also seems that the later the hour, the more highballs your guests will want. Champagne seems to go more with the canapés and hors d'ouevres of the earlier reception.

The type of liquor consumed also varies widely throughout the country. The Atlantic seaboard north of Baltimore drinks Scotch. Bourbon wins in the entire southern tier, and so does rum. There are rye belts and many other local variants. The West Coast seems to be about the same as the East, while the heartland seems more impartial. But a long drink of gin or vodka is nationwide. Thus, we can but suggest that you do as everyone else around you: consult your local liquor dealer or your caterer.

More specialized beverages are often provided. Some people like an aperitif, such as sherry or Dubonnet, light or dark, in the afternoon. However, unless there is a formal meal to follow, cocktails can be omitted. A bartender working at top speed doesn't want to, nor does he have the time to, make up several dozen separate concoctions. The sole exception is the martini. This can be served on the rocks, so have some dry vermouth at the bar. If you are serving cocktails before a formal meal, they should either be passed or there should be a special cocktail bar open only until the guests are seated.

The number of bartenders needed is up to your caterer and depends upon his organization. A caterer's answer to this question is complicated by the peak load landing on the bar right after everyone has come off the receiving line. Then it tapers off. This is just as true when you have passed champagne and highballs and have no bar at all. Many hostesses don't like to see an open bar, so everything is passed. When this is done, the tempo of consumption is definitely slowed down. This is especially advantageous when you are faced with a large unknown contingent and country-road driving conditions. It also prevents the reception from being just another cocktail party and is, in our opinion, a graceful way of doing things.

If you are hiring your own bartenders, you should have one for every fifty guests. Add one barman for each additional fifty. Make certain that one man is put in charge of the bar itself, the potables, glasses, and ice.

Mixes and soft drinks, except in private or public rooms that provide catering facilities, have always been a headache to all concerned. Unless you use the kind in disposable containers, you are going to be left with piles of empties to be returned for credit. Many caterers provide these beverages in the proper varieties and quantities, along with lemons, limes, bitters, and other ingredients. If they don't provide these, they can tell you the correct amounts. If you are your own caterer, your liquor dealer will often send them along; otherwise, he too can tell you what and how much to order. Also, at any reception there will be about 10 percent of your guests who are not in the habit of, have stopped, or never started using alcohol. For them you will need the standard soft drinks and a tangy fruit punch; a sweet one only creates more thirst.

Speaking of thirst, how many of you have driven a long distance to the church, just made it down the aisle ahead of the bride's mother, filed out after the ceremony and made another long drive to the reception only to wind up at the end of a long, hot receiving line? One of the more welcome sights to greet these guests is a table near the line set with pitchers of ice water, iced tea, and lots of glasses. One doesn't have to go to a wedding to become awfully dry. Getting a glass of water in a city, or for that matter in a strange church, isn't easy. In fact, you can usually get anything except just plain ice water in a club, hotel, or restaurant, but how welcome it is when it is available!

Those of you having a home reception must get to know your garbage man, and get him to love you. The morning after the reception, particularly if it is Sunday, is going to find you facing a monumental disposal problem. Very few caterers have either a license or facilities for carrying all the refuse away, although they will clean up and stack everything. Many caterers have disposable containers for wet garbage that they will leave for you, but the disposal is up to you. In addition, you may be in an area where the family dogs are put out at sunup to range the neighborhood. If at all possible, arrange for a pickup the following morning, even if it is Sunday. And be sure the caterer stores everything securely and under cover in some predesignated spot. We speak from bitter experience.

To arrive at a final catering estimate, and to avoid hidden charges, it would be wise to start as follows: The caterer has given you a figure per head for food and service. Ask him if this includes ice, cigarettes, tables and chairs (if he is supplying them), linen, stoves, and other equipment, such as coffee urns. How much are these apiece or per dozen? The cost of the wedding cake is almost always listed separately. Does he include the nuts, mints, petits fours, and ice cream? He usually does, but check it.

Next ask about the following charges if they are not separately listed: overtime, either for all or per man, travel costs, insurance, and tips, which are usually between 10 and 15 percent of the total cover charge only. This charge is usually based on the minimum guaranteed number of people the caterer will feed. You will call this figure in to him at least three days before the reception. You are obliged to pay according to this number even if fewer actually come. However, if you go over this number, you may or may not be charged for the extras. In any event, the caterer usually has enough extra food for fifteen or twenty above the guarantee.

Next, add up the case prices for mixes and soft drinks and the case prices for champagne and liquor. Then, the total of all the sums listed above will give you a figure for your budget.

If you are doing your catering piecemeal, food here, linen there, tables and chairs elsewhere, the items of your budget will still closely coincide with all those outlined above.

Not inappropriately, we leave this chapter on a "left-over" note and with an admonition: Uneaten canapés and sandwiches, even put on ice, look awful and taste worse the next day. Caterers are loath to have anything left behind that might spoil or look unappetizing later on. The last thing they want to hear over the phone is that panic-stricken query, "Is *that* the kind of food you served my guests?" About the only dishes you are safe in carrying over are cooked ham, turkey, beef, and tongue. Those wonderful casseroles and other hot dishes can turn quite rapidly into ptomaine traps.

We hope and urge that you, the mother of the bride,

sample everything that comes your way, even if it kills you. There is an excellent chance that your daughter may never know whether or not she got anything to eat. Not a few of our clients have inadvertently bypassed the entire catering bit only to go out into the kitchen area later on to find nothing but a few very tired canapés. This did not contribute in any way to their day.

Chapter 6

Canvas

THE TERMS USED IN DESCRIBING CANVAS ARE IMPORTANT. The cover under which a reception is held is called a party tent, as distinguished from a commercial one erected, for instance, for a fair or dog show. A canopy, sometimes called connecting canvas, is used to cover entranceways or paths between tents and houses. A marquee is the term used in the Bost-Wash area for a party tent.

Having a reception under canvas, rather than in a building, has several attractive advantages. Decorations have almost unlimited possibilities, tent walls are elastic and expandable, there is no time limit, and a tent allows for individuality. On the other hand, you have a weather problem, a large-scale grounds problem, and often a parking problem.

The first thing you should decide is the type of seating and the type of food you expect to provide. Banquet tables will seat more but tend to limit your guests' freedom. Small round tables afford your guests more choice as to where they sit and with whom they sit. A formal seated and served meal requires the most space per head and a buffet-style afternoon reception, with canapés and sandwiches, the least. Between these two fall the majority of receptions with all their variations. So the number of guests expected and the proposed menu will determine the size of the tent.

Next, where on your grounds can you fit in a tent to meet your space requirements? Let's say that you need a forty-by-sixty-foot tent. You should have at least fifty by eighty feet of clear ground space to allow for corner and sidewall pole guy lines and stakes. Depending upon the height of your side-walls, you need at least eight feet of clearance along the entire perimeter. Some tents have ten-foot or twelve-foot sides. Next, keeping in mind that the center poles give a ridgepole effect, you need at least sixteen feet of clearance. These vertical measurements are very important to the tent man. He doesn't want branches staining or chafing his canvas, so you may have to prune or tie back branches in advance. Tent men are always in a hurry, and if you leave the pruning to them you are going to be left with a bizarre aftereffect. It is better to have him tell you in advance what limbs have to go.

It is possible, as long as the corners remain free, to have the side of a tent up against a tree, or even slightly wrapped around one, provided the seamlines don't meet against the trunk.

As to the land, it is not necessary to have a bowling green, but you should avoid any sharp pitches. Favor an area as close to your house and its facilities as possible. A spot at the far end of your grounds may be esthetically perfect, but to connect it to the house with canopy can be very expensive. If you have a septic tank system with a leaching field, avoid this area entirely. Four hundred milling feet over such a system can bring disaster within an hour, producing howls and pure anguish from the entire neighborhood.

We also advise against picking an inaccessible spot. Tent men usually use dollies or hand trucks to move heavy canvas and equipment. They can, but much prefer not to, back-lug everything in from their trucks. Next, don't cut the grass where the tent is going to be for at least a week before the wedding. Feet, particularly women's high heels prancing around all afternoon, can play havoc with a lawn. But as soon as the tent is down give the whole area a crew cut in the hope that filter cigarette butts will be chewed up, for they never disintegrate. If you live in an area afflicted with flying pests, at the least have all the shrubbery sprayed either the night before or the early morning of the reception day.

Canvas men use various techniques in raising tents, depending on the materials used in the tent's structure. If all the lines are manila, nothing will be in exact alignment, but if the lines used are of metal, the tents can be laid out on a tape as in a parade ground. Raising a center pole can tear up a lawn, so many use a boot-skid under the foot of the pole. Most good canvas men first put down drop cloths to keep their canvas clean. When these cloths are measured to cover the actual tent area, you can then see where the tent is going and adjust it to the best advantage. After the canvas is all up, it is usual to leave some slack if the lines are manila, for rain tightens manila, as any rag boatman knows. The morning of the reception, the crew will tighten all lines, changing stakes where necessary, so don't panic if at first your tent look awfully baggy.

Sizes and colors depend somewhat on the scope of the tent company. Although there are a few odd dimensions, the majority start with a width of twenty feet and go to sixty feet. The length is determined by the number of sections. The twenty-foot width has fifteen to twenty foot sections, while the sixty-foot width may have twenty-five or thirty foot sections. A tent 160 by 30 feet has so many sections, each with its center pole, that the whole layout looks more like Sherwood Forest than anything else. As to color, there is quite a wide variety depending upon the locale. Some are solid, but most are striped. They are usually green, blue, yellow, pink, or red with alternating white stripes. In solids, there is quite a call for green or pink, less for white, and only occasionally for blue. Solid colors are usually more expensive because they show discoloration and uneven fading more easily. The best colors to use under given situations, times of year, and times of day are dealt with in chapter 8.

The bigger concerns have liners in many colors and decorative patterns that are fitted inside the tent. They add a great deal to the "pretty" effect, but they are very expensive. When a liner is used, there is a tendency to pay less attention to the condition of the tent itself; the emphasis is on the inside. This could mean that you may have to put up with a less-than-perfect party tent flying on your back lawn.

You can rent a stripped-down tent. That is exactly what it is. And if you have a very tight budget and are willing to gamble on the weather, fine. Otherwise, specify sidewalls. They come in clear plastic, matching canvas, or a mixture of both. They are equipped with snap hooks that fasten to lines running along the inside of the tent's drop edges. Some drop straight down, and others are cut to tie along the outside of the side guy lines, thus giving you a few extra feet of cover if it rains. If you are enclosing a large area, the canvas man should have one of his men on "standby" duty during the entire reception. If your caterer is used to handling sidewalls, this may not be necessary. You use sidewalls to keep out the rain and keep in the heat. Solid canvas walls are very effective screens against unwanted views or noise. Polyethylene walls are perfect sounding boards when used to enclose a bandstand, for they throw the music out into the tent.

One of the most useful pieces of canvas equipment is the flyer. (See the diagram below.) It comes in several sizes in solid matching colors. Flyers are space stealers in that they can be attached to the tent itself at small open spots. They are useful for getting buffet tables, bars, and bandstands out of the main tent, leaving this large area free for your guests. But you can't fit a flyer onto the rounded sides of any tent so constructed. Nor can more than one side pole and its guy line be removed on any one side without weakening that side.

Most tent companies have photograph albums and brochures in color that illustrate their various layouts and color schemes. These can give you a mental picture of what you are after and where to place it. It is hard to imagine what an erected marquee will look like on your own grounds without some visual aid.

There are at least two unavoidable hazards connected with tents: stakes with their guy lines, and long storm lines leading from the top of the end center poles far out into the area. Most firms have stake covers made of canvas that serve to warn the unwary guest. Still, any stake placed near a traffic area should be greened by the florist as a safety precaution, for greening serves to point out the hazards. (See chapter 8.) This is especially necessary when twilight will be a factor. We find this half-light when everything seems to blend into the background a dangerous period. We have also seen quite a bit of plain and fancy footwork, not to mention some spectacular tumbling, during this witching hour. You don't necessarily have to be bombed to fall over an errant stake.

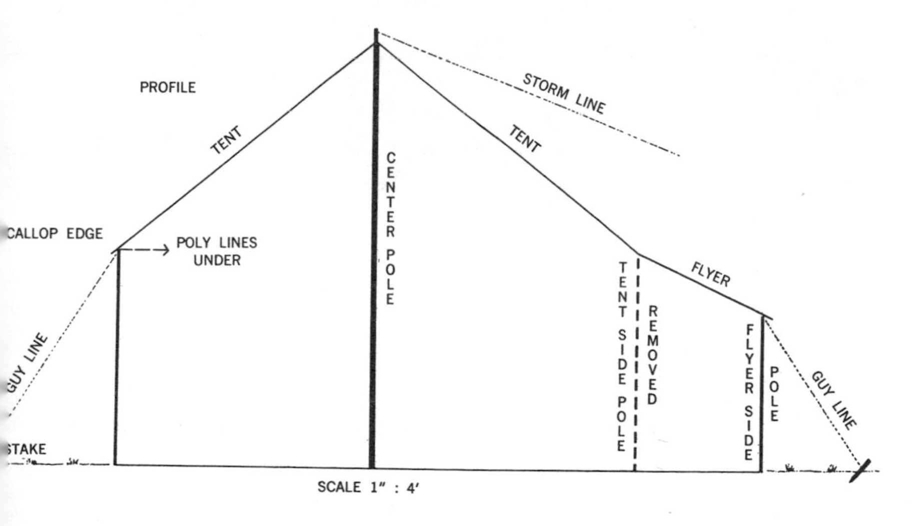

Having placed the marquee to the mutual satisfaction of you and the canvas man, your next consideration is the caterer. The essential element here is to keep the food covered from the stove to the guest. Where will the food be prepared? Even the simplest menu needs a layout place; most menus need a stove. The three most commonly used places are your kitchen, your garage, or a separate caterer's tent, less elegantly called a cook tent. The first creates an uproar in your house, no matter how efficient the staff may be, but the other two remove this entire operation from your already swollen residence. Carrying a tray full of brimming champagne glasses through a clutch of impatient guests and down a flight of stairs to a tent is no easy job. Compound this trip with all the others that will have to be made from the kitchen, and the staff will find it has had an unnecessary workout. Caterers' tents are not that expensive to rent and are well worth the cost.

This brings us to connecting canvas, or canopies, which cover walkways between structures, usually from six to eight feet in width. They are also the most expensive item in a marquee setup. The cost is based on the time and labor at so much a running foot. It is a very picky sort of work even when they are laid out in a straight line, but kitchens and garages are often at opposite sides of the living area of the house opening onto the terrace or lawn where the tent could be erected. So a well-placed cook tent, screened off from the guests with solid sidewalls and requiring only a short connection, will often save you money. Most caterers need only a garden hose and an electrical lead-in to equip it.

Inasmuch as canopies are proportionately so expensive, quite a few canvas companies have arrangements whereby all connections are measured for and included in the estimate. If you don't want one or more of these canopies, the company will accept the cancellation as late as the first thing Thursday morning before a weekend wedding without any charge. This can be true both for your house and the church. It is apt to be the case on noncrowded weekends. Other companies will frame up all connections but not cover them for half the estimated cost. This gives you the option of completion or cancellation as late as Friday afternoon. It is a form of insurance against unpredictable weather. If you decide against them, the frames will be removed before the time of the reception. No matter what you do, you are at the mercy of weather broadcasts and weather maps. So you had best keep an alert eye and ear out that last week.

Besides the expenses saved, we have seen many vistas, terraces, and lawns so visually disfigured by a thin long strip of canopy canvas, plus several tents, that the whole layout begins to look like a midway. Nevertheless we always insist, no matter what the weather may be, that the food be covered at all times. We also prefer not to take any chances either in early spring or late fall on not erecting the necessary connections.

If you live in an area liable to be hit by hurricanes, sudden high winds, or severe rainstorms, take counsel with your canvas man at the outset. He has been there many times before. If you do get a hurricane alert or warning, and nowadays weather bureaus give out fairly precise information, you have time to make an alternate plan.

If very high wind squalls such as are often associated with violent thunderstorms should hit your reception in the middle of the festivities, get everyone out and under permanent solid cover, and let the canvas go down. Once down, it can do little further damage. Never, never try to keep it from going down! Anyone caught under falling canvas should hit the deck near the sidewalls. Only the center poles can be really dangerous. Once flat, a person will not suffer much from the falling canvas alone, for canvas doesn't fall all at once. The windward guy lines give way individually, followed by the windward center pole.

If you are going to have dancing, which most people do,

you will need a dance floor. This your tent man will usually provide. While it is unnecessary to place the floor on a perfectly level piece of ground, the less construction and shimming needed to bring it approximately level, the less expense is entailed. Here again time and labor are of the essence. Needless to say, too much pitch in one direction will result in the guests dancing off the floor into the tables and chairs.

Dance floors are usually made of either plywood or matched hardwood in four-by-eight-foot sections. These sections are shiplapped and screwed down to two-by-fours with flush-type Phillips screws. All leveling construction is inserted under these timbers. Before the reception the floor should be, but not always is, lightly waxed and buffed by someone from the canvas firm. Now, unless that floor is in spirit-level condition, don't let anyone put on much wax. A dipping and glossy floor can be very dangerous.

Most of the time a bandstand is used along with a dance floor. It must not be raised so high that the dropped edge of the tent muffles the music. If you have the space, the best suggestion we have is to extend a section of the dance floor back of the tent under a flyer and put the orchestra there. Not only is this a space saver, but also the enclosed flyer acts as a dandy bandshell. When space is at a premium and the orchestra has to be placed on the grass alongside the floor, save a corner for the drums and/or the piano. Both these instruments need the resonance of a wooden floor.

We believe that, unless you have only one spot under the marquee in which to place the floor, you should wait until the main tent is up before deciding. In chapter 12 we discuss not only where to spot the floor but also where to place other equipment, such as bars, buffet tables, and their flyers if needed. It is very hard, unless you have done it on a weekly basis, to match foot traffic requirements with musical and catering areas and still have a well-balanced area for your guests.

Clients have often inquired about flooring the entire tent area. This procedure is a caterer's dream of heaven, but very expensive. We have done it for deep winter weddings when the family was either unable to get, or preferred not to use, a club or hotel facility. In each case all the important stakes were driven in before hard frost set in. The Tuesday before the Saturday wedding, all the areas were cleared of snow and plywood flooring was laid down to cover the marquee and canopy areas. Over this the tent and canopies were raised, and poly sidewalls were attached and dropped to keep out any more snow. The day before the reception, the sides were securely fastened to one-by-twelve-inch boards running around the entire perimeter of the area to keep out floor drafts. The next morning butane heaters were turned on, so that by the time the guests arrived the temperature inside the marquee was already at 60 degrees. It was a matter of timing. Too much heat or prolonged heating might have drawn the frost to the point where some of the floor timbers would have sunk and produced an undulating effect. Such a reception held behind transparent poly walls, comfortably warm inside with a junior-sized blizzard operating outside, is certainly cozy, if nothing else.

We have used paved courtyards where the canvas was flown over low trees by using gin poles. We have often covered tennis courts, and once we suspended canvas high over a privet hedge-enclosed formal garden. There is also the situation in which a swimming pool, and its immediate surroundings, is the only appropriate spot. This can be very tricky, because you have to floor over the entire pool, and if you put a dance floor over an empty pool, the dancing produces a hollow echo. The pool has to be drained down so that about a third of the water is left in it under the floor.

There are other materials used to cover ground, such as grass or felt matting. The only problem here is to keep the material quiet under a few hundred heels. If your climatic conditions and the shape of your grounds combine to produce a soaked tent area, your canvas man can, by using sidewalls, sandbags, and ditching, keep it dry. Matting won't do much good once it gets wet. Wet or dry, however, when your receiving line is out on the lawn, you should have a felt runner for the bridal party to stand on. Also, if there is the slightest chance that the passageway from the cook area to the guests can get greasy, muddy, or slippery, have an adequate length of very thick coco mat runner handy. The catering staff will be loaded down and in a hurry. And etiquette experts would never approve of a plate of hot pigs-in-a-blanket being presented to guests on the fly because a waitress fell flat in the mud.

Lighting and, often, heating enter into your canvas planning. Nothing is more dismal than a reception on a gray afternoon under unlighted canvas, which, in turn, is down in a hollow surrounded by tall trees. While lighting as a decorative factor is dealt with in chapter 8, there are certain circumstances when it is needed for safety. If your reception is to continue after sunset, or into darkness, you need full party lighting. The types of units that can be used are infinite, but they all derive from spotlights attached to center poles above eye level—ten feet or higher. These spots should be directed up into the top of the tent, giving the effect of indirect lighting, for the canvas diffuses the beams.

For safety's sake, all canopies should be equipped with strings of small bulbs running along under the ridgelines. Since the caterer may need ninety minutes or so to clean up and pack after the reception is over, his facilities should also have adequate working lights. The decorator may need outlets on the center poles and on certain sidewall poles. The band will need at least two outlets behind it; all bands seem to be electrified these days.

Many canvas companies have licensed electricians in their employ who can make these installations as part of the overall operation, or they may have permanent arrangements with an electrical firm on a subcontract basis. Failing this, you should have your own man come in. Whatever else, you must find out the total electrical current required by the caterer and tent man and see whether your fuse boxes will carry the extra load. A caterer once brought in two high-usage coffee percolators without warning us. She blew out the whole spread.

Tent heating is relatively simple. It usually consists of space heaters inside the sidewalls, butane gas tanks with cut-off valves outside, and a man from the canvas firm on standby duty to regulate the amount of heat and raise or lower the sidewalls as needed. Very often the caterer has someone familiar with this kind of operation, thus eliminating the cost of a man on standby duty. But there is one problem in connection with heated marquees that we have never been able to lick: ventilation. If the sidewalls are lifted to provide cross ventilation and eliminate smoke, those caught in the cross draft immediately howl that they are being frozen out. To keep a tent adequately aired but heated means the constant adjustment of heat and flaps. There are always some people who are too cold, others too hot. Finally the poor standby man goes off somewhere to hide, and those who are uncomfortable go home.

You don't necessarily need to have only one tent, especially when you are having a large reception on chopped-up grounds. Often the dance floor is under separate canvas, or you may add one or more smaller tents. But unless all the tents are contiguous with no line-of-sight obstructions, you may end up with several small receptions. The advantage of one large tent, with possibly a separate dance tent, is that the party remains a homogeneous unit. People tend to split up into little cliques anyway as it is, so you don't need to help. A technical note here: In any planning for a multiple canvas layout, remember that, unless you allow at least six feet between tents, the sidewall stakes of one will intrude into the other's main area.

If you are having a garden wedding and reception and have doubts about the weather, you can still have one with certainty in several ways. One is to hold the ceremony under a small marquee and the reception under a larger adjoining one to which a greater number of guests can be invited. Depending upon the setup, you can, by using one marquee for the reception, hold the ceremony in the open, with an alternate plan to fall back upon if it rains. Your home would probably be pressed into service here. Another way is to use the center section of the bigger tent for the ceremony. In this case all the tables and chairs would be set up along the sides. After the ceremony, all those in the receiving line would move to the smaller tent, already set up with small tables and a bar, while the caterer's staff managed the bigger tent. This arrangement is most suitable to those Protestant denominations where standing for the ceremony is either optional or obligatory. Even here, a row or two of chairs should be placed up front for elderly and infirm members of the families. In cases where the congregation is required to be seated, however, you are better off using a smaller tent for the ceremony and forgetting the main tent. Knocking down chairs and stacking them takes time, and makes an awful racket besides.

In all garden ceremonies you will need some kind of aisle marker, such as stanchions and white ribbons. These, as well as white satin kneelers, your florist, or possibly your church, will be able to supply.

Orthodox and Conservative Jewish ceremonies, depending upon the particular congregation, usually need, in addition to seats for all, a *huppah* or canopy, a small table covered with a white cloth, a decanter of wine, a candle, two wine goblets, and a light, fragile glass wrapped in a napkin, all of which may be supplied by your rabbi. In a Reformed ceremony, where standing is permissible, there is usually but one goblet and one candle. In all ceremonies the Sabbath candles that the bride will use in her own home may be used, and one of the goblets may be the groom's kiddush cup.

We have been dealing almost exclusively so far with a reception wholly under canvas, but there are about as many possible combinations of house plus limited canvas as there are houses. We have had many receptions where we utilized the conventional terrace with its awning in connection with cleared-out living and dining rooms, placing the dance floor under canvas beside the terrace. In one instance, where there was only background music but an elaborate seated and served dinner, we used the terrace for cocktails, serving the meal under canvas. In another reception, held in a very huge house whose grounds were suitable only for a small pup tent, we called in the local moving company. It loaded up the entire contents of all the rooms needed for the reception early Saturday morning and parked the van around the corner. That night, after the caterer had cleaned up everything, the van was brought back and all the rooms were reassembled. We have also very successfully, with poly walls and heaters, winterized terraces and those large roofed porches and verandas that many older houses have.

In figuring out how much of your house you can use, turn to your caterer. Knowing your menu, he will be able to tell you how many guests each room will hold. The congregation and movement of people within a restricted area, without the relative elasticity that canvas allows, means that two factors must be considered: individual space requirements and traffic flow. Someday somebody is going to relate the amount of space each person subconsciously wants to have around him in order to feel comfortable to the tenor of the times. Today there is a strong trend toward privacy and seclusion. The reaction to megalopolis, bumper-to-bumper traffic, and housing developments may be the reason. In party terms, people no longer are as happy to be packed in like sardines as they were ten years ago. Add this factor to the mechanics of eating, drinking, and talking, and you will find a room won't hold quite as many as you first thought.

People movement is a fascinating study. They always seem to stand around in clumps at receptions. They tend to block doorways and passageways and spill into small rooms. If there is a dead-end room, that's the one they head for. In using any combination of house and canvas, terrace or porch, each area should lead into another to avoid a dead-end situation.

The area around a receiving line is always the worst. People will clutter it up, and they won't move on. But you can Pied Piper them along if your bar or other refreshment table is placed in full view and as far as possible from the line. The caterer's people who are passing champagne also contribute to this congestion by standing as close as possible to the last bridesmaid in the line. The theory is that the guest should be offered a glass as he or she leaves the line—the epitome of hospitality. It is much better to have the waiter stationed some distance away. No one is that avid for a glass of champagne. Then again, some of our clients, particularly when space permits, have had champagne served to those standing in line. We like this idea. It serves not only to break up the tedium of the queue but also as an icebreaker. However, waiters with *empty* trays should be stationed to receive empty glasses *before* the guests reach the receiving line.

Bathroom facilities are always a problem with a house reception. The longer the reception lasts, the more acute this problem becomes. The minimum requirements are usually one upstairs and one down for ladies and gentlemen respectively. We have no ratio, though, for the number required per X number of guests. The bathroom supplies necessary for a reception are probably best described by the following instructions:

1. Designate room and bath where caterer's help can change into their uniforms. Supply with extra clothes hangers (wire ones will do).
2. Designate bathroom for female guests—two if you can.
3. Supply the following:
   A. Plenty of towels. I suggest attractive paper ones instead of linen because guests, especially the men, hesitate to use them. Extra soap.
   B. Replace usual receptacle for used towels with an extra large one.
   C. Leave plenty of toilet paper visible and handy—at least five rolls in each bathroom.
   D. Stock bathrooms designated for guests with aspirin, antacids, ampules of spirits of ammonia, dental floss, straight pins, safety pins of assorted sizes, Band-Aids, sanitary napkins and tampons, ashtrays, air fresheners.
4. Lock up expensive perfumes and all small bric-a-brac.

While we are on the subject of these facilities, we wish to point out that throughout the United States there are available for rent portable toilets similar to those you see on big construction projects. Few houses are built to accommodate several hundred additional people for several hours. So if the capacities of your house are limited, you can provide complete toilet facilites for both men and women under small tents. Be sure to place them a little distance from the main marquee. The portable toilets should be in place before the tents are erected. Since they are very heavy, awkward, and stand eight feet high at least, it is very hard to fit them under canvas that is already up. Don't forget mirrors, small caterers' tables to serve as dressing tables (two items we have upon occasion forgotten until the last moment), and an ample supply of Wash 'n Dri.

The next thing you must consider is how your guests are going to get from the church to your home. If the house is within walking distance, all those who came by car can simply use the church parking area. If it is not, they will have to drive. This means you are going to have to cope with a parking problem. Now, if you divide the total number of expected guests by two and add a baker's dozen for musicians and catering transportation, you will get a fair idea of the number of cars that will all converge on you at once. In most cases the police can solve this quandary by allocating off-street parking near your home. Failing this, you may have to turn to a designated parking area, using a shuttle system. Renting school buses or other mass transportation vehicles is about the easiest. If this is impossible, then you may have to call in a professional parking service. These companies provide drivers who give each owner a car check at the front door and then drive the car to a lot. When a guest is ready to leave, his number is called by radio to the lot, and a driver returns the car to the front door. A few tent companies provide this service, but if not, either the tent or catering firm will know of a firm with whom it has worked.

While this operation is used only for very large receptions, we have had occasion to use various shuttling methods for as few as seventy-five people. Steep hills, narrow roads with deep gutters, general inaccessibility of the bride's house, and local parking regulations may make shuttling a necessity. If you are having a large reception and such conditions as these prevail, it may be less expensive in the long run to go to a club or inn.

When you are using open fields, your own or a neighbor's, with perhaps a few off-duty policemen to do the parking for you, stake off all low spots. Also be sure that the entrance is on high ground. A heavy downpour can turn an innocent green meadow into a dismal swamp when a hundred or so cars start churning it up. And that means a tow truck.

We don't know how police departments operate in other parts of the United States. In our area a member of the department in each town is designated to look after parties of any size. Standard practice is to assign one or more uniformed men to handle all vehicular traffic on the public roads, both at the church and at the place of the reception. If additional men are needed for parking or to act as watchmen, you make such arrangements directly with the officer in charge. Each police department sets its own fees for these services, some by the hour, some by the job. But wherever you live, you should begin initially with your own police. They are the experts.

In connection with all this, there are two other pieces of canvas equipment that you may want to use. One is a carport that extends from your front door out over the driveway, similar to the old-fashioned porte cochere. This is great for rainy weather. The driver can let all his passengers out under cover so that only he gets wet. The other is the canopy at the church. Many metropolitan churches have their own canopies or use a particular canvas firm on a yearly basis. Check with the church office. Country churches seldom have their own, but most canvas men have the measurements of all local churches on file.

Church canopies, carpets, and white runners seem to go together in our minds, like ham and Swiss on rye. The great majority of ceremonies use a white runner. This will be discussed in detail later, but you cannot put down a white runner on a bare church floor; it is too dangerous. If the church has no aisle carpet, you can usually get a temporary one from your canvas man.

There are two more things for you to check out. Have your septic system, if you have your own, cleaned out before, not after, the reception. One addlepated parent happily had the septic tank service people come the Monday after her daughter's wedding, to the dismay and discomfort of the entire neighborhood. The other matter is your liability insurance policies. Almost all canvas and catering concerns are insured to the hilt for any accident occurring through the use of their equipment. But how about the half-concealed root, the woodchuck or gopher hole?

Taking all things into consideration, a house reception can be perfectly lovely and is certainly your own individual endeavor. It means a lot of work and not a few headaches, but if you have the time and the energy it is well worth every second. Most of our clients who have had one club and then one home reception tell us that if they had a third daughter, they would not even contemplate holding the reception anywhere but their own home.

Chapter 7

Clubs, Hotels, and Restaurants

THE TWO PREVIOUS CHAPTERS HAVE DEALT WITH A home reception. This one will attempt to deal with a reception that cannot be held at home. The usual substitutes for the home are clubs, hotels, inns, restaurants, church parlors, and community rooms. Here again quite a variety of facilities and services is available. The big urban-suburban clubs and hotels and restaurants can provide you with just about anything. Parish rooms or community halls usually can offer little more than the space, the amenities, and a bare kitchen without food, service, or the wherewithal to prepare and serve a meal. These are the extremes. In the case of the former, the club or hotel acts through its manager or banquet head as your caterer and general coordinator. In the latter you have to cope with everything.

Let's take clubs first. Of all the places with fixed walls, they still offer the most flexibility in terms of space. There is usually a terrace or patio that can be winterized with poly sidewalls. In summer a marquee can be erected. This serves to afford you a third room connected to the clubrooms you are using. We know of several country clubs and at least two inns that have season contracts with local tent companies to provide tents, tables, chairs, and so on for every Saturday and Sunday from the first of June to the weekend after Labor Day.

You will have two problems with a club manager: one, space; two, food and liquor. Accept the figure of the maximum number of people he says he can accommodate. When you give him your final head count, try to keep to that figure. If you are nearing a sardine-packed condition, don't compound it and his grief by adding twenty or thirty more guests the morning of the reception. This head count is important. It governs the amount of food, the number of help, and the equipment that he will need to plan for. Getting additional help and equipment on short notice during the busy months is almost impossible.

When it comes to the selection of a menu, ask for his recommendations based on the type of reception you have in mind. He has been serving any number of varied menus fitted to the different receptions that have been held in the several clubs where he has been employed. He usually knows the capabilities as well as the limitations of his kitchen staff. So if he balks at some special suggestions you propose, it is because he knows that his chef can't or won't handle them. This "won't" is important. The troubles any manager has today with staff problems have reached monumental proportions. He is walking a very thin tightrope between what the membership wants and what his staff will do. He may even have trouble finding the number of help he needs to arrange the rooms at your request. For this reason most managers have set notions about receptions, plus several variations.

In discussing liquor and champagne, be sure to specify brands. If the manager wants certain brands unknown to you, ask your local liquor dealer's opinion first. Resign yourself to a high bar bill. The bar is often the factor that offsets the high cost of the snack bar, dining room, or some other amenity. If it didn't, your yearly assessment would soar. You can always ask a member who has had a similar reception what his bar bill came to, thus anticipating one budget item. You can also control the maximum amount to be consumed by one of two measures: limit the total amount to be served and, when that is reached, that is that—not too friendly an idea, but definitely an economical one—or shut down the bars when the bride and groom leave.

Club managers, maître d's, and banquet managers can all serve one very useful purpose. They can take the load of a lot of detail off your back. This is especially true when you use a hotel, restaurant, or inn. However, there are a few hotels and restaurants that have a "pecking order," and your position in that order is determined by the amount you are prepared to spend. In your first interview—whether at a leading hotel, where that gentleman known as the banquet manager will give you a personal tour of the rooms available, or at the smallest restaurant—your financial position will be expertly gauged and there will be a penetrating appraisal of you.

However, you should be able to strike a happy medium between an establishment's most expensive and minimum menus. Banquet managers and restaurant owners can be an enormous help, especially if you let it be known that you are not averse to generous tipping in return for effort and service.

In restaurants that offer package deals, talk about adding a few extras to improve the arrangements or you may wind up with one of those skimpy receptions at which, unbelievably, the waiter asks your guests when they want their *other* glass of champagne as he leans across the centerpiece to pour the first.

The package deal usually includes food, so many glasses of champagne, so many highballs or cocktails, a limited variety of floral decorations, and the smallest orchestra that can still be heard—all at so much per head. Your time of occupancy is often limited; you and your guests must be out at a certain hour, for another reception is coming in. If the per head price seems too high, get the manager to break it down by category, including decorations and music. Then you can get an outside estimate on the last two items, which you may be able to get cheaper. But if economy and freedom from detail are your *leitmotiv,* it is hard to beat an honest package deal—although there are few of them.

Hotels and restaurants are less flexible than clubs as far as the number of people they can hold. They not only have to deal with the physical presence of people, but also, being places of public assembly, they are further restricted by maximum occupancy laws and ordinances. Don't try to go over the manager's maximum; it could mean his permit or license and a fat fine.

When it comes to table arrangements, placing the orchestra—if there is no permanent bandstand—and placing the bar and buffet tables, the banquet manager will have very definite ideas. They are based on long experience with the flow of guests as against the flow of service personnel, and service is going to win. He will tell you, very politely, that's the way it will be. Determined opposition on your part will eventually produce one of his variations more to your liking but less convenient to the help. Also, his advice on setting up the receiving line is very valuable. He knows to the last body the traffic patterns of your guests and how to avoid jams without seeming to. People hate, especially at a social function, to be herded like sheep, but sometimes space restrictions make it necessary.

Long experience enables managers to arrange banquet tables to seat the most people and still leave the staff enough room to serve and move between tables. One drawback in such maximum seating is that almost one-third of the guests will have their backs to the action, i.e., the dance area and the bridal tables, which are usually placed in a center or center-wall position. We have sometimes avoided this situation by setting the tables in an oblique angle, so that only the person sitting at the near end of each table has his back to the epicenter, an appropriate word when viewed in the light of modern dance steps. Then, if you really want to make the manager's day, or, for that matter, his week, ask him to substitute round tables of varying sizes for all his square and rectangular ones. Then hire a bodyguard.

When the placing of the band is not solved for you by a bandstand or stage, the manager will know, either from his own experience or from what bandleaders have told him, what area best projects music. Also, almost all bands now have electrically amplified instruments. Outlets for these have become a necessity and are usually already in place. Several electrical leads snaking along the floor are not only a hazard, but also look messy.

Your final choice for the band in turn dictates where dancing, if any, will be, which in turn has a bearing upon the bride's table if you are having one. You should fit these activities together so that there is but one center of attraction. Try not to diffuse them. We will go into the arrangement of rooms and marquee space in chapter 11. By the time you get there you will have a general idea of how many bodies you have to contend with.

A great many hotels and restaurants have scale diagrams of their public rooms. Some of these are laid out in squares equivalent to so many feet each. From these you can lay out your table arrangements. If you get into any details here (more properly left to the maître d') you should allow two feet for each chair. Thus a four-foot-square table would really take up an eight-foot-square space. Then, by allowing a foot and a half around this unit for service and guest passage, you can juggle the units around until you get the arrangement you want.

Some of the big tent companies provide charts of standard-sized tents laid out to scale. They also include cutout cardboard figures representing, let us say, forty-eight-inch round tables or eight-foot banquet tables. Such a set will come in handy when the tent finally goes up. Then you can check your horizontal layout with the vertical appearance of the tent and its background.

Restaurants and hotels are apt to be more amenable to your decorative ideas than club managers, as long as their normal operations are not impeded by a flood of interior decorators and florists. However, some hotels do specify the florist you should use. From previous working experience the banquet manager knows the requirements of the particular florist and that this florist will make his installations efficiently, disturbing normal staff operations as little as possible. Others don't care so long as the florist gets finished, doesn't mess up the ballroom, carries away his trash, and leaves enough time for the staff to give the place a quick "once-over-lightly" before the bridal party comes in the door.

There may be other facilities available for your reception. Many areas have community houses with assembly halls and kitchens. Some private country clubs have only snack bars. There are many "association" buildings that prove perfectly adequate. The latter should be treated more as you would a home reception, subject to the particular bylaws or house rules regarding decorative installations, what caterers can come in, and so on. Some, but not many, may have a time limit, after which the premises must be cleared. Most of them have the same fire and occupancy regulations as do hotels. They usually have adequate parking facilities, which many hotels do not. In any event, you can normally bring in your own florist, caterer, orchestra, and liquor. Obviously the overall cost will be lower and more flexible than that of a hotel. You can add or cut to meet your budget. In using an association hall or a community house assembly room you may, in effect, be substituting a small rental fee for a large canvas bill.

Speaking of ways to accommodate a larger number of guests than your home can handle, don't forget the church parlor or parish hall. These very necessary additions to churches have recently burgeoned throughout the land. But what you can do, and how you can do it, is a matter between you and the appropriate committee of the church body. Generally speaking, you can bring in your own catering, whether or not you use the kitchen facilities. Within certain broad limitations, the normal floral decorations would be sanctioned. Few churches would ban background music, and most churches would permit dancing of the less ultramodern variety. But when it comes to anything stronger than fruit punch, you may have a problem. We have had one or two such receptions at which champagne was permitted. We have heard of but have not personally been present at a reception in a parish hall at which the hostess was permitted to have hard liquor passed from the pantry. We have never heard of or encountered an open bar. But see your minister, priest, or rabbi; something new is always happening these days. Besides, practices, viewpoints, and customs of many churches and sects may well be less restrictive than those outlined above.

Now we would like to discuss the relative advantages and disadvantages of the reception at home and the one away from home, along with the relative costs. The home reception permits you to exercise your decorative talents to the limit. You have all the time in the world, and you can, within reason and a proper regard for the neighbors, do just about anything you wish: complete individual freedom and flexibility in numbers, food, and liquids. A reception held in any place outside your home is going to be restricted in one way or another. You can be limited as to numbers, decorations, and time. You are up against bylaws, house rules, public laws, and so on. No matter what the management may do for you, they, not you, are kings of the castle. Try as both you and the manager may, the reception will still look as though it were cut out by one of several cookie cutters. You can do only so much to any room. There are exceptions to this, but whether the party is held in a luxury hotel, a big country club, or a little community house, putting your stamp of individuality on it is going to be expensive.

As any housewife knows, the preparation for and the cleaning up after just a small cocktail party entail work, as well as stress and strain. When you put this entire matter into a manager's hands your job then becomes one of supervising rather than producing. The home remains undisturbed, the grounds don't need major or minor landscaping, there is no parking problem, and you don't have to call in the interior decorator. You are able to enjoy relative peace and quiet. If you go back over the details in the previous two chapters with a view to making as few piecemeal arrangements as necessary, the desirability of putting everything and its coordination into some other, competent hands becomes apparent.

There is also the matter of family pets. We once had a fairly large country reception held on an erstwhile colonial farm. The hostess, a widow, had several large dogs, the kind that don't recognize a fence and barely tolerate a door. Off to the vet they went. When the reception was about to begin and the last of eight lovely bridesmaids had been placed at the end of the receiving line, five assorted sizes and breeds of neighboring dogs arrived, sat down in line next to the last bridesmaid, and stayed there. Real scene-stealers they were, and they knew it. The guests all cooed, "How perfectly wonderful and so in character with dear Mary to have included the family dogs."

The family cat is going to take a dim view of any home reception and will make a point of getting lost for the day at least. We have heard of several that used the general upheaval as an excuse to go AWOL for as long as a week. You might conclude that we consider the family dog and cat to be obstacles in the path of the home reception. Actually, 98 percent of the four-footed occupants present no problems at all.

As to comparative costs, the do-it-yourself home reception without canvas is the least expensive. Next most reasonable and in order of increase are the church parlor, the community house where a rental is involved, the hotel or restaurant package deal, and the formal dinner at a top hotel. At the far end of the scale is the seated and served evening reception at home under canvas. The hotel is cheaper because the bar bill is less than the cost of canvas, there is no parking charge, and you need one less musician because it is indoors. The country club reception, by the way, stands about midway. If you would have to use canvas at home, the total costs of a club reception may run between 10 and 15 percent under those in your home for the same number of people.

If your guest list is so large that it is beyond the capacity of any nearby club or hotel, you will be forced to use your home or to borrow a friend's for the occasion. We are thinking of those receptions that run to five hundred or more guests, although these are very much the exception today. However, you will find that the per head cost of catering, canvas, decorations, and music will noticeably decrease beyond the three hundred point: that's one consolation.

In conclusion, we personally feel that whenever possible a home reception is the best, as we said in chapter 6. It is the most intimate, the most pleasant for everyone—even the hostess—and the most memorable.

Chapter 8

Decorations

In this chapter we are going to use the term "florist" to mean a person who works professionally with flowers, foliage, and greens of all kinds, fresh and artificial, and the term "decorations" to cover all flowers, plants, shrubs, foliage, and trees used where the marriage ceremony takes place, as well as where the reception is held.

Most women well understand that floral decorations give individuality to any wedding or party, and are the single element most remembered. But most men couldn't care less about them. Some are even hostile especially when they have to pay for them because flowers can't be eaten or drunk, are expensive, and just die.

If the father of the bride gives you, the mother of the bride, a hard time about the cost of decorations, tell him to concentrate on that list of the brands of whiskey he wants served at the reception and leave the decorations to you. The cost of flowers, if you live in the Bost-Wash area, will stun you. And if you are planning the wedding immediately after Easter, around Mother's Day, Thanksgiving, or anytime around the Christmas holidays, an estimate from a florist will send you into shock. Prices during these times, when the demand far exceeds the supply, are at their highest. If you are working on a strict budget where each and every penny has to count, avoid these periods, which, unfortunately, are so popular with brides-to-be.

As for finding a florist with talent who can be trusted not to cheat you, there are many around the country, but *discovering* one is a lot harder than you may realize. If you live in or near an urban area, you can afford to be more selective in the choice of a good one. A "good florist" is defined as one who understands, both by instinct and experience, the value of understatement and practices it in his work. The florist who can capture the feeling of a particular interior, whether it be church or home, and can achieve an effect that enhances it by means of decorations is an artist. The ones we work with are artists, and they go to the wholesale flower market in person not once but several times before any wedding or party decorating they do under our supervision.

A florist with taste and a discerning eye can pick up the beautiful fresh and *different* flowers and greens by going from specialty house to specialty house, early in the morning, until he finds the blossoms in the colors he will need to fill your basic order—or finds alternate flowers for your arrangements. Those early morning shopping tours in person are what make the difference between a "good florist" and one who is interested primarily in the amount of his bill. The latter will suggest to a customer those "easy" run-of-the-mill flowers like glads, snapdragons, belladonna delphinium as opposed to the quality hybrids, carnations, and some varieties of roses he knows he can store in his refrigerator and unload to his regular trade if he overorders for your wedding.

The best course to follow to find the most qualified florist for the job is to check him out in every reasonable way possible, ask all the questions that come to your and your daughter's minds, agree on the general overall color scheme, discuss the flowers of your first choice—and give him the latitude to switch to alternates when your first choices are not available. Get an estimate *in writing,* agree on costs by putting a ceiling on what you will spend, and then delegate to him the authority needed to carry out the plans.

Most florists will send you an estimate that is itemized but does not show the total cost at a glance: They leave the addition to you. Get the total cost added up before you even think about the items listed. You could be carried away by the thought of each lovely arrangement. Don't be. Try to think of those items in terms of what you really need and see what you may, on second thought, be able to delete. We have the estimates for decorations that are submitted to a client list first the items and arrangements we think are basic. Then come additional suggestions, including substitutions, for optional arrangements we and the flower arranger think would add to the basic plan. In this way the client is left to make her own decisions as to what she would like to delete, add, or even substitute. This seems to be a fairer way of going about the financial details concerned with decorations—and the total costs are added up by the flower arranger.

We advise working with only one florist if possible, for by doing this you cut down on conflicts arising from temperaments, differences in taste, skills, and methods of working, and professional jealousy. Remember you are going to be doing all the work on the wedding without the assistance of a social secretary to act as buffer. In order for you to enjoy the wedding, it's best to eliminate the probable disaster areas in advance. You will see later on why working with two florists is sometimes impossible to avoid on prime dates. If this proves to be your situation, keep the two florists completely apart. These people are engaged in one of the "ulcer professions," as are most people in the firms and services used for weddings and parties. Consider for a moment what happens to a florist on those prime dates we have mentioned:

Roman Catholic churches usually have several wedding masses scheduled, with little or no time in between even to carry in already fixed arrangements to set on the main and side altars, to take care of attaching aisle markers or white pew ribbons, or for the florist and his crew to pick up after themselves and flee before the guests for the next wedding begin to fill the church. All of this is difficult enough at best, but if someone in the parish has died in the middle of the week of *your* daughter's nuptial mass, the funeral mass for the deceased will have to take place on that prime Saturday, too, and all this *before noon*. So, along about Thursday, the poor florist, who has been sweating out the possibility of a funeral to further complicate the logistics, starts calling the church to find out how bad Saturday is going to be. Usually only the priest can tell him definitely.

Besides this funeral possibility, there may be short marriage ceremonies in the early afternoon or one very large one scheduled for 3:30 P.M., the usual hour for mixed marriages.

In Protestant churches, sometimes three or four weddings are scheduled on a prime date, usually with one and a half hours between ceremonies.

Synagogues or temples usually will have only two weddings on the same date, one with a luncheon or buffet reception following it and possibly one in the evening with a ceremony at six-thirty or later.

The only sensible answer to these problems of prime dates is for all the brides and their mothers, whether or not they are acquainted, to meet well in advance of the big day to see if they can agree on one florist, the flowers to be used in the decorations, and the cost, and share the basic expenses. If one bride wants a more elaborate plan, it might be completed between ceremonies by adding other arrangements, just as aisle markers have to be changed or put on at the last minute before the guests are ushered into the place of worship.

But at least all would have a basic plan that a good florist could work out so as to avoid the nearly impossible between-wedding mad dashes.

Often such agreements cannot be reached by the various brides and their mothers because a bride whose ceremony is scheduled earlier or later does not plan to have any but the simplest, most inexpensive decorations. If this is so, the bride (and her mother) who is having the larger, more elaborate wedding should ask if her florist may decorate the church early in the morning so that all the other brides can enjoy the setting for their ceremonies. If this is refused, the tactful gesture is to invite the others to pay your florist whatever amount they had in their budget for decorations. Give a little. We have known many instances where a very young couple being married with only twenty people present, or a middle-aged widow and widower who have invited only their children and grandchildren, have had the full benefit of the most beautiful decorations available without the uncomfortable feeling that they were taking a free ride on a wealthy family. Occasionally, a bride wishes only the simplest kind of floral decoration. If so she will have to pay for removal or arrange a different time for the ceremony. It's all in the manner in which you present this sensible compromise plan to a less fortunate bride than the one in your household. Almost every minister, priest, and rabbi has at some time or other found his place of worship turned into what looked like the inside of a florist's refrigerator. As a result, most of them have evolved rules governing decorations. One cannot blame them in the least. You should find out what the rules are in your place of worship before you meet there with your florist.

If you are a member of a church that has an altar guild, talk to its chairman and get her ideas of what looks best. Most churches and other places of worship have very definite styles of their own that should be taken into consideration by a florist. The ladies who work in altar guilds are well aware of this as a rule and know what goes best in the containers that belong to the church and what is in scale to the altar or the mensa behind it. For this reason, many altar guilds insist on having a member present when you meet in the church with your florist, especially if he is not familiar with that church and its rules about decorations. If this is your situation, be sure also at the same time to discuss lighting, the number of pews you plan to reserve (if any), the type of aisle markers, the number of them, the white ribbons for the main aisle, and check to see if the church has a carpet and a canopy available for the main door if you need one. Large city churches, synagogues, and temples usually have printed lists, which they give you at the time you reserve the wedding date, of such items and the rental charges for them. If yours is a church without these items available, your florist will be able to rent them for you.

In New York City, many churches and other places of worship have an "official florist," or a choice of several, whom they expect you to use. This does not mean, of course, that you have to use these florists for the bridal bouquet, bridesmaids' flowers, corsages for yourself, the groom's mother, and grandmothers, or for the boutonnieres for the groom, best man, ushers, and fathers. It would simplify things if you could, but you just might find yourself stuck with some official florist who's great with funeral pieces, skimpy on decorations, and hasn't had a new idea about a bridal bouquet in thirty years. If you should find yourself in this position, just tell him that all flowers for the wedding party are going to be delivered to the bride's room (if there is one in the church) forty-five minutes before the ceremony and that his responsibilities are limited to the church decorations only. Be firm. This could very well happen if you are sharing the costs with the families of other brides being married on the same date.

Have your own chosen florist take care of the wedding flowers for the bridal party and forget that "official" one.

Yours will send an assistant along to show the bride and the bridesmaids how to hold and carry their bouquets in a relaxed and graceful manner. By then the church florist will have done his work and be long gone and "never the twain shall meet."

One question is often raised: "What do we do with the flowers at the church, or at both the church and the reception, afterward?" In cities and the larger suburbs, a florist's footwork has to be fleet, and a staff of three, four, or more veteran assistants, plus a deliveryman, is a must, so to ask him to deliver the flowers from the church and the reception to a hospital after the guests leave can be the final straw on one of those prime dates. However, go ahead and ask him, but be prepared to pay him extra for the time and those papier-mâché containers he will have to substitute for the good ones he uses for his decorations, or those that belong to the church. Remember the flowers belong to you, but the florist's containers are merely rented to you. Of course, you might wish to buy them. He will tell you that each one costs him between $1.75 and $5.00 wholesale, and that the cost of labor involved in having two of his men pick up the flowers, transfer them to papier-mâché containers, deliver them to the hospital of your choice, and return to the shop would end up being as much as sending a whole new order of fresh flowers directly; that his flowers and greens were cut and arranged for particular containers and that, once removed from them, packed in florists' boxes, and delivered to a hospital, they would be about as welcome as an outbreak of measles on the maternity floor.

In short, whatever you have in mind for the flowers *afterward* should be worked out well in advance among you, your minister, priest, or rabbi, and your florist.

Many people have the happy notion that what they call "simple" decorations are less costly than others. This is one of those misleading half-truths that cause confusion and acute disappointment to many brides and their mothers on the wedding day. To achieve a successful look of "lots and lots of daisies and field flowers appearing not to have been arranged at all, but to have been freshly gathered in the morning dew" is not only one of the most difficult to create but the most expensive because of the labor involved and the lack of staying power in the flowers themselves. It takes masses of them so that they are not lost in bridesmaids' bouquets, and, worn in the hair, they can take on the appearance of wilted lettuce before the day is half done. The heat generated by the human head, incidentally, is a fast killer of flowers, except for carnations and the dianthus family in general.

The large, firm Majestic daisy, if well conditioned and arranged, is lovely for the bride whose heart is set on daisies, and it can be combined with cornflowers, or bachelor's buttons, provided they are used in their natural full size, together with great big ones formed by binding eight or ten regular ones together. This is done about the same way one builds up a "cabbage" or "Duchess" rose. Pretty as they are, they are just as expensive as any other flowers you might choose. Also, this combination has become very trite because it has been beaten to death by repetition everywhere for so long.

For those of you who live in benign climates where many types of flowers grow in profusion, the choices are greater, and the costs are less than in the New York area where—even in June, when our gardens are in bloom—wedding flowers have to be trucked, or flown in by airfreight, from long distances. To be sure, we New Yorkers can get just about any kind of flower, but the cost is great.

Even geraniums, unless bought before Memorial Day and tended in pots with lots of expert loving care, are seldom available for June weddings. Peonies are on the way out, bouvardia is hard to come by, and so is lily of the valley. There are no camellias, but gardenias are with us always, as are the orchids of most species and their ever present mate, stephanotis.

Since this book is for people everywhere in our fifty states, it would be folly to try to go into the various kinds of flowers available regionally. All we can hope to do here is to pass along to you some of the broad, general bits of knowledge we have gleaned. One of the most important is to decorate at eye level or above. However, keep table arrangements low enough not to interfere with across-table visibility. Proportion is very important, too. A thirty-six-inch round table with a centerpiece, no matter how lovely, that is too large or too small (like those bud vases with spindly bases) can look terrible. Centerpieces, no matter how delicate, should always have firm bases and be in scale with the table on which they are to be set. This is especially true for a formal bridal table where members of the wedding party are seated according to plan and place cards are used.

The centerpiece in front of the bride and groom should be low enough so that they may be seen. This is, after all, the day when they are the center of attention. Frequently we suggest that no centerpiece be used in front of their places at the bridal table and the space left available for the bride to lay her bouquet down, facing out. In this case, it's attractive if a pair of family three-piece silver candelabra are used (plated ones *newly polished* may be rented, too) on either side of the couple's places. We have the florist remove the bobeche from the middle of each candelabrum and replace it with one we have, which is glass and can be fitted in firmly. These can be used for delicate arrangements set in oases, which cannot be seen if string smilax is used with them properly. They may be made of bouvardia, tuberoses, lily of the valley, stephanotis, small camellias, gardenias, or white roses —any type of little flower. Two eighteen-inch slow-burning candles may be used in the outer holders of the candelabrum and should be lit just before the bridal party is seated. Other flower arrangements—usually three to seven, depending upon the length of the table—should also be low. If fewer arrangements are used, each bridesmaid should place her bouquet, also facing out, on the bridal table when she arrives at her place.

For the afternoon reception at which no meal is served, a formal bridal table, in our opinion, is out of place. It seems silly to have one all set up and then watch waiters pass canapés to the bridal party. Nor can they very well be served different food from that of the rest of the guests. Our solution is to have one very large round table—sixty or seventy-two inches—with a skirt in white, made to match that of the cake table. Use all-white decorations on it. Ten, twelve, fourteen, or more chairs may be used with such a table, but no place cards. It is never formally seated, but it is a table reserved for the bride and groom and any members of their wedding party who may wish to sit down, or for grandmothers and grandfathers who may want to sit with them for a while before moving on to join other guests. These "reserved for the bridal party" tables are becoming quite popular in this time of easy informality, and they, too, can have a centerpiece, with space left around it for the bridesmaids to leave their bouquets.

There are many ways of treating a bridal table or one of the reserved round tables just described. If a meal is to be served, then the formal bridal table with place cards is a must. Our flower arrangers make various skirts that can be pinned around three sides, and the table is formed by combinations of four, six, eight, or ten-foot-long rectangular tables, which are usually thirty inches high and thirty inches wide. These dimensions are pretty much standard all over the country now, and the tables used for gifts, buffets, and bars are the same. In making up such a bridal table, which has seating on one side only plus a place at each end, it is important to avoid having a table leg just where someone has to put a leg. This is why we use tables of various lengths. The chairs are lined up and put in place before the basic tablecloth is laid. Then the caterer, the club manager or whoever is in charge of setting it up, *and* the florist all know exactly what they are working with. Good linen or damask should be used for the top, big enough to form an overhang of at least three feet on the inside, where the bridal party is to be seated. Then the florist attaches the skirt around the three sides. It may be made of satin, white organdy, nylon net, or any of the materials that can be pleated or shirred loosely to fall to one inch above the floor, ground, or lawn. The skirt should be even all the way around and not transparent or it will look like a sheer skirt on a woman who has forgotten to wear a slip. (This can happen in clubs where no prior provision has been made by you and the florist for an undercloth.)

Often there are fine linen or damask banquet cloths in a bride's family that seldom see the light of day except for special occasions. If there be any in your linen closet, by all means get them out and use them for the bridal table. (Check for those telltale yellow marks along the folds.) The cost of having these lovely old banquet cloths laundered by hand is becoming frightfully expensive, but if you can't enjoy using them for a wedding in your family, why are you keeping them?

You may not have a lace cloth long enough or large enough to drape over a basic cloth of your own, the caterer's, or the club's, but you may have one that the florist could drape around the cake table. We like to use a separate thirty-six-inch or forty-eight-inch round table for the wedding cake, and our flower arrangers make a skirt matching that of the bridal table for it. These small round tables, whether on casters or not (two waiters can carry one easily), have the mobility we like to count on so that they may be placed near the bride and groom on the dance floor when token slices of the wedding cake are cut. Then the table is moved off to the side where the help can cut and serve the cake to the guests.

Another way to handle the cake table is to have all the bridesmaids wheel it to a predetermined position in front of the bridal table for the bride and groom to cut their token slices. This makes for a rather pretty ceremony of its own, for it serves to keep the bridesmaids all together around the bridal couple in a circle to which may be added both sets of parents and the small-fry among the guests for whom this is the moment they have been waiting for all afternoon.

If there is to be a toast, this is the time when the best man gives it. With the help of the orchestra, he will have everyone's attention so that what he says can be heard. (Please see chapter 14 for further details.)

As for the guest tables at receptions, we always prefer round ones. If this is not possible because of space limitations, then we like to use a combination of rectangular—in the corners and background—and round ones, at least to outline a dance floor. Linen in a color on these tables can go a long, long way to aid in the decorations. Most clubs have a linen service or can rent colored cloths for you. They are well worth the cost, for even very simple arrangements of various greens —without flowers—can be used against colored cloths to cut costs if your budget is a tight one. So can the use of tall candles firmly set in holders in the middle of a centerpiece of foliage. If you are using colored tablecloths, the bars and buffet should also be covered in the same color. This leaves only the formal bridal table, or reserved table for the bridal party, and the cake table all in white and puts the emphasis where it belongs.

Brides and their mothers are always concerned about where the receiving line is to be, and they usually choose the place that will make the prettiest setting. This is fine, provided the receiving line is as far away as possible from the entrance for the guests. And this goes for summer, spring, fall, and winter weddings at home in the living room, under a marquee, at a club, or wherever you have the reception.

The very first choice of where to receive is in front of a mantelpiece, or at least that is what everyone seems to want.

We call it the "mantel syndrome." If the mantel you have in mind is of shoulder height (about five feet) you are fortunate. But if it's one of those that are just above head level or higher, forget about it. The latter is the deadly type because any decorations placed on it—even simple combinations of greens—will make the members of the bridal party in the receiving line look just like those beautiful Grecian caryatids *holding up* the Erechtheum on the Acropolis.

The mantel in most homes and clubs has a painting or a large mirror above it. Both are deadly enemies to the candid photographer. If the mantel you have in mind as the background for the receiving line has either of these objects above it, have it removed for the reception. This will leave you with a picture hook and perhaps some discoloration on the wall. Think nothing of it; your florist can cover it with greens or a garland of greens in which flowers of your choice may be inserted after the greening is completely secure. These flowers should all be in plastic tubes, or water picks, so they will remain fresh.

Or, if the reception is in a club, the mantel may be one of those baronial beasts that hasn't been cleaned properly since Coolidge didn't choose to run. These tend to "swallow up" mere humans standing beneath them, and they need massive, expensive arrangements. Also, what will it look like decorated *after* the receiving line has moved away from it? Probably pretty stiff and empty.

One way of getting around this mantel syndrome is to have the bridal table, either a formal one or a reserved one, set in front of a mantel that is decorated. The receiving line is formed in *front* of the table. This is often a happy solution to the problem—and the expense—of decorating two important places. But what should guide your choice of where to receive is not a mantel, but the side of the room or marquee that is on the left and located as far from the place where the guests enter as possible. The reason for this is that if your guests approach you on their left side, the receiving line moves along in the best way and it automatically places the bride where she should be standing, which is before the groom and on his right side. You should see to it that your receiving line is placed so that your guests have room to wait in comfort, can check wraps in winter, and use the necessary facilities before they line up. If you have any choice whatsoever, never have the guests approach you from their right.

Be guided by your florist as to the size of flowers to use for the larger, above-eye-level arrangements and decorations. Your favorite flowers may not be in scale for the area, or even compatible with its feeling. Any good florist knows that a combination of round and spiky flowers used with two shades of greens and long delicate flowers to give height is best for this kind of decoration.

We think that, whatever the flowers, the kind the bride chooses for her own bouquet and for her bridesmaids should not appear again in other arrangements or centerpieces. Finding a favorite combination of flowers and repeating it over and over again is dull, but selecting other flowers that are complementary both in feeling and color but different in size and texture from those of the bride and her attendants makes for a more beautiful effect without detracting from the principal floral statement.

Lighting is one of the most important parts of any decorating scheme and can make it or break it in a place of worship or where the reception is held. A great many people think that "all candlelight" is beautiful. It isn't at all, unless thousands of candles are used. What is beautiful and gives the effect of all candlelight is a subtle combination of electric light and candlelight. This is particularly true in places of worship. Nowadays most of them have lighting that can be controlled by rheostats. Be sure you have a lighting rehearsal as well as a regular one or a combination of the two. Have a lighting plan that will include directions for both a bright sunny day and one that is dull and overcast (naturally, the light level is a great deal lower inside a place of worship than that outside under any circumstances), and also one for the evening. Ask your minister, priest, rabbi, or the cantor what he thinks is the best lighting. Just remember that the most exquisite decorations can be completely lost unless the lighting is right. Rent standing candelabra from your florist if necessary, but do work out *in advance* the combination of candlelight and electric light that is right for the space.

Lighting in a great many clubs across the country is so dim that it's depressing. House committees are notoriously lax about spending money on lighting fixtures, except in kitchens and bowling alleys. A torchère that can be moved about to give indirect light where it is needed for certain occasions, like wedding receptions, must be the item in their budgets they eliminate first. Investigate this lighting angle with your club manager. Usually he can speak with deep feeling on the subject, if you give him a tactful opening while you are planning the menu with him. Dark and lugubrious or bright and nerve-racking seem to be the two extremes in club lighting—with little choice in between unless you are willing to provide it.

You can have your florist supply candles, the long, slow-burning, eighteen-inch type, and fix them firmly into the middle of the centerpieces, or even supply three to five glass holders that can be grouped around centerpieces on forty-eight, fifty-four, sixty, or even seventy-two-inch round tables. It's a good idea to have candles on "standby" for luncheon receptions in case the day is overcast and the interior darker than expected. The candles and their holders can easily be removed by your florist at the last moment if they are not needed, but whatever you do avoid having unlit candles anywhere. Nothing is more lifeless than an unlit candle in the middle of a centerpiece. Light it and it can produce diamond-like, dancing reflections on the surface of glass, silver, and china; unlit, a candle merely stares back at you. In short, if something is not both beautiful and functional, forget it.

In marquees, the lighting is the most important adjunct to their decoration, especially for late afternoon and evening weddings and receptions. When shades of blue are being used under a solid blue, solid white, yellow and white striped, blue and white striped, or green and white striped marquee, blue will go black or blah on you like a poor sapphire if the lighting has not been properly worked out. If your canvas firm has a licensed electrician on its staff, he should be able to help you and your florist with the necessary and most effective lighting for the colors you are using. If not, and you are spending a considerable amount of money on your daughter's wedding, it would be to your advantage to call in the best electrician available. Correct lighting is not only an important factor in the decorative plan, it is a safety factor in and around a marquee. Discuss it at your first interview with the man from the canvas and equipment firm.

Depending upon the number of center poles in a marquee, we suggest a basic number of baby spots. Any electrician either has them or he can get them. They should be placed on the poles in such a manner that they will be pointed up into the peak of the marquee to give indirect light. There are many ways of decorating around and under them safely. We have used metal cones covered with flameproof fabric and placed them on the center poles at a minimum height of sixteen feet from the ground. Greening starts just below where these cones are attached and covers any construction or attachment work. Either artificial or fresh flowers—they should all be in water picks if fresh—or a combination of both may be used, keeping the artificial flowers up high and the fresh ones just above head level, or at seven or eight feet. This is a great way to cope with guests who find the flowers so beautiful they just have to pinch them to see if they're real.

Strings of small Italian lights (all in one color; otherwise your marquee could look like the Ginza), which are now available to florists all over the country, are most effective for late afternoon and evening weddings, and they give an amazing amount of light when used around the rotunda, or scallop area, of a marquee. New lighting elements come on the market all the time, and there are all types and kinds of wrought-iron (you can have them sprayed any color) carriage lights, Spanish lanterns, giant Mexican, Japanese, and Chinese paper flowers and lanterns that can be used safely on center and sidewall poles to cover raw lights under marquees. In fact, the world of lighting possibilities combined with decorations can be the joyous expression of your own and your florist's imagination, unlimited except by your ability to pay.

The sidewall poles behind a receiving line under a marquee should be decorated to complement whatever natural background of evergreens or shrubs is behind it on the outside. If the receiving line happens to be where the rays of the morning or afternoon sun will slant into your guests' eyes so they will be looking at the bride against them, do, for heaven's sake, have the canvas man provide a backdrop to prevent this from happening. This is one of those little but most important details that can be overlooked. Be sure he will provide a pristine section of canvas either white, or in a color of the marquee you are using. If the natural background you have is attractive and there is no sun problem, then ask him to use a clear section of *clean* poly instead. These backdrops are most useful on cool, drafty days when you may not wish to have the sidewalls dropped all around, or on three sides of the marquee. Again, lighting is important, so have rented standing torchères that give indirect lighting held in reserve in case the day is dark and overcast.

Good lighting is a must for all evening weddings and receptions under marquees, and light that gives clear visibility is no more expensive to work out than inadequate light. It just takes preplanning and a little effort. If you have a bridal table or a buffet table or tables, have the areas where they are placed lit. The use of a backdrop as described earlier may be indicated for both bridal and buffet tables. Also, wherever there is an entrance to a marquee, the sidewall poles should be greened and for an evening wedding, lighted as well.

If the dance floor is raised, and some have to be in order to get them level, guardrails are a necessity along with clearly marked places to show people where to leave or approach the dance floor. These rails may be made very simply from plain two-by-fours that the canvas firm can supply and install. They may be painted to match the marquee. Your florist can green them or decorate them in any way you choose. Low dance floors, those six inches or a step above ground level, should be greened by your florist to cover any raw wood or signs of construction. This greening is done on only three sides, for the orchestra may be placed on an extension of the floor on the fourth side, which may not be visible. If there is a bandstand, this too should be greened, of course.

Whether the reception is at home or elsewhere, the place where the bride plans to throw her bouquet before she leaves to change into her going-away clothes should be decided upon in advance and decorated. Many brides do not wish to toss their bouquets or have their grooms throw their new wives' blue garters to their unmarried groomsmen or ushers. We have frequently had brides tell us they preferred to present their bouquets personally to a close relative in a hospital who was too ill to attend the wedding. Other brides care very much about where and how they will throw their bouquets. Some have very definite ideas about a staircase at home where, perhaps, they played "bride" as children. This part of any bride's wedding reception is a very personal one and the construction of the bouquet should be discussed in advance with the florist.

Often a bride has no bouquet at all, but carries instead a family prayer book tied (so it will not fall open) with white satin ribbon to which is attached a spray of delicate little flowers of her choice. Such a spray can be detached easily by the maid of honor as soon as the bride indicates that she and her groom are ready to leave for the respective rooms where they will change into their going-away clothes. Then it can be tossed to her unmarried attendants. And, if the bride has elected to wear a flower or a corsage when she and her groom leave, the maid of honor should be in charge of getting it from the home or club refrigerator where the florist has left it. Many brides prefer to have no going-away flowers at all because they think of them as "just married" labels. Whatever is done, however, the details should be worked out in advance.

By this time, mother of the bride, you will either be numb with happiness and full of ideas about what to do with other weddings in your family or your central nervous system will be permanently damaged. We hope the latter won't happen, and we wish you luck. Have fun: decorations should be the most enjoyable part of your work of planning the wedding!

Chapter 9

Music

EXCEPT FOR A CEREMONY PERFORMED IN A JUDGE'S chambers or before a justice of the peace, music is, in one form or another, almost universally played at a wedding. There is a large body of traditional church music for weddings subscribed to by almost all denominations. The only exception to this that we know of is the Quaker service.

Whether or not you are a musician, you should consult with your church organist or pianist (some country churches do not have organs). If you wish unusual selections played, he may need time to prepare them and to determine whether his instrument can even play them, let alone do them justice. In such cases, you will also need permission from the minister, priest, or rabbi. Otherwise the organist will have quite a wide selection to offer. At this point you should also arrange for the prelude, which begins one-half hour before the ceremony, the processional that starts the ceremony, the music to be used during the ceremony (such as a doxology, solos, and choirs), and the recessional.

Our clients frequently ask us to suggest music to be played before the ceremony and for the processional and recessional. We feel that this question should be addressed instead to the choirmaster, organist, or cantor. But we could not write this chapter on music connected with weddings without passing along the following comments, which will be understood by brides and their mothers who know something about music.

Anyone who has ever attended a performance of Richard Wagner's opera *Lohengrin* or read the libretto would never dream of requesting that the Wedding March from it be played at a wedding. Yet we have had mothers, and even fathers of brides, say, "But it's traditional—it was played at our wedding."

If a tragic piece of music has been allowed to become a tradition by a mere fluke, then it's time to start a new one. The first time the Wagner Wedding March was used for a processional was at an oh-so-social church for the marriage of an American heiress and a poverty-stricken nobleman, probably at the suggestion of Ward McAllister, who may have attended the first production of *Lohengrin* in Weimar in 1850, before he returned to the United States and set out on his career as the arbiter of the New York social world of the 1860s. This was a world of newly rich, amusical people to whom anything composed by Wagner *had* to be right, for it was new, and all were told that Wagner's music was the coming thing.

With the great wealth of church music available, it seems too sad that this Wedding March from *Lohengrin* hangs on.

We give here two samples of musical selections for a marriage ceremony. You will note the inclusion of a very popular processional, Purcell's Trumpet Tune. In fact, Purcell wrote two trumpet voluntaries, but the one that is so popular and is attributed to him was actually composed by Jeremiah Clarke and not by Purcell. This is the Trumpet Voluntary in D major called "The Prince of Denmark."

Roman Catholic

Church of St. Augustine

Second Organ Concerto, in B flat major ....Handel

A tempo ordinario e staccato

Allegro

Adagio

Allegro ma non presto

Deck thyself, my soul, with gladness ................J.S. Bach

Ich folge dir gleichfalls (from *St. John Passion*) ....Bach

Rhosymedre ....Vaughan Williams

Bist du bei mir ....Bach

PROCESSIONAL:

Bridal Chorus from *Lohengrin* ....Wagner

Marche Pontificale ....Widor

RECESSIONAL:

Now Thank We All Our God ....Karg-Elert

Protestant

St. Matthew's Church

Prelude

A Mighty Fortress ....Pachelbel

Sheep May Safely Graze ....J. S. Bach

Preludio ....Bach

Jesu, Joy of Man's Desiring ....Bach

Flute Solo ....Arne

Panis Angelicus ....Franck

Adagio ....Vivaldi

Air (from Suite in D) ....Bach

Trumpet Tune ....Purcell

Bridal Chorus ....Wagner

Hymn 479

Dresden Amen ....Wagner

Wedding March ....Mendelssohn

If you are interested in using any of the three Purcell voluntaries, there are some excellent recordings of them, so familiarize yourself with them prior to talking to your choir-master, organist, or cantor. Having a trumpeter at the ceremony adds greatly to a processional or a recessional and is easy to arrange. You merely have the musician, provided he is a real pro, who will play the trumpet in the orchestra at the reception come an hour earlier to the church, synagogue, or temple, and get his signals straight with the organist before the ceremony.

Episcopalians are missing a real bet if they fail to consider using the full choir, or the boys' choir of their church when it has a choir school. Nothing can be more beautiful than a full choir leading the ushers and the rest of the wedding party up to the chancel steps and coming to a dramatic stop as the bride and her father reach the place where the groom steps forward to meet her.

We don't wish to expand further on this; the variations in customs and church regulations throughout the country are too diverse. But we remember one beautiful ceremony for which the entire musical score was written especially for the bride and performed by the composer's own quintet. We have assisted with numerous garden ceremonies at which a modern portable electric organ was used to good effect. Now, if any of you ever have to use an old-fashioned harmonium or melodeon, make very certain your man knows his instrument intimately. We once used a harmonium whose blats, squeaks, and squeals came in a very close second to the actual music.

Once in a great while we are asked, "Do we have to have music at the reception?" This question is posed by families who feel that the interjection of music into a sacred occasion constitutes a profanity or that it detracts from the purpose of the reception. Everyone is assembled to honor the bride and groom. Friends and relatives of both sides are there to become better acquainted, thus connecting more firmly the bonds of the new alliance. Therefore, to them, music is nonessential. One thing is certain, however: It produces a much briefer reception, and it is the simplest and most informal way to shape a reception.

For that element of celebration and jubilation, music is a must. For instance, as small a unit as a strolling trio that can play good background music gives the assembly a lift. Music gives tempo to the whole reception. It serves to highlight certain events, such as the cake cutting, and cues the guests as to what is happening by the use of certain universal melodies.

Dancing is another matter. We have found a few families that balk more at having dancing than at having background music. Dancing at weddings goes far back in history. It was frowned upon and frequently banned during the Cromwellian Ascendancy, whose effects seem to linger on to this day. Before that, especially during the Middle Ages, merry England danced at every wedding, although there was little enough to celebrate in those days. To dance or not to dance depends entirely upon your particular customs and the dictates of your religious faith. While we have yet to be told in so many words that dancing is the work of the devil, in one or two instances we have indirectly been made aware of this feeling.

Only once were we told that dancing went hand in glove with overindulgence. As far as a wedding reception is concerned, that is pure tommyrot. If anything, dancing diminishes the effect of alcohol. You go to a booth at the corner saloon to tie one on, but never to a wedding reception. If you do, you are going to be very conspicuous.

So when it comes to that question, "Do we have to have dancing?" the answer is no. If you really don't want it, there is no dictate of good form we know of that says you must. But we urge you to have background music if at all possible. We just hope that you are not up against a situation in a church parlor or parish hall where all kinds of music are banned.

If you are going to have music, however, make it good music. The Boilermaker Six may be fine for a clambake, but they might well ruin a reception. So you should, if possible, call several leading orchestras and have them send you estimates. They will even quote prices over the telephone. The variations will depend on whether or not they are including the personal services of the big name leader and whether the music is to be continuous or not. Always buy continuous music. Unless you do, the musicians may be taking their break just as your party is getting off the ground or the bride wants to cut the cake or throw her bouquet. A well-known leader is not essential for a wedding reception. He is only as good as the individual style he has developed and passed on to his first men. It is this leader or his first man who will pick up the other players needed at the union hiring halls that are found all over the country.

Everywhere in the United States there are small orchestras that are seldom known beyond their own locale but are, nonetheless, excellent. Usually they are composed of part-time musicians, or the players are members of an association. They usually are able to practice and play together a great deal more than the "name" organizations, so what they may lack in individual professional virtuosity, they make up in cohesion. While they may or may not belong to the local union, they will at least be much less expensive. Also you won't have to pay for a name or for travel. Remember: more than one big name in orchestras started out in a small local band.

Combos spring up almost overnight, especially around centers of higher education. This is one way to pay college expenses. A great many of them are surprisingly good, and not a few stick together after graduation to go on to the big time. So if you hear one, or know of one, why not use one? They may not be familiar with the procedures of a wedding reception, and they are seldom geared to play continuously, but you can always give them a schedule.

We are often asked, "What will be played?" This is the bride's day, and her preferences should be heeded meticulously. This is especially true of the selection for her first dance. The leader should be given the title of this song ahead of time, along with the titles of her other favorites.

Almost all leaders are adept at judging the guests. They can make an educated guess as to the various age groups and so tailor selections and tempos to gratify each one. But the music should still be mainly as contemporary as the bride.

For very large receptions we have used two separate bands, one the so-called society orchestra and the other a trio, a modern combo, or a calypso or merengue band. In spelling each other, they provide variety.

To talk instrumentation with a band leader, unless you know his field, is rather futile. He knows what instrument each of his men can play best and what musical effect he will get. But if he asks for one extra man, one more than is absolutely necessary, it is because continuous music needs that extra man to rotate rest periods. This is not true of the orchestra that plays for, let us say, twenty minutes and then takes a ten-to-fifteen-minute break before continuing. Then, too, most leaders have their favorite combinations for a given location and for the type of function at which they are playing. Electronics, incidentally, have not served to decrease the number of musicians needed. They only affect the individual piece.

When a piano is being used in a club or hotel, be sure the manager has the action checked and the instrument tuned to international pitch (440), and have this done the day before the reception. Most of the bigger hotels and clubs have contracts to have their pianos tuned at least twice a year by professional tuners. Tuning should also be done in your own home or the community house assembly rooms. A piano under canvas presents more of a problem. When you are using your own, have it moved onto the dance floor the day before the reception, if possible, and then have it tuned. The act of moving makes the pitch drop. Cover it with rugs or something else to protect the case from the damp. Or, better, rent one from a music store, thus placing on the store's shoulders the burden of getting the piano in place in perfect shape.

One of our favorite instruments, which so often is viewed askance, is the accordion. Not only is it an excellent "bridge" instrument, but it is highly mobile. There are also the "sweet and sour" notes of the balalaika and the lively music of the concertina. If you are looking for something really different that will serve as a conversation piece, ask your bandleader to get you a cimbalom and someone to play it. Several of our clients have dined out all winter on their use of this Hungarian instrument at a wedding reception.

Aside from actual instrumentation, we would like to suggest a few combinations that we have found to be very effective. First, as we have said, there is the solo accordion. Then, for a small background trio there is the piano-accordion combo plus either a violin or a tenor or alto wind instrument, depending on how lively the music need be. A standard quartet for both background and dancing uses the above and adds drums. A good bass fiddle can at times replace the "cocktail" drums. A quintet will add another horn, a bass drum, or a steel guitar. For more than a septet, the orchestra leader will include full drums, a bass fiddle, and increase his harmonic and melodic sections proportionally. When you get to twelve men or more, you are moving into the area of the full orchestra guaranteed to overwhelm any but the really big reception of five hundred and more.

Having decided on the orchestra, its composition, and the price, your next consideration is time. When you are dealing with a band that does not belong to the musicians' union local, the time it plays, hours or fractions of hours, and overtime are matters strictly between you and the leader. But under union rules, a contract is for three or four hours, according to local regulations, and the men are in place and ready to play at a certain hour, such as 4:00 P.M., but never at 4:15 or 4:30. Contract time runs by the hour on the hour, and for any part thereof. We know this is true of Local 802, New York, and we are not aware of any deviations from this practice elsewhere. However, ask your leader and read your contract.

Normally the orchestra is present and ready to play the bride and groom into the reception area when they arrive from the church. It will play for the length of the contract, but if it is released before the expiration time, generally there is no rebate. In contrast, if you want it to play for an extra twenty minutes while the bride and groom are leaving, you will pay for one full hour of overtime.

There is one way to cut the cost of music when you are having dancing (most applicable when the reception is of such size that it will take the guests at least one hour to go through the line). Have a trio play the couple in and stand playing near the receiving line for the first hour, then move the trio onto the dance floor where it can be joined by the balance of the band for general dancing. This means that a large part of your music time will be billed at trio rates. The reverse—having a few musicians remain after the full orchestra has left—can also be arranged, but you will have to make the arrangements in advance, especially on a prime date.

If you are going to any large hotel in a metropolitan area, you will find that the union has set a minimum number of musicians for certain rooms in these hotels. For instance, if your reception is held at the St. Regis Roof in New York City, Local 802 has set the minimum number of musicians you must engage at eight. The banquet manager of the hotel will know all about the requirements of the musicians' union local in your area.

While you are going over all the details with the leader, be sure to ask about the method of payment. Established orchestras will normally bill you for the entire amount within ten days. Part-time bands and combos may ask for a check in advance for half the amount, the balance to be paid by check when they leave or within the next few days. Usually the leader has to pay his men off the day of the reception, and since he doesn't carry very much operating capital, a delay can cause him some financial hardship.

The customary dress for men in the band is a dinner jacket with soft turndown collar and black bow tie. Some orchestras wear red, white, blue, or plaid jackets as forms of advertising. We have occasionally had a few adverse comments concerning overemphatic visual displays. It was felt that a large billboard placed in front of the leader, where the dancers could not fail to fall over it, carried things too far. However, there has never been any objection to small signs off to one side, or to the name of the band being painted on the bass drum. As with any other business, orchestras have to advertise, and when their music is their best advertising, everyone should know who they are.

One final note: The orchestra gets hungry and thirsty, just like everybody else. So be certain that you arrange with your caterer to take care of the musicians. By and large, club managers see to this automatically, but occasionally we have had to flag down a waiter to give him a bar order for the orchestra, or to go out into the kitchen to make certain there was food set aside for the musicians.

We have only hit the high notes concerning dance music for the reception. Preferences, styles of dancing, and modes of music are as varied as are the segments of the conglomerate mass of our people. Not only is there a divergence because of locale, but there is the generation gap or gaps. Tastes at one gathering can encompass everything from "Tea for Two" to a medley from *Hair*. Whatever band you select, it is going to have to know the topical songs of the seventies as well as the big-band tunes of the thirties.

Until now we have been considering live music. However, there is also "canned music," which is sometimes appropriate but not particularly recommended. A stereo system can be used in a small home marriage ceremony. There are quite a few recordings that have the standard processional and recessional music. There is excellent recorded prelude music as well. You would need someone standing by in a position where he could see what was happening to man either the turntable or the volume control of the amplifier. In the same way you could use a more elaborate system for a home reception, possibly a tape deck. Volume control in this case would permit the pauses necessary for the cake cutting, toasts, and other occurrences. But unless you have a good, in fact an excellent, system with several loud speakers, recorded music is not very satisfactory under canvas, unless it is used strictly for background. And by the time you finish getting all the necessary equipment, or if you are already a buff buying additional parts, a live orchestra might prove to be cheaper. We have used recorded music for a small home ceremony, and we have heard of one or two garden receptions where it was used. Also, if you check around, you may find one or two parish houses or other assembly rooms where such a system may have been installed.

Some hotel ballrooms have amplification, which can be a mixed blessing if there is no one from the hotel to handle the individual speakers, especially those installed in the ceiling. Initially the crowd of people absorbs the full volume, but as it thins out, the loudspeakers can become overpowering. Also, there are blind or silent areas when you have a full crowd and small spots where the dancers can hear nothing. Usually the hotel's maître d', if the question is raised, can see to it that he has someone to regulate the volume. But he can do little with dead areas, unless they are in places where he can set up tables.

Another special situation will come up if you are using an

electric organ in a garden wedding. You should determine the distance from the nearest house outlet to the spot where the organ is to be placed. Then have the firm from which you are renting it tell you what size heavy-duty electrical cable you should use in order to get the maximum effect out of the instrument.

Chapter 10

Photography

A BRIDE WOULD DO WELL TO BE VERY NEARLY AS SELECTIVE about choosing a photographic studio as she is about her groom-to-be. Formal wedding portraits and that album of candids are presumably going to be with her for a lifetime, too. As with men, there are photographers, and photographers, and. . . .

Don't let your daughter's choice be guided only by the reputation a certain studio enjoys, nor should you be taken in by the lure common to them all: the package deal. Just remember that a photograph is only as good as the skill of the person who takes it. Finishes, while important, are secondary to the man or woman with control of the lens. Some of the greatest photographers whose genius lies in catching the essence of the personality of the subject in a posed portrait—or formal, as it is called—are quite inadequate when it comes to taking candids, and vice versa. In the many years during which we have worked with most of the top photographers, we have met only three who were equally good at formals and candids. The techniques needed for each are so very different that this is quite understandable, but it is something that seems to be little understood by brides and their mothers when they are shopping for a photographic studio.

Unless you are fortunate enough to have one whose work you know and admire, the best way to line up good photographic work for your wedding is to ask your friends for personal recommendations. Look at the photographs they have in their homes and, if there are recent brides you know, ask to see their wedding albums. Be hard-nosed and objective in your appraisal of the work.

Knowing *when* the photos were taken is important, too, for there are constant changes and feuds in the various studios, and at the top of this profession, where the best talent is paid the most for their work, it becomes a very, very small world. It's a whispering gallery world where the competition is fierce and one prestigious studio thinks nothing of stealing good formal and candid men from another. That's why you must know *when* the work was done for your friend, for the man who took the formal and the man who did the candid coverage for her wedding—like chefs in better restaurants—may have been lured away to another studio whose name is quite different from the one imprinted on your friend's work. If she can recall the name or names of the men who photographed her, half your battle is won, for you can go to the studio and find out if either of them is still there.

Before you make a final commitment to a studio—and give them the deposit they require—find out *who* is going to take your formal portrait and *who* is going to be assigned to the candid coverage. The reputable studios may not like your questions—they want to ride on their reputations alone—but they will have more respect for you, and you stand a better chance of not having some last-minute "free lance" show up the day of the wedding. When you make a commitment to a studio and pay a deposit, get a commitment in return—especially if your date is one of those prime ones.

There's another fail-safe you might employ before you commit yourself: have the photo for the engagement announcement press release taken by the studio you think you'll use for the wedding work. This is an excellent test run.

Every so often we are confronted with a photo of an engaged girl that was taken for her school or college yearbook. It's the kind that should be on a passport, but she has an idea she would like to use it for the press release "in order to save expense." Unless the yearbook photo was an absolute dazzler, don't use it. First of all, it's probably dated as to hairdo and clothes. Secondly, the photographer who took it may be located at some distance from your hometown or, because he likes to eat regularly, has gone to work for one of the "macaroni factories."

The latter are studios with old established names that continue to operate under them but are owned and controlled by giant companies that have applied the techniques of mass production to wedding photography. They have vast finishing plants all over the place where the negatives for both *your* formal and candid photographs—and thousands of others—are turned out like so many cookies. With all due respect to mass production, we do not think it should be applied to so personal and individual an area as wedding photography. We also know that photographers have to have a lot of capital behind them to survive financially until they become established, or else they have to get on the full-time payroll of a solidly established independent studio to make a go of it. Few of the top studios bother with yearbook assignments because they are money-losers unless the school or college is an Ivy League one.

If your daughter is having "engagement" photos taken, let someone in the studio guide her as to hairdo, dress—usually a plain shirtwaist is best—and makeup. The person who can help with these questions is usually the woman who sets up the appointment. In the top studios, these gals really know their business and can be of great assistance during this early stage. They have blouses and various materials that can be used for drapes. Before the appointment the bride should be sure to talk to one of them, or to the photographer himself. Also, she should get a good night's sleep, go easy on the makeup, and try not to sandwich the sitting in during her lunch hour if she has a job.

As for the formal wedding portrait—and it is always called this instead of a photograph—it is usually taken at the time of the bride's final fitting on her wedding gown, and in the bridal salon. In New York, all of the first-rate shops are prepared to have photographers work in them. The bride should tell her photographer what flowers she has chosen for her bouquet and give him some idea of its shape and size. He will then provide a "pretend bouquet" as nearly like it as possible. Or the formal photograph can be made in the studio. The main advantage of having the formal sitting in the bridal salon is that you will have a pro on hand—maybe even the bridal consultant herself—to drape the veil and train in the best way, even if the gown is only pinned in places and not finished. Also, many bridal salons have "pretend" bouquets made of silk or plastic flowers (no greens are used, for they photograph black) which may be preferable to the one the photographer provides.

The other way of having the wedding portrait taken is one that many brides prefer: at home. A lot of girls "freeze" when a lens is even mentioned and therefore feel they will be more relaxed in familiar surroundings. Talk over these alternatives with the man who will wield the lens and be guided as much as possible by his working requirements and preferences. There are great photographers who, because of the lighting they use, and because they do not have control of their milieu in a bridal salon where the static of organized confusion distracts them in their work, will not consider working anywhere except in their own studios.

If you must have a studio sitting, have someone who is responsible for its care transport the wedding gown and veil there, wait until the sitting is over, and return both to the bridal salon. This is a "must" even if you have to pay extra for it.

The delicate question of whether to have her mother present before and during the formal sitting is a highly personal one that the bride will have to cope with as she sees fit. Some mothers have a built-in cluck or a fluttering quality, either of which can make their daughters so nervous that it's far better for these mothers to be under a hair dryer or on a golf course when wedding portraits are taken. A top photographer usually prefers to be alone with his subject, so if an otherwise adorable mother tries to get into the act, let *him* tell her he works best when he is alone with his subject.

The photographic studios we most enjoy working with are those whose owners are modern minded. They are realistic enough to know that if an engaged girl needs photos for the press release her parents are sending to the newspapers, she and her family are not going to be interested in ordering a lot of prints of it when their minds are on the wedding pictures—and expenses. Therefore, they make a charge for the sitting only (which can be adjusted if you do want to order their minimum number of prints) and for the glossy prints you need for the newspapers. You can make this type of arrangement with any good studio, but you have to be fair with them, too, by giving them the formal and candid order for the wedding. And giving one studio in which you have confidence the entire assignment is better all the way around for everyone concerned. Yet there are brides and their mothers who think they are ahead of the game if they have a well-known studio take the formal portraits only (for the sake of status) and give the candid order to some lesser studio that is not so expensive. This is poor economy, just as it is to have "a dear friend with a Polaroid who *adores* to take pictures and will be a guest at the wedding anyway" counted on for the candid coverage.

Limited or split orders are one of the main reasons that the cost of formal sittings, minimum orders, finishes, and glossy prints for wedding press releases has risen so sharply in recent years. If you will think of wedding portraits as food in a fine restaurant, and candids as liquor, then you'll better understand what we mean.

Working with a reputable studio, and being frank with them at the outset, can result in your getting the best possible coverage for the engagement, formals, and candids. You can even arrange to pay only for the formal sitting and the glossy prints for the wedding press release and have the minimum order held in abeyance until several weeks after the wedding when you can see proofs of the candids. With the improvements in the techniques of natural color photography, many brides prefer it today both for formal portraits and candids. If you are having candids in color, you just might end up having pictures of yourself, or of you and your groom, taken on your wedding day that you would rather have than those formals made at your final fitting with that "pretend" bouquet in your hand. It's certainly worth considering, so talk about it with the studio gal when you are still making arrangements.

In discussing the art of candid photography, we are dealing with a rare talent. A good candid man appears to the guests as though he were floating around casually, sighting and shooting pictures effortlessly. He must be quick on his feet as he moves around, always with his eye on the bride, in order to get what his trade calls complete coverage. What this really means to him is being in the right place at the right second. If he's good, he knows intuitively—and from long practice—where and when something interesting is about to develop. But he has to be discreet and selective even though at a large wedding he may take between eighty and a hundred shots, many of which do not deserve to be preserved for posterity.

We have several criticisms that apply to certain candid men with whom we no longer work:

They are underfoot too early at the reception, and when they are wanted most they can't be found.

They sulk because we won't let them hold up the guests when they first arrive while they fiddle around getting group photographs of the parents and members of the wedding party that can better be taken when the guests have finished passing by the receiving line. We like to start the guests into the line as soon as the first fifteen or twenty have come on the scene.

When we need him, the candid man is off in some obscure corner, eating, resting, or changing films.

Then there's the character with his eyes on future business, who is greeting people he knows and taking shots of former clients with younger daughters rather than asking members of the wedding party what special shots they would like. This type always manages to miss the bride's aunt from Anondale, New Jersey, who has dressed with great care, been sent a corsage by the groom, and has been diligently turning her best profile toward his camera whenever she sees it. The corsage alone would give the clue to a good candid photographer and he would get a shot of this lady early on.

Possibly the worst offender in the brotherhood is the candid man who knows it all and is incapable of following suggestions and instructions about not flashing shots like a meteor in certain churches that have firm rules about taking pictures other than time exposures. Another beef we have is against the candid man who is so thorough when shooting the wedding party that he tries their patience to the point where all he gets is a picture of mass pouts, sulks, or outright dislike. That "just one more" to a bride standing in the hot sun is maddening. We had one bride who threw both her flowers and a glass of champagne at the camera man when he made her pose with various people in every possible group combination, facing a July sun, for some thirty-five minutes. Before each shot, he fussed and adjusted interminably. A candid man in name only.

A good photographer has a number of chronologically set pieces that he must cover. Briefly they are: the bride leaving home, entering the church, the couple leaving the church, entering the place of reception, preliminary toast or glass of champagne before forming the receiving line, first dance if there is dancing, cutting the cake, throwing the bouquet and garter, leaving for the honeymoon. The candid man should be told the approximate times for all these events.

There are other photographs that he should get, but there is more latitude here. For the group pictures—wedding party, family, and other posed pictures—the time sequence varies considerably, depending upon the type of wedding ceremony and reception. We prefer to get these all done immediately following the receiving line activities and before the wedding party and the families have scattered too widely. In any event, you should delegate some younger male member of your family to check with the photographer and then to notify all concerned where he wants them and when he wants them. The younger member is going to have to herd them like sheep if the pictures are delayed too long. Watch out for the father of the groom: he usually manages to disappear first. While you are at it, you should have this young man initially tag along with the photographer to point out all those whom you want photographed. And be certain to check with the groom's side as well.

The site or background for all group pictures, unless you have a strong preference, should be left up to the photographer. Indoor shots of large groups require a wide lens and a long axis. They can be very difficult, particularly when a guest gets half his body and head into the side of a picture. The photographer will need all the help you can give him to photograph twenty-four members of the wedding in a small assembly hall. Outdoors is a different matter. There light becomes his chief problem.

In the case of a large church ceremony, but with only the immediate family and friends invited to your home or a restaurant afterward, you may wish to have the family and group pictures taken outside the church after the ceremony. This has the advantage of having everyone you care to have photographed still available. Not all of them may be going on with you. However, any group photography in this case depends upon two factors: one, the weather; two, whether or not there is another wedding following on the heels of yours. If it rains, use either your home or some part of the church building. If there is another ceremony, the photographer will have to pick a spot, if he can, where there won't be strangers wandering in front of his lens.

Most of the set scenes mentioned above are routine to the professional. He will find a spot from which to get the best results. But there are at least two special situations. When the bride throws her bouquet, she should be standing on some sort of elevation facing the receivers—on a chair if nothing else is available. The other situation is flash pictures inside the church or synagogue. Most of them do not object to stills inside, but you should check beforehand as to whether or not flashes can be used and to what extent. Be sure to pass this on to the photographer ahead of time.

Any good candid photographer has his own time schedule. He usually arrives at the bride's house, or wherever she is dressing for the ceremony, at least an hour before she leaves. He follows her to the church, often riding in the front seat of the limousine carrying the bride and her father. He is either with the newlyweds or ahead of them as they arrive at the reception. He keeps them in sight, or knows generally where they can be found, during the entire reception. His work is over once the "getaway" car has pulled away from the front door. He can usually be found covering the entire receiving line as the guests reach the bride and groom. After the group pictures are taken, he circulates, but makes certain to be in position ahead of time for both the cake cutting and the flower throwing. All in all, he is a busy man.

Now a word about color. Until quite recently, color candids were expensive, but now we recommend them over black-and-white. This is something you should discuss with your photographer. Get his price lists. Quite a few studios shoot both color and black-and-white on speculation. This means your candid man will be going around with two cameras, which is no great hardship with modern equipment. If you specify color, he may get some black-and-whites in places where he knows color won't come out well.

As with formal portraits, candid albums are getting smaller. Very few people, especially young marrieds, have the space for big albums. That is why eight-by-ten, or even five-by-seven albums—which are the smallest possible—are becoming increasingly popular. They fit comfortably in the hand, in the bookcase, and in airplane luggage. This is not quite so true for the eleven-by-fourteen or sixteen-by-twenty variety.

Almost all studios have a minimum candid album price guarantee, which means that you must order the album with so many pictures for such and such a price. Over this number, candids are sold individually. Additional album pages usually are included in this price. All studios have price lists according to size and finish, color or black-and-white. If you are very strong-minded you can hold your expenses to the minimum shown on the list.

Most studios will mail proofs to you, usually three to four weeks after the wedding, depending on the backup of orders to be filled. We have known of instances when the candid proofs took three months to complete. There may be one or two studios left that send out proofs which fade out to sepia blobs after a certain length of timc. The idea behind this practice is to expedite an order and to prevent the proofs from being kept and used in lieu of an order. Of course, by the time the candid proofs do finally arrive, the parents of the bride are feeling so impoverished that even the loveliest color photograph doesn't generate much enthusiasm.

Other studios may notify you that your proofs are ready and ask you to come in immediately to make your selections. They are perfectly capable of mailing them out, but they have a fancy line of accessories such as albums with which they want to tempt you. They are probably going to have to mail samples to the groom's family, anyhow, since each side often buys its own set.

Still other studios send a representative to your house by appointment to show the proofs and, if possible, to get an order completed. Actually this method is far and away the most pleasant and the most satisfactory. You are going to have questions and need some technical advice. The whole thing can be settled then and there with the least amount of inconvenience to you. You will then also be given a final price, the bill payable on delivery of the finished albums.

We have a pet aversion to one or two fashionable photographic studios that force you to come in personally with proofs. They have a by no means "loss leader," the "free photo album," which is apt to be made only for eleven-by-fourteen prints and wouldn't stand up for as long as a year. Any demurrer on your part may elicit a vague implication from the salesperson that you must be from the sticks and that you need her expert guidance. Get all the information and leave. Tell her it's a buyer's market, your market, and she will, under protest, deliver exactly what you want. The better the studio, the more it needs to protect its reputation in making up your finished order to your satisfaction.

Chapter 11

The Last Roundup

IT HAS BEEN OUR EXPERIENCE THAT ABOUT FOUR WEEKS before a wedding, an otherwise well-organized mother wakes up one morning, looks at the calendar date, goes straight up in flames, and calls us for reassurance. Anything could set off this panic, but it is apt to be the bridal gown more than anything else. In the meantime, daughter is calm and serene. Her time for blast-off comes much later. If you have no one to call to restore composure, the chronological checklist you have made out should serve to bring you back to earth.

There are some things that you can't do until the last week, but there are others that you can get out of the way before this. One thing you must do is to make certain all your invitations have been mailed. The timing for this has been mentioned in chapter 3, but for the sake of emphasis allow us to state again that they should go out a full four weeks before the wedding, and preferably be mailed on a Wednesday or Thursday. Here are some other things that you should do: make reservations for those coming from quite a distance; establish where the bridesmaids will dress; establish how their clothes will get to them; unless you have a big house, farm these bridesmaids out; establish where the ushers will dress (again, anywhere but your house) and select someone to collect the ushers and bring their clothes to a central spot.

Then there is the matter of gift tables if you have decided to show the gifts. In certain sections this has been quite a subject for debate lately. Lack of space and the rising incidence of breaking and entering have often decided a family against following this old custom. In surveying what some five hundred clients have done about gifts, we find that if the reception is at home or nearby, the majority set up gift tables about three weeks before the wedding. If they are available, get regular banquet-type tables, which are steady, rather than bridge tables. Either a rental company or a canvas company will measure for and install them.

Another method some use when there are a good many valuable presents to display is to call a local moving company, especially one affiliated with a long-distance van lines outfit. Arrangements can be made for the local company to lend and install gift tables with the understanding that it will do the final packing, storing, or moving later on. This has the advantage of all gifts being fully insured from the moment of packing until final delivery.

Displaying the gifts is really an individual matter. There are only a few general rules to follow: only one unit of a set is shown; separate amounts that the couple receives in cash or by check are written on white cards and placed in a series to one side, such as "Gift of $50.00 by check" (in no case does the name of the donor ever appear); whenever possible, the inner boxes the gifts came in should be placed under the gift table.

Most stationery stores carry a special book in which bridal gifts can be recorded. These books will have duplicate stickers, one to be placed on the bottom of the displayed gift, the other to be pasted in the book. In chapter 3 we have gone into the various stationery items the bride will need. She should start writing her thank-you notes immediately and keep up to date as much as possible. We have known brides to be so swamped by the amount of notes to be written that they have let as much as six months go by before thanking the donors. The least she should do, if she can't do better, is mail out gift acknowledgment cards so that the donors know their gifts actually arrived.

If the refurbishing and redecorating of the home has not been completed, bring all such efforts to a conclusion. That is one uproar you can well do without. The same goes for your grounds if you are having a home reception. In chapter 6, mention was made of trimming or making other preparations for the canvas man. You should get this done early, particularly if all plans were made when the trees were bare. Leaves make quite a difference. If you can, get your canvas man over to see what additional work has to be done.

By now the wedding party should be completed, in numbers and names. It is not at all unlikely that many of the prenuptial affairs will land in your lap, especially when the groom's family lives far away. They may shoulder the financial burden of a rehearsal dinner, but you are often left with all the details. The sooner these arrangements are made and out of the way, the better.

As this month progresses, you are going to become completely involved in "who is and who isn't coming." No caterer or manager will expect an accurate head count as yet, but the number of people who have not replied will bother you. This is where the "rude box" comes in. In your shoebox invitation file, make three divisions: acceptances, regrets, and no answer. This last category becomes the "rude box."

Generally speaking, regrets come in first, then acceptances. You can usually count on the latter as being firm, but you may be fooled on the regrets. If, for example, you are in an area where many of those "regrets" go up to the mountains for skiing and a January thaw occurs near a Friday, quite a few of them will show up at the reception, despite their regretting, on the theory that they won't eat anything or that the club or hotel always has extra food. In the winter of 1969 one of our clients gave her club manager a guarantee of 275 on a Wednesday for a Saturday evening reception. The whole of New England was hit with a heavy rainstorm on Thursday and Friday. Over 400 came, causing near panic among the club staff.

Another client of ours sent invitations with reception cards to people all over the country on the theory that long distances would deter all but the most hardy. But she hadn't taken the New York World's Fair into account. During the last ten days she was deluged with acceptances. Panic again. Reunions can make for unpredictability, too. One bride's father, whose alma mater was located nearby, had his twenty-fifth college reunion fall on the same day as his daughter's wedding. No one had anticipated that five chartered bus loads of happy warriors complete with boaters, blazers, and half-empty flasks would arrive just in time for the first dance. A lot of them he had never even known.

A lot of the people in the rude box will live nearby. They may meet you downtown, wave, and tell you that they are looking forward to Marybelle's wedding, but they don't answer the invitation even though they may send a gift. You should note them as coming in the rude box file. Ten days before the day, count all the heads in the file. Then eliminate all those who live more than two hours' travel distance away, take 30 percent of the balance, and add that figure, together with the neighborhood wavers, to the acceptance head count. You won't be far off the actual head count at the reception. We have found that there are a surprising number of people who for one reason or several, none really valid, don't answer invitations, and there is nothing anybody can do about it.

Don't worry about the unexpected houseguests of close friends: they are usually offset by those who have accepted but are detained by an equally unexpected emergency.

Next on your worry list should be the publicity. Elsewhere we have described how press releases are written (chapter 2) and how you should insure that the glossies and the stories are as firmly hitched together when they hit the editor's desk as you hope your daughter and her groom will be. So often the fly in this ointment is the bridal salon, which has not completed the dress for a final fitting on time. If the dress is really late, it is almost impossible to get a formal portrait taken. When you are faced with this unfortunate situation you have only two choices: forget about running the picture and get the editorial matter in; or find someone, possibly your husband's advertising firm, who has sufficient pull with the editor of the society page to reserve space against the picture's arrival. This really takes some doing. Most editors are very independent. They are all bound to observe the ratio between engagement announcements and wedding releases and the advertising necessary to support them. In the big metropolitan papers on a prime Sunday, there are few photographs but many releases, so even if you have done everything according to Hoyle, Susie's picture may not appear with the release. Chances are that the omission is pure happenstance. The layout calls for five photographs and the editor has to choose from fifty.

Note: Until quite recently the large advertising firms and other publicity media could be of help in getting a release published. In the last two years, however, we have been told that using these firms has become the kiss of death. However, almost all our readers will have some way of checking this out.

While we are on the subject of publicity, we have on occasion had a client ask to have the staff photographer of a newspaper come to the ceremony. For various reasons a picture of the happy couple descending the church steps after the ceremony with the paper's by-line credit underneath lends additional cachet to the whole affair. This is a request we have never made, because we feel it to be an unwelcome intrusion on a paper's editorial judgment. If it feels that Susie's wedding warrants sending a staff photographer, and there are few enough on tap as it is, it will call ahead of time and ask permission. But, as we have said, a newspaper is an independent operation and apt to resent pressure.

About the time you are mailing out the invitations, you should also have a final wrap-up session with your florist or decorator. You have already decided on your overall color scheme and the effect you wish to achieve. But there are still questions of what flowers and foliage may be available, whether the cost may be prohibitive, and whether artificial flowers may be substituted in places. If you are using a club or hotel, you may want to get the manager in for a few moments. In any event, this is the time when the decorative plans should be gone into in detail, and it can't be done sitting in an office or a living room; it should be done on the set, as it were.

Among other things your florist will want to fix definitely is the position of the cake table and, if you are having one, the bridal table. You should complete the entire layout of the banquet rooms at this meeting and get it out of the way. A bride's table takes up quite a lot of space, and it should never be obscured. It is impossible here to tell you specifically where to place it; we can only suggest a spatial relationship: the table, the dance area, and the band should be generally so grouped that they form, as a unit, the center of attention. But put some space between the table and the band. If the orchestra grows enthusiastic, guests sitting near it can get up and move about. But those at the bride's table are often in a captive situation and thus have their ears assaulted. Sometimes a bride wishes to have her wedding party away from the floor to give them a sense of privacy and to get out of the limelight. A manager can often create the illusion of privacy by using a corner where the composite table is set up at a right angle.

Another position you should fix is the spot for the receiving line. You can always ask the manager for his suggestions, but you don't necessarily have to follow them. The chances are that the place he designates has been used by every bride before you and is calculated to produce the least interference with his staff. Esthetics never enter into his scheme of things.

Another detail you can take care of before that last week is the limousine or car arrangements, i.e., the transport. You certainly don't have to use a livery service, particularly if you have friends who will lend you a station wagon for the bridesmaids, but you do have to have drivers who are free to stay with the cars. This is one order of transport that we have found to work: Car number *one* takes the bride and her father to the church, stays, and takes the newlyweds to the reception. Car number *two* takes the bridesmaids to the church and on to the reception. Car number *three* takes the mother of the bride and any extra bridesmaids or family. This car stays and takes the bride's mother, joined by the groom's mother and, ideally, his father, back to the reception. Getting both mothers back is the key to getting a reception off on time. We once had a groom's mother, an independent character who knew exactly where the reception was to be held a few blocks away. This distance she elected to walk. We waited for forty-five minutes for her to arrive, then started the line without her. She was happily waiting for a line to be set up at another club on the same street. When she did finally arrive her only remark was that she had never seen so many strangers gathered in one place.

Actually, two cars and drivers are the minimum number you need. From then on you are on your own. It is nice to have both families chauffeur-driven in big black Cadillacs equipped with everything but hot and cold running maid service, but it is not necessary. The only male to get in on the action is the father accompanying his daughter to the church, and the groom when they leave the church. Ushers, the best man, the father of the groom, and the groom on the way to church are on their own. Even the father of the bride fends for himself after the ceremony unless he is to be in the receiving line. Then he should ride back with his wife and the mother of the groom. Often the father of the groom will drive his car to the reception alone or take other passengers with him—perhaps the father of the bride—so that it will be there for his wife and himself after the reception is over.

There is one other transportational arrangement that you may wish to make. Have some responsible person chosen, or a limousine, to drive the couple away from the reception. It doesn't matter where they are going—station, airport, hotel, or just to their own car, which has been well hidden beforehand. An impersonal third party at the wheel tends to inhibit a herd of frisky ushers.

Before the start of the last week, which should be reserved for emergencies, delays, and details forgotten or omitted, most of the arrangements and other coordinating conferences will be completed. You and the club or banquet manager should be as one regarding food, liquor, table placement, band, and everything else. All he should still need is a fairly accurate head count. Check your bandleader as to time and place. If he needs travel directions, write them out and mail them. Does your photographer know where and when he is to be on hand? What about the church, or synagogue, the music, choir, soloist? Are you and your flower arranger agreed on what is to be done at the church? Have your ideas been cleared with the altar committee? Have you made up a pew seating list? Have you decided on the number of reserved pews? Will you have ribbons? A canopy? White runner? If the latter, what about carpeting under it? Who arranges for a traffic cop on duty at the church entrance—you or the church office? What about traffic control at the place of the reception? In the event of foul weather, can the bridesmaids dress at the church? What are you going to have to do about the ushers, if anything?

In other words, by the Saturday or Sunday before your daughter's wedding you should have all situations under control. This leaves you free to cope with numbers of heads, individuals who must have special attention, and the myriad household requirements. The services needing numbers are, in order of importance, the club, hotel, or restaurant manager, your caterer and your liquor dealer, your flower people, and, finally, the firm supplying canvas, tables, and chairs. You really should hold off any final fixed commitment until the last Wednesday. You might even have to add to or subtract from the number of cars required.

There is one monumental headache you can alleviate, although it is never completely cured until the receiving is half over. This is the seating procedure or method when you are having a large formal seated and served meal. We suggest that the following system (or one of your own) be started at least ten days ahead, when the majority of the acceptances will have come in: Take paper pie plates, each representing, let us say, a sixty-inch round table for ten. All around the bottom of each pie plate cut neat double slits—ten of them—and in each slit insert a stiff, narrow piece of file card. The name of a guest is written on the slip, and for every slip two corresponding cards should be made: a place card that goes on the dinner table and a card with the number of the table written on the inside. The place card is placed unfolded in an envelope (place cards are not folded until actually set on the table) and the envelopes are stapled to the bits of file cards. The envelopes should not be sealed in case changes and substitutions are to be made. The second set of cards is alphabetized, and arranged in rows by letter and facing out on a table so that the guests can find their own names readily after their arrival at the reception. A butler or caterer's assistant should be stationed at this table to remind the guests to pick up their table number cards. The reason for the pie plates is that they allow for better visualizing of the dining situation and space to make notations and changes.

This may sound complicated, but we have tried nearly everything, and this is the easiest way to deal with last-minute changes. Keeping the pie plate intact also enables the club manager or the caterer to seat people who had previously sent regrets or never answered, but have decided to come anyway. There will be blank spaces at some tables. You may even have several "rude tables," to take care of the unexpected guests. Don't be shocked; this happens more often than is realized. In all fairness to those who do show up in this manner, they usually had no idea that the reception was to be a formally seated affair. Naturally this pie plate system is equally applicable to long banquet tables. Just cut the holes in the pie plates to correspond with the number of places along the banquet tables.

If your daughter is having a bride's table, she doesn't have to prepare so elaborately as in the above manner. She merely works out a seating chart on cardboard or white paper, places her wedding party in selected seats, and makes out her place cards. Have someone give this packet of cards to the club manager or the caterer the morning of the reception and he will set them up. We advise "morning of the reception" because this doesn't allow much time for the cards to be lost. In seating her party the bride may well wish to follow a scheme like the one below. This was made for a sixteen-member group, which is about the average number we have encountered. In this case we had to use a modified U shape. With smaller groups, the arms can be eliminated, one member facing in at each end if necessary. Ideally, all members of the party should be in line facing the guests. If it can possibly be avoided, don't seat even one or two of them with their backs to the guests.

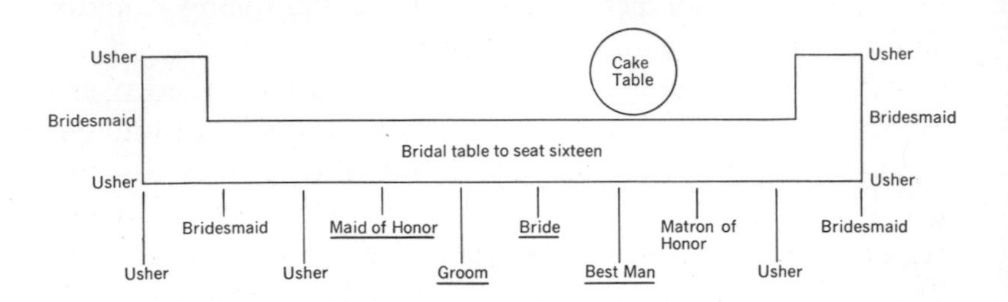

Note that we have underlined the positions of only the four main members of the party. These are the only ones that good form insists upon. It is entirely up to the bride and groom where all the others are placed. Chances are that during the reception they will all shift around anyhow.

Most of what we have been discussing immediately above is equally important for the small wedding and home reception for seventy-five people. When you are doing everything yourself, it is a good idea to get all the nonperishables ahead of time, including your liquor, and set aside a room or closet where you can lock it up. You are still going to have to check out the music, photography, livery service, and all the details in connection with the ceremony. The only difference is that while you may have as many services to deal with, you have a lot less of each to worry about. When you have no caterer or club manager to help you, the more you get behind you before the week of the wedding, the better.

Ten days before the ceremony you should mail out the pew cards that you have taken from your reserved pew lists. At the same time, if you live in a maze of unmarked roads, you should enclose driving directions, in map form, directing guests to the church or synagogue and then on to the reception.

Let us get back for a moment to those lists of people

to be seated in front of the ribbons. You are going to know exactly who is coming from your family, including those male members who would much prefer to watch the Amazin' Mets, but you have heard nothing definite from the groom's mother. We have found this to be a not uncommon situation in view of the tremendously wide dispersal of the young attending college today. She may well be trying to find out herself what family is coming.

You can, however, start making up your own pew seating cards for the ushers and set up a master list. We have never kept track of the average percent of those to be seated ahead of the ribbons who either forget their pew cards or leave them behind in another purse or pocket. But it seldom fails that a couple arrives in a complete dither just before the mother of the bride is to be seated. They tell the ushers they are to be seated with the family, but where? Luckily they do usually remember their own names.

Just as a reminder, the bride's family sits on the left side of the church as you face the altar from the back of the church, and the groom's family sits on the right. Some churches have highly polished brass numbers on the pews, but these numbers should be ignored, for the ushers are probably going to be completely unfamiliar with your church. They are probably not going to know much about ushering either. Your list and the ushers' cards should have two columns—Left Pew 1, Right Pew 1, Left Pew 2, Right Pew 2, etc., with 1 designating the first pew of the church. Under each number are written the names of those to be seated in that pew. Now if the first row of pews has no rail in front of it, forget it even exists and start your numbers with the next rows back. The first row of pews is also left vacant at a nuptial mass, especially when there are quite a few attendants. In this case, the left-hand pews are reserved for the bridesmaids and the right-hand ones for the ushers.

If you have to, leave the cards for the groom's side blank

until the very last moment, and that moment very often is the rehearsal dinner. You still have time to get someone to fill in the master list and the ushers' cards. When you are faced with this last-minute seating, have one of the bridesmaids or ushers fill in the master list (type or print), make a card for each name, put the cards in envelopes and take them with you to the rehearsal dinner. This dinner is usually seated by the groom's mother with place cards—when she and her husband are the hosts—so it is an easy thing to leave pew cards beside the place cards where they will be found easily.

The combined reserved pew lists should be typed so that there is a copy for each usher, including the head usher if one is given this courtesy title. Then there should be a duplicate set, plus a set for your wedding file. The first two sets should be put in separate envelopes and taken to the rehearsal by the bride's mother. One set is given out then so that the head usher and the others may familiarize themselves with the names on the lists. The second set should be given to the clergyman to be left in his study, where the ushers can find it on the wedding day.

In making up these reserved pew lists, don't forget the household help, particularly those who may have had a hand in bringing up the bride or groom. Some families have one entire pew reserved for household help, former nurses, baby-sitters, cleaning ladies, and so on, while others simply tell their help to ask an usher to seat them on the appropriate side of the church on a first-come, first-seated basis and do not have them in the reserved pews.

Many people seat the the family doctor and his wife—and their children if they are invited—with the minister's wife in one of the reserved pews. If any emergency calls are made to the church, the ushers and the sexton or janitor can locate the doctor quietly and quickly. Both of the latter should be told about this possible necessity at the rehearsal.

In the case of a bride who is close to both parents, but

these parents are divorced, on bad terms, and could not conceivably be at the same church or reception together, there is a solution that only she can work out. If her mother and stepfather are paying for her wedding and reception, she arranges with her father to give a bridal supper at his house after the reception. The supper is set to begin when she would otherwise be ready to change into her going-away clothes at the end of the reception. Instead, the couple in their wedding clothes, together with all their attendants, slip away to her father's, where their street clothes will have been previously brought. It is from this supper that they actually leave for their wedding trip. Her father sends out his invitations the same day as the regular ones are mailed. Such an invitation might read:

Mr. Elijah Wilmuth
requests the pleasure of your company
at the wedding supper of his daughter
Tabitha
and her bridegroom
Sergei Orhloff
Saturday, the twentieth of June
at seven o'clock
131 Piscatawney Road
Hardscrabble, New York

There will probably be some neutral friends who will be included from the earlier affair. In view of all the food available prior to this supper, something simple and in buffet style would probably be in order. If the father is remarried, the wording follows the usual form, i.e., Mr. and Mrs. Elijah Wilmuth, etc. What is sauce for the gander is equally sauce for the goose. The reverse situation is equally correct. The bride's mother can also give her a bridal supper.

Let's look now at a few protocol situations where there is an armed truce between divorced parents. If you are living with your mother and stepfather, who is giving you away and paying for everything, your father watches unseen and leaves the church. He does not go to the reception. If, however, your father is giving you away, he retreats to Left Pew 3. He also does not attend the reception. Reversing the situation—you are living with your father and his second wife, and he is giving you away—your mother is in Left Pew 1 and in the receiving line with the groom's mother, while your father and your stepmother stand near the front door greeting guests as they come in. If no real truce is in force, your stepmother does not attend the ceremony, but she is still the hostess of the reception. If your mother has also remarried, her husband is in Left Pew 1 and should act as escort for your mother at the reception. How long they remain at the reception depends upon the amount of tension. In many cases your mother and her husband will leave after the group photographs have been taken or after the first dance. If she chooses to be part of your first dance program, the groom, when cut in on by your father, should lead her out on the dance floor. Her husband should then cut in, and lead her off if she so desires. Anyway, once he cuts in they are on their own.

A bride who has an infirm parent, possibly a father in a wheelchair, who will give her away arranges it so that he is wheeled in by a side door in front or off to one side of the first left pew. (In most Roman Catholic churches, the first four pews are indented from the others to allow for a casket, while other places of worship with narrow main aisles will usually have some space available for the same purpose.) The bride may be escorted up the aisle on the arm of a brother, if she has one, or the head usher, who stops at a place, designated in the rehearsal, where the groom steps forward to meet her. The minister then directs his question of "Who gives this woman to be married to this man?" to the father in the wheelchair, who responds, "I do" or "Her mother and

I do." (This latter response is being used more frequently now—even in Protestant Episcopal churches.)

If a bride's mother is a widow, wishes to give her away, but doesn't wish to walk up the aisle with her, any male member of the bride's family, a godfather, or the head usher may escort her. Her mother can then make her response or nod her head from her place in the first left pew facing the altar.

Many brides are given away by uncles or older brothers when the inclusion of the father will cause real trouble. Usually it is a case of a father not being able to get on with a stepfather anywhere or anytime. Here recourse to the bridal supper should be made.

Embattled parents are bad enough, but what about four sets of warring grandparents let loose in the confines of clubrooms or under canvas? About all you can do is to assign each set a corner with firm instructions to stay put. It won't work, we have found out, but at least you can start them all out that way. As far as seating them in church, you are going to have to reserve four extra pews and then assign them by drawing lots.

In certain sections of the country, the South and the Midwest, and more recently in the East, there exists the delightful custom of having the groom's family fete the entire wedding party several days before the ceremony. This is not necessarily the so-called rehearsal dinner, but it could be. It also includes friends of the groom's family who are specifically invited to meet the bride. These guests are not necessarily invited to the wedding or the reception. If the groom is faced with an interparental state of war, his father easily can follow this custom and finesse the wedding entirely. This serves to eliminate any partisan strain existing among former neutral friends, and the bride will meet all her father-in-law's friends on neutral ground.

It takes time, tact, and serious deliberation to arrive at

the best possible solution to these many ticklish problems. There is nothing to prevent you, the bride, from making several alternate plans long in advance for all the services you basically need. Then you can sit back and watch the players act out their parts or leave the stage for good as the situation develops. In every case, the truly viable *modus operandi* does not become evident until you approach the final few weeks. This is especially true of the ceremony. The basic question of who is giving the reception and where, since this is a question of that most sincere commodity, money, will usually be solved before the last month, but questions of protocol may not be solved until the day before the wedding.

Not so long ago one of our brides was married during the throes of a particularly acrimonious divorce. Her father was paying for everything and giving her away. Her mother would have no part of the proceedings under any circumstances, but she showed up at the church in full regalia, without so much as a warning telephone call to her daughter. We had left pew Left 1 vacant on the lists against this possibility, and had reserved an outside place for her father in Left 3, just in case. As the mother left the church she announced that she wouldn't be seen dead at the reception. About twenty minutes after it had started, she showed up and took up a stand at the head of the receiving line. Not only did she stay for the reception, she was almost the last person to leave the hotel. So you see what can happen.

Speaking of situations outside the customary wedding and reception, there are two that are infrequent but should be mentioned. One occurs when the bride is an orphan without any close relatives. If she can find a friend who will act as hostess for her reception, the normal procedure obtains. In this case, though, she is most apt to be footing the bills herself. The other is when a bride's family is utterly opposed to her marriage and refuses to have any part of it whatsoever. Here, too, she will have to make all the arrangements herself.

In both cases the reception should be given in a hotel or restaurant. Certainly, in the latter case, the bride should not involve any outsider, no matter how good a friend. Nor should she involve even her close relatives. It would only exacerbate a bad situation. Also the size and elaborateness of the reception should be kept in check. As far as the receiving line is concerned, we suggest that there be none. This does away with the necessity for the guests to appear to take sides. If, however, the bride feels she must have one, the order would be: the bride, the groom, and the maid or matron of honor. In the case of the absolute orphan (and in this category we would include those girls whose parents either cannot or are not permitted to come to her wedding) there is more latitude in planning her reception. In fact, since World War II it has become increasingly acceptable for orphan and refugee brides, especially when they can't afford the extensive entertainment that the groom's family wants, to have that family give the reception.

However, when the bride's parents remain completely hostile, we think that the best solution is to get married either by a magistrate (no wedding dress) or in the parsonage or parish house. In either case, the couple may go on to a friend's house or restaurant to have lunch or dinner. To save her parents' displeasure from increasing and involving even more the groom's family, the couple should have only their own friends with them on that day.

If you as a bride fall into one of the two above categories or their variants, we suggest that you consider yourself *in loco parentis* and carry on as your family otherwise would. However, there is no real necessity for anyone to give the bride away, even a young bride. This question may be deleted entirely from the marriage ceremony. But you should talk it over with your clergyman.

In the case of hostile parents, time might bring them around. And because both ceremony and reception have been planned initially as modest and simple, a month would suffice to put everything together, if the parents do indeed relent. The invitations can even be of an informal nature.

In this era when the population is restless and given to frenetic movement, many a bride's family sees very little of the groom until the last month. Most never meet the ushers until the last week. Therefore, we would like to review briefly just what the groom does up to the moment when he assumes, in theory, anyhow, full responsibility for his bride.

Obviously he is in the process of arranging for some sort of bed and board for his bride, although today that is usually a joint effort, often involving painting and redecorating. He also has to figure out some way, usually with the help of the bride's parents, of escaping from his ushers when the couple leaves the reception. If he has a responsible job or is trying to complete a doctorate, for example, he will need an "executive officer." That's usually the best man. (In Appendix B is a list of specific expenses that are his responsibility.)

One thing he must get is the marriage license. In most states this involves physical examinations that must be taken within thirty days of the ceremony and within the state in which it is to take place. Many states also require that the license be issued in the town or city of the ceremony. Once that piece of paper is in your hands, run, don't walk, to your minister, priest, or rabbi, and give it to him. We have known of several weddings held up while the best man galloped all over town trying to find the marriage license. The clergy has the same outlook regarding this matter as the Chinese laundry: "No tickee, no washee." What happens if the church loses the license we don't know, but we suspect this is a matter that belongs properly in the hands of the deity. If the need for a passport is in the groom's plans, he had better apply for a duplicate as well.

There is no question that the groom pays the minister, priest, or rabbi, but most grooms as well as most brides' families are in a quandary as to the amount and the method. The general rule of thumb is a *minimum* of twenty-five dollars, but it could vary according to what is customary in the bride's church. This amount is sometimes hard to find out because, unless there is a church secretary who is frank, no one wants to say. Usually it is the mother of the bride who is left to come up with the facts. If the bride's family are supporting members of the church where the wedding will take place, the groom can get off with a smaller fee, but if they are not members and the wedding is a large one, the groom may give the most he can afford, and should do so.

If all else fails, the amount and method of giving the fee might be discussed—by the groom and the clergyman—ahead of time. Some clergymen will not accept any fee whatsoever for officiating at a marriage ceremony; others count on receiving one. If the groom finds that the former is true, he can draw a check payable to the church as a donation. This is always acceptable, and tax-deductible besides. The best man usually presents the fee, or donation, when he and the groom are waiting offstage with the clergyman for the processional signal to be given.

We would like to note here that if there is a family minister, priest, or rabbi who is to assist at the ceremony, the bride's family or the groom's family, as the case may be, pays for all his travel expenses, including hotel accommodations and meals.

It is a matter of local custom, and by personal arrangement, whether or not the groom pays for his bride's bouquet, her going-away flowers—if any—and those for both mothers. Usually he is responsible for these costs, and the bride's florist bills him directly, for this florist is, of course, the one who supplies these flowers. For the sake of tact, the groom should order, and pay for, flowers for any stepmothers who are to attend the ceremony. He always pays for his best man's, ushers', and fathers' boutonnieres. In some parts of the country the groom's mother offers to pay for all the bridesmaids' flowers.

Sometimes we wonder what a best man actually does. We know more or less what he is *supposed* to do, and that includes being responsible, as stated, for handling the minister's fee. Also, he is to get the groom to the church on time, properly dressed and rehearsed. He has the ring with him. But before this, if he is on his toes, he has acted as packer and valet to insure that the groom has the right clothes in the right suitcase at the right time. He runs all the errands in connection with the wedding trip, such as reservations and accommodations, in such a manner that the newlyweds don't arrive at the first stop, hotel, train, or airport looking like a bride and groom from a comic movie script. Finally, he should help the couple to escape the ushers and other friends at the end of the reception. Incidentally, it is not necessary for the best man to be responsible for the initial toast.

And now, here comes that last week, and no matter how much prior planning and checking have been done, circumstances beyond control, even beyond imagination, are going to conspire to leave loose ends to be tied up, problems newly arisen to be solved, and all the prima donnas to placate. This is the moment, maybe Friday or Saturday night, when the bride's mother should snare her husband, whose nerves are almost as frayed as hers are, and say, "Take me out to some new, strange, lovely, bright spot for dinner—someplace where we are unknown, where there is no chance of meeting anyone, especially a prospective guest."

Chapter 12

The Last Week

SOMEHOW YOU HAVE MADE IT TO THE SUNDAY BEFORE the wedding. Let's say it's late afternoon and raining, for which you are grateful. You hope it rains every day until Thursday. You're sitting in the small TV room opposite your husband who has his feet up as he reads the paper. On your lap is a clipboard firmly holding the notebook—with the checklist tucked into it—that has become a part of your body for the past four months. You take out the checklist and run through it again to reassure yourself that nothing has been forgotten. Satisfied, a great sense almost of peace and well-being pervades your soul, and you feel you might even close your eyes and indulge in a little nap. Then you hear it: the sound of the front door closing, but not with the usual bang. This is an odd sound somewhere between a bang and a definite click. Put your shoes on, for this could be it. Get up quietly and go out into the hall. If you don't see your daughter, the bride-to-be, call to her, "Who just went out?"

If she tells you it was the groom, whom you had been expecting to stay on for supper, follow the sound of her voice. You may not reach her before she locks herself in her room. Never mind. Do nothing but listen for several seconds. If you hear her crying and her tears reach the pitch of rending sobs, play it cool. Wait. Then try to get her to open her door or at least to tell you what has caused her anguish. If she blurts out that she can't go through with the wedding and never, *never* wants to see Peter again in her life, you'll have to persuade her to open the door and let you in.

You may be able to achieve this by insisting that she tell her father in person just what she's told you. You must refuse to do it for her. The very prospect of having to tell her father may be the icebreaker. Go into her room and stay there. Listen to her. Find out if this is just a very bad case of bride's nerves or the real thing. Both of you know that you're her mother, but if you can add a new dimension to this relationship by shifting into another gear, this could be your finest hour. Talk to her woman-to-woman now—as if you had never heard of the generation gap. And do it before either of you disturbs that poor, long-suffering man in the TV room who's probably taken a real beating in the market by selling stocks and bonds in anticipation of wedding bills. In short, madam, get the facts, and get them fast.

If you have any lingering doubts as to the firmness of your daughter's intention of calling the wedding off, try this one on her: ask her to give you her engagement ring then and there; tell her it must be returned at once. Should she give it to you, try to get her calmed down enough to have a family conference within the hour. It's far better to call the whole thing off than to have your daughter go through with the wedding on Saturday only to head for the divorce court later. Just be sure she isn't fooling herself—and you. The engagement ring test will be a real one. Take it from her and put it away. See if you can locate your family doctor and fill the prescription he will undoubtedly order for your daughter, your husband, and you. You will all need a night's sleep. If on that Sunday before the wedding you find yourself in this position, it may be heartbreaking, a welcome relief, or only a false alarm—even if she does give you the engagement ring. Whatever it is, don't do anything about canceling the wedding until the following morning. There isn't much you can do late on a Sunday afternoon anyway—and the wedding might be right back on again by Monday morning. One way or the other, you are going to be a very busy person.

If the wedding has to be canceled before the invitations are mailed, how much will it cost? This will depend in part on how much time the various firms and services have to find a replacement for your patronage. It would be most unlikely that they could find another wedding at this late date, but there are always parties of one kind or another and company business that could replace the wedding you have to cancel. The caterers and canvas firms usually consider a broken engagement just another business hazard if they are notified six or more weeks in advance. Any deposit made is generally refunded. This is equally true of the orchestras, although few ever ask for deposits. Hotels, restaurants, and inns follow the same pattern, unless the wedding date was on one of those prime ones, in which case the matter is open to adjustment. Practices vary widely.

You are stuck with the photographer if the formal portrait has been taken and you have proofs, and possibly glossy prints made up for the newspapers. You will have to pay for the sitting, the glossy prints, and probably the proofs—which no one will ever want to look at again. If you have been working with one good photographic studio and have given them the order for the candid coverage also, this is now very much to your advantage. Most reputable studios are very understanding and cooperative, for broken engagements and even last-minute cancellations are not unusual in their experience. Most of the studios take the long view: your attractive daughter will either marry Peter at a later date or some other young man, and it's better to have your goodwill and loyalty than to make any but necessary charges now.

As for the decorations you have ordered, it is only the occasional florist or designer who will ask you to pay for anything unless it be some special fabric that, though still in the bolt, can't be used for anyone else because it was a special dye job for your decorative scheme. We have had this happen to a client, but the matter was adjusted between the client and the decorator, who was able to unload the fabric later on to someone else who loved weird colors.

You are stuck with the cost of the wedding invitations, of course, whether they were mailed or not, and with the announcements unless you can reach the engraver in time to cancel the order. In rush periods engravers often do not make up the announcements until two weeks before the wedding date, although they send you the envelopes ahead, as they do with the envelopes for the wedding invitations. We occasionally have had these "splits" in engaged couples in time to return all envelopes before they were addressed. It's not much of a saving, but everything you can add to the total does help.

Any silver that has been engraved with what were to have been the bride's new initials can become a problem. Talk to your silversmith and find out if the initials can be removed and the silver buffed sufficiently to hide any marks. Here we are talking specifically about family gifts of silver (from the bride's family) that may have been made between the time of the engagement announcement and the sending out of invitations.

Linens or towels that have been marked as part of the trousseau could be a dead loss if the bride has used what were to have been her new initials. (Those old-fashioned girls whose silver and linen are marked with their maiden initials only are a lot smarter than modern brides give them credit for.)

All gifts from showers, as well as wedding gifts that may

have been received before the invitations were sent out, must be returned, too.

The bridal gown and the veil, if purchased with it, and all the bridesmaids' dresses and each and every accessory are total losses, which, under these circumstances, the bride's family should bear unless the girls whom your daughter has asked to be her attendants wish to buy their dresses to wear for other occasions. There are exceptions to both losses: we have known two brides who kept both their bridal gowns and veils and wore them at their marriages to other grooms; and we have known bridal salons to sell all or most of the bridesmaids' dresses for other weddings. Both of these exceptions are rare, but you could be lucky.

As for the newspapers—unless a wedding release and glossy print of the formal wedding portrait has been sent out—you may decide to do absolutely nothing. Or you may send out a release to all the papers to which you sent an announcement of the engagement. (Please refer to chapter 3 for the correct form.) The decision about this must be a personal—and intuitive—one on the part of the bride's parents. We have known far too many engaged couples whose wedding plans were canceled just before the invitations went out to make up and either elope or set a new date. We advise parents to play this one by ear.

When the wedding is canceled the week before the ceremony, the problem is far tougher. It's also much more expensive—and a more frequent occurrence than any bride-to-be and her parents might like to contemplate. Whatever the reasons or circumstances may be, the hard fact is that it can and does happen. So what do you do first, and what will it all cost?

The first step is to notify the newspapers that the wedding will not take place. This can be done by the bride's father or mother early on Monday morning. Use the form suggested in chapter 3, and read it over the telephone to the society editor or to the editor of the women's pages. If need be, follow up the telephone notification with a written one. Send copies to all newspapers to which you sent wedding press releases and glossy prints.

That invitation file system we urged you to set up will now be pure gold to you, as will several intimate friends of both the bride and her mother. Call them and see if they will help you now (they'll be only too glad to be in on a dramatic situation), but you need give them no explanation whatever beyond the fact that the wedding is being called off. The reasons are personal ones, and if there is anyone so tactless as to inquire into them, she isn't a friend, so don't ask her to help out. Your good friends will stand by. Have as many of them as you can make local calls on their own telephones (so your line won't be tied up) to let the guests know that the wedding has been canceled. Give each woman twenty or more cards and have her return them to the file later.

The rest of the guests may have to be notified by telegram. Make out a form, use your invitation file system, and go through it alphabetically until you have covered every person. The would-be recipients of telegrams could be away from home and not get them as planned, so it would be wise to have someone delegated to be at the church, synagogue, or temple a half hour before the ceremony was scheduled to begin to let any guests who might appear know that the wedding will not take place.

You and your entire family will be in for a tough week at best and then, like any other five-day wonder, it will begin to die down and become old news. You, your husband, and your daughter should plan to be away from home on the wedding date and at least during that week. Don't hang around in the midst of reminders of the wedding, especially all the gifts, which will have to be returned as quickly as possible.

With this job ahead of you, a weekend of rest and diversion is very definitely indicated.

Quite a number of gifts arrive late, that is, after the scheduled ceremony. All of these should be returned unopened to the shop that sent them, together with a note requesting that the card enclosed giving the name of the donor be sent to your daughter so that she may write them. In your note tell the shop that the wedding has been canceled and that you will appreciate its cooperation in either having the gift credited to the account of the person who sent it or in getting the donor's instructions as to its disposition. If gifts that have been insured are opened, the shop's insurance policy no longer covers them. As for gifts that have been opened, they should be packed by a professional packer and returned to the shop or to the donor if sent directly to your daughter. The gifts from relatives and friends in your community could be packed by you or your daughter and returned to them personally or by a delivery service if a good one is available to you. We suggest making up a form note, taking it to your engraver, and having him make up as many as you need. Raised printing is great for this type of note, which your engraver usually can help you word.

We urge you and your daughter to take care of these details as soon as possible. If she has a job she was planning to keep after her marriage, let her apply herself to it with all her interest and energy. If she doesn't have a job, now is the time for her to find one, or to take the trip to Europe she had been dreaming about until Peter came along. Do whatever you can to get her away until the air clears and she gets a new perspective on life.

And while we are on unpleasant subjects, what exactly does a bride do when she is left standing at the church without a groom? Let's say an ashen-faced best man comes into the rectory five minutes after the processional is due to begin with a note from the groom saying that he is "sky-jacking" a plane to Cuba and will never marry the girl, that day or ever. This calls for a hurried conference between the minister, the girl, and her parents, followed by an announcement from the minister that the wedding will not take place. This is a rare situation but one in which we were involved some years ago.

Then there's the other stinker of a situation in which the groom does not show up and there is no message from him or his best man. Nothing! Just deadly mounting tension! Finally, the silence in the church is broken by the organist, who begins to play over again all the music that had been chosen as the prelude to the processional. We had one of these horrors to contend with, and the reason for it was that the groom and his best man had been seriously injured in an automobile accident en route to the church on a stretch of parkway where no telephones were nearby. A call to the hospital confirmed that both the groom and best man were out of danger but that the wedding would have to be postponed. After some lightning consultations with the bride and her parents, the minister made the announcement of what had happened to a crowded church. Everyone present was invited to proceed to the reception, the bride left to change her clothes and go to the hospital, and her parents went on to the club to greet the guests. They had the wedding cake and bridal table removed while they welcomed everyone as they would at a cocktail party. The bride-to-be joined them later for what turned out to be not her wedding reception but a real bash just the same.

We hope you and your family will be spared any of these troubles, but we decided to mention some of the things that can be just as upsetting as the sound of your front door closing on the groom. So now, back to the clipboard and the checklist, for you have work to do during this week of the wedding.

You're going to spend quite a bit of time with the card

file you set up in the beginning for the invitations and the announcements. We hope you're good at addition and subtraction, for you'll have many last-minute changes to cope with, both at the church and at the reception. This is why we suggested that you get everything possible nailed down firmly, and as early as possible.

We have been stressing the final head count you must give the caterer or the club manager on the Wednesday before the wedding—after your mail has been delivered and that day's acceptances and regrets taken into consideration, and *after* making due allowance for the contents of the "rude box." The rude box is now more important to the determination of what your final head count will be than any other part of your file. Taking a count of acceptances and regrets is an easy matter, but one needs a crystal ball, if not a computer, to tell how many of those guests-to-be, or not-to-be, who have not had the decency to reply will show up at the wedding. Their names jump out at you now as you run through their cards in the rude box. Whether they are your friends or the groom's, you hate them one and all, as you promise yourself to answer all future invitations promptly.

If you are using a marquee, give the total head count to the canvas firm. The man in charge may want to add a flyer if the number exceeds your earlier estimate. If your count is below the original one, he may be able to reduce the size of the marquee itself. Except under certain conditions where there are seated and served meals, or where you have already reached the limit of comfortable tent coverage (there is usually an allowance of at least twenty-five heads either way), he may advise you to stick to the original plan for the marquee. Twenty-five heads *less* in the event of a downpour on the wedding day could mean more elbowroom, but a reduction in the size of the marquee might produce an atmosphere akin to that in a packed sardine can.

If the reception is at home, you will have overordered

champagne, liquor, and mixes, we hope, so the addition of twenty-five heads merely reduces the amounts you will send back to the liquor dealer for credit. If you are using a club, hotel, or restaurant, it will make the necessary adjustments in its calculations when you report the final count.

For the same reasons the florist should be given the count, for he may have to provide more or fewer centerpieces, since you may need more or fewer tables, and there's no use paying for anything you don't need. On the other hand, it would look miserable if there were tables without centerpieces. Incidentally, don't forget to include in the final count all the members of the bridal party, including the bride and groom. Believe it or not, several mothers of brides have forgotten this.

No matter how detailed a picture you may have in your mind, always wait until the marquee is up before you try to make final decisions as to where certain things are to be placed. Usually the first consideration when working under canvas is where to place the dance floor, assuming your grounds permit a choice. The dance floor is both the greatest center of attraction and your biggest block to traffic. Ideally, it should be centered on the long side of the marquee opposite the entrance that leads from your house, or at one end of an oblong marquee. But whatever you do, don't ask to have it placed in a spot where extensive shoring up or a lot of extra building is necessary. Many women are apt to do just this for what they think will result in perfect balance. Often it just isn't worth the extra time, labor, and materials. Besides, once a marquee is decorated and starts filling up with guests, no one will ever notice any of the things that might bother a hostess as she stands under a bare marquee which has just been erected. We often say to our clients that we wish they would see the marquee on their grounds for the first time *after* they return from the church on the day of the wedding.

After you and the man from the canvas firm have fixed

the locations of the dance floor and the bandstand, if any, you should decide on where to place the bridal table or the smaller one reserved for the bride if she prefers it. Do be sure, however, that enough passage space is left for the special service and attention a seated bridal table merits. Equal consideration should be given to the location of the cake table. It should be where it may be seen, out of the line of traffic, but near where the bride and groom will cut the cake. The bride may want to have the cake table carried onto the dance floor so that all the guests can see the cake cutting. If so, do have the cake table placed where the caterer's staff can move it easily onto the dance floor when the couple is ready for it instead of in some distant spot from where they will have to carry it the length of the marquee and run the chance of dropping it en route.

Some brides like to receive in the house no matter what the weather is; others have a favorite background outside that can be used if it will be shaded at the time the guests arrive. Inside the marquee is an excellent location for a receiving line because it affords your guests ample space, in good weather or bad, to check wraps, greet one another, and form in line under conditions of optimum comfort.

After these decisions have been made, let your caterer take over. He will most likely already have picked out the best spots for his bar (as far from the receiving line as possible) and the buffet and food serving tables, because the thought uppermost in his mind will be to have sufficient passageway space between the tent and your kitchen, garage, or the caterer's tent. If you are having a seated meal, or a buffet where you have allowed tables for about a third of your guests, ask for his ideas about placing them. We have a running battle with just about every caterer with whom we work concerning the way he sets up guest tables. Given a free hand, a caterer will line up those tables as though he were preparing for army inspection. Straight lines can be so dull, and they usually do not square with the irregular sides of a marquee anyway.

After you have done all this, you should go over the entire canvas layout with your florist and your husband, with the following questions in mind: Where are the solid canvas sidewalls, or drops, needed to insure privacy from the road or from the neighbors? Where should poly sidewalls be used against cool winds or the possibility of slashing rain? Where will the sun be during the time you are receiving your guests? Your husband is more apt to know the answers to these questions than anyone else. When he has given them to you, let him leave; it makes a father of the bride nervous to be in on any discussions between his wife and a florist at this stage of the game. But you and the florist have to decide what areas need emphatic greening to accentuate the background for the receiving line, the bridal table, the main entrance to the marquee, the dance floor, and the bandstand. All this sounds like a time-consuming task, but it shouldn't take more than an hour if you can get the florist, the caterer, the canvas man, and your husband together at the same time for this final mop-up.

Failing this coordinating meeting, you'll either have to draw up a ground plan for the caterer or be there when he is setting up before the wedding. The latter you won't be able to do, for you'll either be under a hair dryer or coping with some *crise* having to do with dressing for the ceremony.

We suggest that you take some small cards, print on them "Bride's table here," "Receiving line here," etc., and thumbtack them to the sidewall poles where you want specific things placed. And it would be a good idea for you to make a tour of the marquee—in housecoat and comfortable slippers—just before you finish dressing to go to the church. This eleventh-hour cruise insures your finding caterer, florist, and canvas man—and probably your husband—all under the marquee at the same time and will enable you to see that everything is working out according to plan.

Now is the time, too, to make any changes in the chronological schedule of reception events. Be sure you inform the key people involved with your schedule, including the orchestra leader, of these changes before the reception. Doing this will relieve you of most of the supervisory details later when you want to be free to enjoy being with your guests. Some hostesses rely heavily on the orchestra leader to be their surrogate emcee—a good idea if you have a top leader who knows his business and uses a microphone sparingly, if at all, for cues. Others rely on their caterer or the club manager. The main thing is to get the details taken care of smoothly so you can have a good time.

You will need a personal "runner," another pair of legs to spare yours. This runner or messenger could be a son, if you have one, or you could appoint one of the ushers. His job is to be the liaison between you and the key members of the services who are present, particularly the photographer, as well as between you and the bride, groom, and other members of the wedding party. Save your feet whenever you can. If there are a number of ushers, they could spell each other in the job. Since the mother of the bride often meets them for the first time at the rehearsal, appoint them here, or have the groom do this. Your "extra feet" merely have to be on the alert for a signal from you to come wherever you are and carry out an errand for you.

Before we leave the subject of marquees, we want to remind you that there's a way to make very full use of the one you've rented for the wedding: it's a great place to have a buffet supper or a small seated dinner after the rehearsal. And this is so whether the groom's parents, you, or one of your relatives or best friends are paying for it. Your caterer will provide whatever menu the groom's mother wants, if she is indeed giving the party. Contact her by phone or letter and offer her a choice of linen in a different color from what is being used for the reception, find out her preferences in liquor and other beverages, whether she wishes to have one large table or several that seat eight, with one seating four for the bride, groom, and their two honor attendants, and give her prices. Then telephone your florist and have him either write or call the groom's mother to choose a color scheme for the centerpieces (again different from that of the reception). One more call, to the office of the orchestra to have them give the groom's mother an estimate on a musician to play an accordion, or on a trio if there is to be dancing, and you are in business. Other than the telephoning, there's no work for you involved because the groom's mother will do her own seating and get her own place cards.

This additional use of a marquee is well worth considering. The dinner usually turns out to be more personal and enjoyable than one in the grillroom of your club or in a restaurant, and having one or more men from the orchestra that will play at the reception gives them an opportunity to know the bridal couple's tastes in music, thus creating a far warmer rapport with them at the reception.

Seating arrangements for these dinners vary greatly, and since the mother of the groom may be the hostess—even under your marquee and on your grounds—the choice is up to her. We should say here that, except in the South and the Middle West, it is not necessarily customary for the groom's parents to give a prenuptial or rehearsal dinner, although for many years there has been a growing trend all over the country for them to do so.

Regardless of who gives the dinner, the question of whether to invite the minister and his wife, or the rabbi and his wife, or the priest, or another member of the clergy who will officiate or assist at the ceremony, is always raised. Our answer is to invite them by all means if they are close friends, but do not unless they are. Pity the poor members of the clergy if they had to attend all rehearsal dinners, as well as wedding receptions! As for clergy who are to assist at the ceremony (from the groom's hometown, for example), they usually arrive about an hour before the wedding. If the bride's parents wish to have their clergyman present—and the groom's family is paying for the rehearsal dinner—then it's up to the groom's parents to decide whether to have their own clergyman (and wife, if any) present too.

Whether you live in a city or a suburb, telegrams and cablegrams may be telephoned in and tie up your line, making it nearly impossible to receive or make phone calls. You should call the manager of the Western Union office and request that no telegrams of a *congratulatory* nature addressed to the bridal couple be telephoned to your home. Ask him to have copies made and mailed to you. In this way the newlyweds will have the actual telegrams for a scrapbook or their wedding file instead of bits of paper on which whoever answered the phone at your house tried to write down the telegram. Often there are two shifts at the Western Union office, the second taking over after 5:30 P.M. Check this with the office manager, and be sure to get him personally; don't leave a message. Do this no sooner than the Tuesday before a Saturday wedding; if you notify the office earlier, your instructions just get lost.

A number of your good friends will ask if there isn't something they can do to help you. You bet there is, so give them each a specific job:

Have one take a large thermos of ice water and a carton of paper cups to the church one hour before the ceremony, unless yours is a church with a new addition that can be reached by the bride and her attendants without being seen by the congregation. Sometimes there is a refurbished basement with a kitchen and all its facilities available, connected by stairs to the narthex where the ushers, bridesmaids, and the bride and her father line up for the processional. Frequently, all such modern conveniences are located in the "new building" and are totally useless for weddings unless some genius of an architect remembered to add a covered passageway between it and your dear old church.

Ask two other friends, whom you can rely on to remain calm, to stay within easy calling distance of the place where, before the ceremony, the bride, her attendants, you, and the groom's mother have been told by your clergyman to assemble. Have them stand by for last-minute help. You should equip them with a "panic bag" containing such items as bobby, hair, safety, straight, and corsage pins, spirits of ammonia, sewing and first-aid kits, a styptic pencil, a hand mirror in a leather case, cleaning fluid, small packages of tissues, sanitary napkins, cotton pads, combs, hair spray, pliers, screwdriver, green florist's tape, paper cups, Scotch tape, nylon stockings, white gloves, flasks with one ounce each of Scotch, brandy, and vodka, three silver wedding rings, peppermints, tranquilizers, suspenders, collar buttons, ascots, pin-striped ties, extra white kid and pearl gray gloves, and one portable container of oxygen.

Unless you are using a limousine service, you will probably have to rely on the husbands of friends to drive the bridesmaids and the honor attendant, or attendants, to the church, wait, and then drive them to the reception. (Station wagons are great for the bridesmaids, but put some sheets over the seats.) The drivers may be relatives or the husbands of members of your family, and you would like to have them seated in the reserved pews. Don't do it. Seat their wives, if you like, but the husbands who are drivers should remain in the back of the church near the door so they can leave just before the recessional, get into their cars, which should be parked in front of the church, and be ready to drive away as soon as the wedding party comes out. This is merely common sense unless you plan to form a receiving line just inside the church entrance. This is done when a simple luncheon or dinner for the immediate families only is to follow the ceremony. Otherwise, have the drivers where they can get out ahead of the wedding party.

In certain sections of the country it is customary for the best man not to walk out with the maid of honor in the recessional but to leave the church by a side door and make a dash for the front of the church, where he sees the bridal couple into the car—and possibly drives it himself—that will take them to the reception.

It is wise to have your telephone answered promptly all during the last week. There are always eleventh-hour crises of one kind or another that your cleaning lady or day help should not be expected to cope with. Have your friends work out a schedule among themselves so that your phone is answered. Many newspapers have a policy of checking out the press release on the Wednesday or Thursday preceding a Saturday wedding, *before* they make up the society pages for that day. They are anxious to know whether the wedding is on or off or if there have been any important changes regarding bridesmaids, ushers, etc., since the press release was sent in. Few of us these days can *find,* let alone *afford,* live-in help, and cleaning ladies of otherwise robust health and vigor have a strange way of being brought down with the first major illness of their lives during the week of a wedding. Better line up some friends to cover the telephone.

If you are having a home reception—under a marquee or otherwise—and are renting a piano, call the rental source and remind them to deliver it by noon if the ceremony is in the afternoon, or by ten A.M. the day of the wedding if there is to be a nuptial mass.

Wear your wedding shoes around the house for several hours each day. Assemble your clothes and all of the accessories, including the underpinnings, for the wedding and give *yourself* a rehearsal. Do this early in the week before the bridesmaids, out-of-town relatives, and those delightful friends who like to drop by to see the gifts the day before the wedding begin to arrive. And they'll do it every time. Enlist the aid of one of your friends to act as their personal guide.

Check out hair, manicure, and pedicure appointments for you and the bride to be sure there is no foul-up with any of them.

If the reception is to be away from home, you and the bride should check out everything she needs for her going-away clothes, take them to your club on Friday, and have them locked up in the room where she will change. The groom should do the same. Also, take along a garment bag and a box for the wedding gown, veil, and all her wedding clothes so that they will be available for your convenience *after* the reception. The maid of honor should take this detail off your shoulders, but sometimes it doesn't work out that way.

The bride would do well to have all her luggage packed by Friday and in the trunk of the car in which the couple will leave the reception, or have a *reliable* best man check the bags into the hotel where they are going to stay on their wedding night. All the bride will need—if she packs right—is, in addition to the rest of her luggage, one small case for her makeup, which should also contain a duplicate set of keys for the luggage, her jewelry, passport (if the couple is going out of the country for their wedding trip), "mad money," a small supply of informals with her new initials, envelopes, and stamps.

If your church is one that provides each newly married couple with a small wedding book containing a page signed by the minister, the bride, groom, best man, and maid of honor (almost like a copy of the marriage license), a place should be left for it in the bride's case. One of the duties of the best man is to have this book signed by all members of the wedding party and have it put back in its envelope and sent up to the room where the bride is to change so that she may take it with her. If the couple is going out of the country, you should arrange well in advance for your clergyman to have a true copy of their marriage license made so they have an official document to take with them. The little white wedding book is a keepsake and may not serve the purpose if the couple should need proof of their marriage in certain foreign countries.

We also suggest that you take the club manager a cake knife, if the bride has been given one, with which she can cut the wedding cake at the reception. At the same time check with him on the time of delivery of the cake, the cakes in small boxes if you have ordered them, the matchbooks with the initials of the bridal couple and the date of the wedding imprinted on them, and the rose petals. Be sure the manager has the name and telephone number of the shop that is to deliver these items. If they are not delivered at the appointed time, the club manager can then do something about it; you can't, for you'll be at the ceremony.

If the bride has been given one of those silver cups for the first toast (they are charming items to look at but require contortionists to drink out of without spilling champagne down the front of the bridal gown), you might give it to the club manager along with the cake knife. Unless this type of silver "his and her" cup has been bestowed upon the bride by some very special relative or friend, we suggest that you tell the club manager to give two *regular* champagne glasses to the florist so he may decorate them with string smilax and a few blossoms of bouvardia or stephanotis when he is doing the same for the cake knife.

And while you are at the club, look in your purse for the list of the last changes you have for the reserved tables for families. Give it to the manager. Give him the bridal table place cards and seating chart and any other charts and place cards you may be using for tables reserved for families.

By now you will know how many small children—if any—are coming to the reception with their parents, and how many teen-agers. The latter usually take care of themselves by picking a table as far from parental eyes as possible (behind the band is a favorite spot if they can work it out). The problem of ankle-nippers (all small-fry under ten) can usually be solved by having a reserved table for them if they are relatives or members of your immediate family. Such a table should be under the supervision of a paid baby-sitter, preferably an attractive young woman whom some of them know and one in whom you have confidence. A table of properly supervised ankle-nippers can add to the fun of the daytime reception, but one that is not well organized can quickly get out of hand. In any case all very small children should be taken home on the early side, be they family or not.

You might also check with the club manager to see whether he has made provision for one more reserved table. This is the one we call the "fifth wheel table," and it is for the wives, husbands, fiancés, and best beaux of the wedding attendants. They are always, or nearly so, the forgotten guests at wedding receptions and have a miserable, lonely, left-out feeling unless some provision is made for them. This is only fair, especially if they know few of the guests. The "fifth wheel table" should be placed as near the bridal table as possible. If only one table is reserved for both sets of parents and the immediate families, the "fifth wheel table" could balance it on the other side of the bridal table. The bride should remember to indicate ahead of time those whom she wishes to be seated at it. The rehearsal dinner is a good time for this because they will all be present. Otherwise, we suggest using place cards for this table, too.

The bridal salon should deliver—to the predetermined dressing place—each bridesmaid's dress with a ticket on which is printed the name of the wearer. Often the bridesmaids bring their own slippers with them because they have had to have them dyed where they were purchased. The same may be true of headpieces, unless these are being made by the florist.

The men's rental firm should also have the name of each usher pinned to his suit. This saves much confusion when the ushers are dressing. If possible, the best man should check out this detail for the groom, but if he can't, then you might delegate your husband to do this.

He will probably stay home from the office on Friday to help you, so give him something to do. If the poor father of the bride has been your tower of strength for weeks, the day before the wedding is the time he'll probably have an attack of nerves. So get him out of the house. If you have relatives who have to be met at the airport or station, this is the perfect job for him. However, if you have any really complicated errands left, he's not your man, for he'll either forget them, try to do everything over twice, or "improve" on your directions because he's a nervous wreck but won't admit it. He's probably apprehensive, too, about every last detail of the marriage ceremony that concerns him. If you were able to get to the core of his problems, you'd discover that his chief concern is that rented cutaway and how he will look in it. The other one is the fear that he will step on his daughter's train, trip on his way back to pew Left 1, and fall flat down in the church in front of everyone. And there's nothing you can do about him except to keep him busy until it's time to leave for the rehearsal. So, again, let him get out of the house. You take a nice warm bath and try to relax.

Chapter 13

The Rehearsal and Marriage Ceremony

HERE YOU ARE WITH LESS THAN TWENTY-FOUR HOURS TO go, so be stouthearted and plunge on bravely. When you and your husband leave for the rehearsal, be sure to take with you an envelope with a check for the organist, one for the soloist—if any—and one for the sexton. Take *all* those beautifully typed lists showing where each person is to be seated (by pew number) in the reserved pew section. You should have two sets of lists: one to give the head usher, and the duplicate set to be left in the clergyman's study or some place he designates that will be known to the ushers so the lists can be found easily on the wedding day. And bring one more envelope, the one that contains the order of the "first dance" at the reception, with reminder cards for the groom, best man, father of the groom, and head usher. In addition, you should take with you three "pretend" bouquets, which can be made out of the ribbons with which wedding gifts are tied. (The maid of honor or one of the bridesmaids could run these up for you ahead of time. They are most useful and take no time at all to make.)

The one thing we suggest you don't take is the drink someone always urges on the mother of the bride before the rehearsal—usually vodka. Far from leaving you breathless at this particular time, it will have the general aroma of embalming fluid. Settle for Scotch and water or, better yet, a couple of aspirins, and try to keep off your feet until it's time to leave.

Also stay off the telephone except to call those two friends of yours who are going to the church one full hour before the ceremony and remind them about the thermos of ice water, paper cups, and the panic bag. Ask one of them to check out the number of attendants' bouquets in the big box in which they will be packed in tissue paper. The bridal bouquet, or prayer book with a spray of flowers, will be in a separate box, perhaps inside the big long one, which should contain the boutonnieres for the groom, best man, ushers, and the fathers, along with smaller boxes with the flowers for you and the groom's mother. If flowers have been ordered for grandmothers, they may be in yet other boxes. Give your friend the florist's telephone number and tell her to call him immediately if she finds anything missing.

Most city florists send someone to the church to give out the flowers, but in the suburbs and in the country few florists can spare an assistant for this purpose.

Ask those two wonderful friends to remind the ushers where the "facilities" are located so they can direct guests to them when asked—and they certainly will be by those people who have driven long distances to come to the wedding.

Also ask your friends to be sure the ushers get the set of lists showing the names and pew numbers of all those to be seated in the reserved section and that they know where the Mass books are (you will have ordered them through your church if your daughter is having a nuptial mass). Usually the Mass books, among which are two special ones for the bridal couple, are delivered to you directly from the printer, although the order for them is placed through your church. If they are delivered to you, be sure to take them to the rehearsal. The priest in charge will show the ushers where the Mass books are to be kept overnight. Before the ceremony, one usher should take the two special ones for the bride and groom, and two others for the honor attendant and the best man, and place them on their kneelers himself, or give them to an altar boy to place. The others should be placed in the pews reserved for the bridesmaids and ushers, and the rest may be given out to incoming guests by the ushers, or placed in every pew, if time permits, before the ceremony.

If there are copies of directions to your home or club, they should also be taken to the rehearsal. Ushers should be instructed to place them where the guests can find them easily. The first arrivals should be given copies by the ushers so that subsequent guests will see them and will pick them up on the way out.

Ask these last favors of those pals of yours who are going to the church early: Pin on the ushers' boutonnieres. They always get them crooked with the pin showing if they do it themselves. They should be pinned on *under* the lapels and up near the head of the boutonnieres, generally wired and bound, hardy and firm carnations. If the ushers are wearing ascots, see that the pearl stickpins are lowered (from just up under the Adam's apple, which is where they are when delivered from the clothing rental firm) to a position in the upper middle part of the ascot that shows. And see that a black-headed pin is inserted straight across under the collar in back and through both the vest band and ascot behind the necks of all ushers. Tell those gals that two pins are necessary sometimes. The same should be done for the groom and best man. This is a simple but important detail and prevents the jacket from leaving unattractive, gaping spaces between the shirts and jacket collars. We suggest you also try this out on the bride's father before you leave for the ceremony.

Rehearsals are necessary whenever there are more than two attendants at a wedding, and the time set for them is usually five o'clock—an unrealistic hour for the ushers and bridesmaids to be present if they work for a living. Nevertheless, many ministers both in New York City and in the suburban communities have a rule that rehearsals must be scheduled for this hour. The consequence is, of course, that in town most members of the wedding party cannot arrive at the church until five-thirty—if then. For those who have to take a train or drive out to the suburbs, particularly in Friday traffic, the situation is very nearly hopeless. Therefore we have in recent years suggested that rehearsals be set for eleven-thirty on the morning of the wedding if it is on a Saturday out of town. This is all very well for Protestants who may be having a late afternoon or evening ceremony, but for Roman Catholics it is usually impossible. Members of Orthodox, Conservative, and Reform Jewish congregations have more flexibility about setting the time and hour for wedding rehearsals.

Neither of us can remember attending during the past sixteen years a rehearsal that began on time. So if your rerehearsal is late or if not all the bridesmaids and ushers are able to take part in it, don't panic. Most of them have probably been in weddings before, and those who do rehearse can tell the others. Have each usher leave a place beside him for his absent partner. Do the same for the bridesmaids if they are walking in pairs. Insist, however, on every usher being present at the church *one full hour before* the ceremony, even if there is an earlier wedding. This will give time to those who were absent, assisted by those who did rehearse, to have a dry run. This can be done quickly, just as long as they know where they are to stand.

If there are to be white satin ribbons used, or plaited ropes that belong to the church, be sure that two of the ushers present at the rehearsal are appointed to pick them up and run them down the aisles, laying them on the top of the pew backs just inside the pews, *after* the mother of the bride has been seated.

If you are using a white runner, two more of the ushers present should be appointed to pick up the runner—it is either folded, or "flaked," at the foot of the chancel steps or is to be unrolled by means of a handle—as soon as the white ribbons or the ropes have been placed along the inside of the pews. These are the two last details that must be taken care of by the ushers before they get in line for the processional, which they lead as they walk in pairs ahead of the bridesmaids, who may also walk in pairs, or singly, as the bride wishes.

The maid of honor always walks alone, as does the matron of honor, but the maid of honor takes precedence and walks in just before the bride and her father unless there are a flower girl and ring bearer. If you have one or both of the latter, they may walk together until they near the chancel steps, where they separate—the flower girl walking to the left side and taking a position between the matron and maid of honor (if there are both) or beside the maid of honor, and the ring bearer walking to the right and taking a position beside the best man. If the flower girl and ring bearer are very young (four or five years old), it may be advisable to have them precede the bride and her father only as far as the second left and second right pews, where each may be gathered in by parents and allowed to sit in the aisle seats. They need not take part in the recessional if there are signs of fidgeting.

Whether to allow very young children to participate is a decision that should be made by their parents. It depends greatly upon the individual child. We have had ring bearers and flower girls as young as three and a half who performed their parts to perfection. The decision, in any case, should be made well in advance of the rehearsal. If you do have either a flower girl or a ring bearer, or both, in your wedding, be sure to let them get all the way to the reserved section before the bride and her father walk up the aisle, otherwise the oohing and aahing will still be going on and the grand entrance will be missed. If a bride can't make one on her wedding day, when can she?

And play it cool with these little people. Don't over-rehearse them. They should be brought to the rehearsal just to see the church, and to fix in their minds to which positions or pews they are to walk. Then they should be taken home. In their case, practice does not make perfect.

About one bride in every three or four hundred feels that she must have a stand-in at the rehearsal. Unless a girl has been raised from childhood on the old wives' tale that it's bad luck to take part in her wedding rehearsal, she would be wise to rehearse. If she is truly superstitious and her fear is real, then she had best have someone—possibly her mother—take her place, but then she must follow closely each and every cue of the minister for the whole procedure.

If the bride is going to wear a face veil, she should be sure to tell her clergyman at the rehearsal. And this is the time, also, when those "pretend" bouquets of ribbons will come in handy. The bride should carry one, and so should the maid and matron of honor or the bridesmaid who will stand nearest the maid of honor if there is to be only one honor attendant. If they are used at the rehearsal, the bride and each of her attendants will know exactly what to do with the real bouquets on the big day. Many members of the Protestant clergy forget about mentioning the bride's bouquet, and the Roman Catholic clergy don't give any thought to it at all, usually because their altar boys assist with this detail.

The way we suggest dealing with the matter of the bouquets is as follows: If there is a matron of honor, she goes up the aisle alone, turns left, and takes her position at the side of the chancel steps, leaving a space for the maid of honor, who follows her up the aisle and stands nearest the bride when she arrives in place. The maid of honor hands her bouquet to the matron of honor as she reaches her position, thus leaving her with two free hands so that the bride can give the maid of honor her bridal bouquet immediately upon her arrival in position for the betrothal part of the ceremony. This now leaves the bride with both her hands free to manage her skirt as she and the groom follow the clergyman up to the altar where the marriage ceremony takes place.

If the bride and groom are using kneelers, the bride rises at the end of the ceremony, usually with the groom's left arm under her elbow as he also rises from the kneeler. This is following the benediction. The maid of honor should then place the bridal bouquet in the bride's *right* hand, and not in her left hand, which will be the nearer at this moment, *before* the bride turns to face her husband. The decision to kiss or not at this time is a personal matter between the couple. In any case, the bride will make a half-turn, slip her left arm through the groom's right arm, and they will lead the processional from the chancel down the main aisle to the door. The wise bride does all of this very slowly, and is able to avoid the awkward jerky motion caused by having to switch her bouquet from her left hand to her right because the flowers are already where they should be.

The bride's slow half-turn will give the maid of honor the time needed to move and straighten out her train and veil. The maid of honor then joins the best man who gives her his right arm as they follow the bridal couple to the chancel steps, where the matron of honor should step forward and return the maid of honor's bouquet to her so that she does not have to reach over for it. This gesture is both graceful and functional, for it tends to slow down the best man and maid of honor and keeps them from treading too closely upon the heels of the bridal couple. Nothing looks worse than a wedding party rushing out of a church at a dead gallop.

We use very nearly the same procedure if the bride is wearing a face veil. In this case, she would rise from the kneeler and turn to her *left* to face her maid of honor, who, using *both* hands, raises the veil and places the bridal bouquet in her *right* hand. Then the bride turns and the couple kiss, if they have agreed beforehand on this gesture. A fail-safe for the maid of honor who forgets to give the bride her bouquet in the above manner is to give it to her *after* the bride has placed her *left* arm in the groom's right arm and they are about to begin the recessional. However, if there is a court train and a cathedral-length veil, the first system is better for the poor maid of honor who has to cope with arranging yards and yards of fabric.

A variation on the raising of the bride's face veil sometimes is used at Roman Catholic weddings: the bride, walking on her father's *left* arm, will stop with him just a step ahead of the first pews, where he will lift her veil and kiss her *before* the groom moves forward to join her and the ceremony begins.

The question of which arm a father escorts his daughter on in the processional, his right or his left, should be resolved at the rehearsal. The ultimate decision is the clergyman's in all cases.

Here are some suggestions for the ushers: for the processional, keep your hands down at the sides of your bodies, and start up the aisle on the *left* foot, your shoulders nearly touching those of your partner. Walk with dignity and slowly take your designated positions by means of a semipivot that is nearly a half-turn. This allows you to keep your attention on the bride, and then on the bride and groom, at all times without turning your back on the congregation. Do not try to march to the processional music, but walk to it naturally, keep in step with your partner, and leave a minimum of four pews between you and those walking before you. There is a happy medium between a dirge and a fire drill pace that should be worked out at the rehearsal with the help of the organist.

Always offer your right arm to a lady when escorting her to a pew. If she has a male escort with her, he follows behind. Men alone are merely shown by an usher to a pew, and an arm is not extended to them unless they are infirm and need assistance. If several ladies arrive together, the usher should offer his right arm to the eldest and indicate to the others to follow him, or offer to come back later and escort them—if there is time. We always instruct the ushers to seat the church as evenly as possible on both sides and not to ask that awkward question, "Friend of the bride or the groom?" but to say instead, "We are seating equally on both sides. May I seat you?" If the guest has a pew card, she will produce it, but if she begins making a series of quick pelicanlike dives into her purse, ask her name, consult your reserved pew list, and seat her. But if an older woman says firmly that she wishes to be seated on either the bride's or groom's side, do so. Seat the main aisle first, starting in the pews behind the reserved one, then the side aisles. You will have to do this because the early arrivals will never, *never* move over. At large weddings of three hundred guests or more, the ushers should use the main aisle in seating the guests, proceed up toward the altar, turn, and go back to the entrance by the side aisles. This helps to avoid unnecessary crowding in the main aisle as the hour of the ceremony nears.

At a large wedding where there may be ten or more ushers, we station two at the beginning of the reserved pew section, where they remain until the ushering is over. Other ushers who are given pew cards by incoming guests escort them to the two ushers at the front of the church, who then seat them. This also helps cut down on the traffic jam in the main aisle. And when the time comes to bring up the white runner, the two ushers who have been stationed in front of the church merely walk forward, turn, bend down, and get a firm grasp on either the two edges of the runner if it has been "flaked"—folded neatly at the chancel steps—or on the handle of the roller. (We do not like handles on white runners for two reasons: they are apt to make a creaking noise that can be heard when the organist is not playing and they are not always pristine in appearance.)

If the two ushers who are to bring the white runner to the back of the church will follow these few instructions, it will not turn on them like a crooked snake: Pick up the edges of the runner—this is actually a piece of white duck or canvas—and wait a second to be sure your opposite number is ready. Then walk toward the back of the church *without once turning back to see how the wretched thing is going.* The motion of your bodies as you turn is what makes the runner get twisted. As you near the last third of the aisle, walk more slowly. All that's holding the runner in place at the chancel steps is a strong iron bar over which it has been folded many times. Too hard a yank by two hefty ushers will pull the whole thing out of place. Unless the runner is old and thin from countless washings it should not get twisted, but if it does, you and your fellow usher can straighten out the worst places. There will be time for this because the organist usually has a mirror, or some means of seeing most of the main aisle, and will not start the processional without a signal.

Exactly what signal is to be given to the organist, and who is to give it—whether it is an usher or not—should be made crystal clear at the rehearsal. Sometimes there is a button to be pressed beside one of the doors inside the church that will activate a signal light beside the organist, but other times an usher has to make a fast dash up to the organ loft and back down in time to take his place for the processional. In large churches, the sexton gives the signal.

If your church has a bell tower and you would like to have the bells rung just after the benediction has been given at the end of the ceremony, make arrangements for this. In some modern churches, the bells are rung electrically, but there are many lovely old ones where the bells have to be rung manually.

As much as possible should be spelled out clearly for ushers at the rehearsal, especially the detail of how and when to remove the white ribbons after the ceremony. If your church has a sexton, it is part of his duty to instruct the ushers about ribbons and white runners, but many churches do not have sextons. In this case, the clergyman will have to take over.

Before the ceremony, when all members of the wedding party, including the bride and her father, are ready, the groom's mother—followed by his father—should be seated in the first right pew facing the altar by the head usher, or by someone appointed for this honor at the rehearsal. She may have two sons who are serving as ushers and prefer to have one seat her before the ceremony and the other escort her out of the church after it is over. Work this out at the rehearsal.

The last person to be seated by an usher before the ceremony is the bride's mother, who is escorted to the first left pew facing the altar. If white ribbons are being used, two ushers then go down the main aisle, pick them up, and run them to the back of the church by laying them flat along the tops of the pews (there is usually a raised ridge on the edge of pews that keeps them from falling off). The ends of the ribbons are dropped over either the last pew on each side of the main aisle or two up from the rear. At large weddings we prefer to leave open the last two pews on either side for late arrivals, so they do not have to find their places by the side aisles. No one, however, should be seated by an usher after the bride's mother has been escorted to her pew, where she leaves the aisle seat vacant for her husband, who will join her after giving the bride away.

While the two ushers who have been appointed to take charge of the white ribbons are putting them in place, another pair of ushers should go up to the chancel by the side aisles, take their positions on either side of the white runner, and be prepared to bring it to the back of the church. If there is time, the second pair of ushers, the white runner men, could wait at the back of the church until the white ribbon men reach them. Then they could go up the center aisle for the runner.

The ushers should then line up as they have rehearsed, one being prepared to give the signal to the organist.

After the ceremony the bride and groom, followed by their entire wedding party, walk out of the church to the music of the recessional. The head usher or the usher appointed to escort the mother of the bride then *immediately* goes up the main aisle to escort her out of the church. (The bride's mother may also have two sons in the wedding party and want one to take her in and the other to take her out.) The bride's father follows behind.

When the usher who is to escort the mother of the bride out starts up the main aisle to get her, the usher who is to take out the mother of the groom should start up the side aisle—if there is one. If not, both ushers walk up the main aisle together. The groom's mother's usher waits until the bride's mother and her usher are nearly halfway down the aisle, and then he extends his right arm to the groom's mother. His job of offering her his right arm is more difficult than that of the usher who escorts the bride's mother out because the groom's mother is on his left in the pew, so she has to cross in front of him in the main aisle.

The usher for the bride's mother, to make the escorting out as smooth as possible, should walk slightly past the first left pew, turn so that both parents may see him leave enough room for the bride's father to step out into the main aisle to the right and slightly behind the usher. He then steps forward and offers his right arm to the bride's mother and escorts her out. The bride's father follows.

The usher for the groom's mother waits in front of the first right pew until the bride's parents are nearly halfway to the narthex. He then moves in as close as he can to the end of the first right pew, extends his right arm—this will remind the groom's mother to cross in front of him—and escort her out, followed by the groom's father. If she is lost in reverie and fails to get his signal, the usher shouldn't make an issue of it, but may have to escort her out on his left arm. The procedure of escorting the mothers in before the ceremony and out afterward should be practiced at least once at the rehearsal, and the usher who has been given the honor of escorting the groom's mother should remind her a few times to cross in front of him.

As soon as both mothers have been escorted out of the church, the other ushers should be massed on either side of the first left and first right pews to escort out any ladies seated in them—grandmothers, possibly—and in the rest of the reserved pews. Then the pair of ushers who handled the white ribbons before the ceremony should stand at the last pews of the reserved section—now empty—to release the ribbons, which are to be gathered in by a pair of ushers at the back of the church. The whole operation takes but a few seconds when done properly, and the key to it lies in the coordination of the two pairs of ushers. This detail should be explained well in advance to the four ushers responsible so that it is completely clear to them. The removal of the ribbons is the signal for the balance of the guests to leave. The white runner will be taken up later by the florist.

If the bride and her bridesmaids have dressed at the church, ushers should be appointed at the rehearsal to stay after the ceremony to pick up whatever suitcases, dress boxes, wraps, handbags, and other items may have been left and to take them with them to the place where the reception is being held. If the ushers have dressed at the church, they too must not leave anything behind. These days places of worship are locked up at a certain hour—usually as quickly as possible after the last ceremony—by a tired sexton, janitor, or custodian, who will not appreciate having to be routed out to unlock the church because the bridesmaid—the one who has flown in from Tacoma and plans to leave on a night flight after the reception—has forgotten her suitcase.

An alternate plan used to empty the church after the ceremony is for the mother and father of the bride to wait until the last members of the wedding party have reached the halfway mark out during the recessional, and then rise and walk out arm in arm. The groom's parents wait until the bride's parents are about halfway out, and then follow them arm in arm. Two ushers stationed at the first left and first right pews nearest the altar move forward and "bow out" the rest of the ladies and their escorts in the reserved section one pew at a time, from left to right, until all are empty. The pair of ushers then stop at the end of the reserved section and indicate to the rest of the guests that they are to leave, or they can "bow out" every pew.

Whatever system you use, be sure the ushers understand at the rehearsal exactly what they are expected to do. This goes for any special orders concerning relatives or friends who may be infirm or in wheelchairs and will arrive at a side door needing assistance, both in arriving and leaving. The question of whether the best man will join in the recessional or leave by a side door should also be settled. In our area, the best man joins in the recessional and escorts out the female honor attendant (the maid of honor if there are two honor attendants, the head usher taking care of the matron of honor).

A few suggestions for the bridesmaids: *Walk naturally!* That ghastly walk known as the hesitation step makes you look like stupid, lopsided penguins and, in our opinion, should never, *never* be used at a wedding. Where this unattractive custom had its origin is another one of those mysteries never to be solved. We suspect it grew out of an old Hollywood "C" movie or was something a crazed choreographer ran up for a Ziegfeld chorus line. Forget it. Lead off on your left foot and walk normally, smile, and don't look down at the feet of anyone in front of you. When you arrive at your designated place, which will be assigned to you at the rehearsal, use the simple semipivot to get into position, and do keep your feet together, not pointed out. As with the ushers, your attention should be focused on the bride, then on the bride and groom, all during the ceremony.

In the days of spiked heels, the best-laid plans of brides and the Bryants sometimes went awry because one bridesmaid would start to teeter and lapse into that hesitation step, and, to our horror, the ones behind her would follow suit in chain reaction, thereby turning the processional into a social secretary's nightmare. Don't let this happen to you unless, of course, the bride admires the hesitation step and her clergyman will allow this nonsense in the church he serves. Perform your duties slowly and gracefully, and don't rush out during the recessional, even though its timing will be somewhat quicker than that of the processional.

An important reminder to the bride's mother: Do not leave the rehearsal until you know exactly when you are to be seated, when you are to rise, and if the congregation is to stand or be seated throughout the ceremony. These details should be discussed with your clergyman at the end of the rehearsal if he has forgotten to clue you in. You, as the bride's mother, give the cue to the rest of those in the church during a wedding, so be sure of your role and then tell the groom's mother, because she will most likely not attend the rehearsal.

We have discovered that the small, obvious customs with which most of us seem familiar are the ones first forgotten by the bride's mother during a wedding. Either she draws a complete blank or becomes confused because of fatigue and emotional involvement.

It is customary in Protestant Episcopal weddings for the bride's mother to rise when she hears the first notes of the music of the processional, to remain standing throughout the entire ceremony, and to sit down again only *after* the last member of the wedding party has passed her pew during the recessional. This allows the congregation to be seated (they will have been standing for approximately eighteen to twenty minutes) while the ushers return to escort out the bride's mother, the groom's mother, and each of the ladies who occupy seats in the reserved pews and then, finally, to release the white ribbons.

In other Protestant churches that have the option of being seated throughout the ceremony, the minister will indicate by gesture or word when the congregation is to be seated following the betrothal part of the ceremony (the giving away of the bride).

The old question about being able to see is always raised. Just as many people claim they "can't see a thing" if they stand as make the same claim if they are seated. If you do have the option of standing or sitting be sure to work it out at the rehearsal with your clergyman so that you will have it fixed firmly in your mind at the wedding.

When this problem is straightened out, we suggest you give out the list (first copy) for the reserved pews to the ushers. If there is a head usher, give the list to him and let him instruct the rest. You might tell the ushers to familiarize themselves with the names on the bride's side and the groom's side of the reserved section, and that there will be a duplicate set of lists for them available at the church before the ceremony. The location of this duplicate should be firmly established. Have your clergyman tell them to arrive *one hour* in advance of the ceremony; coming from him, this instruction will have more authority.

The simple diagrams that follow are like those we give many brides so that they can go to their rehearsals with a clear picture in their minds of how their attendants will walk in the processional, where they will stand when the ceremony begins, and how they will walk out in the recessional. They serve, also, to help a bride line up her attendants by height—shorter ones first—and, if she knows them, the ushers. Again, the shorter ones lead and move into their positions as indicated by the numbers in the drawings. In this example, there is a total of eighteen (about average for the weddings with which we assist) in the wedding party, including bride, groom, flower girl and ring bearer, and two extra ushers. We always suggest having at least one extra usher over the number of bridesmaids

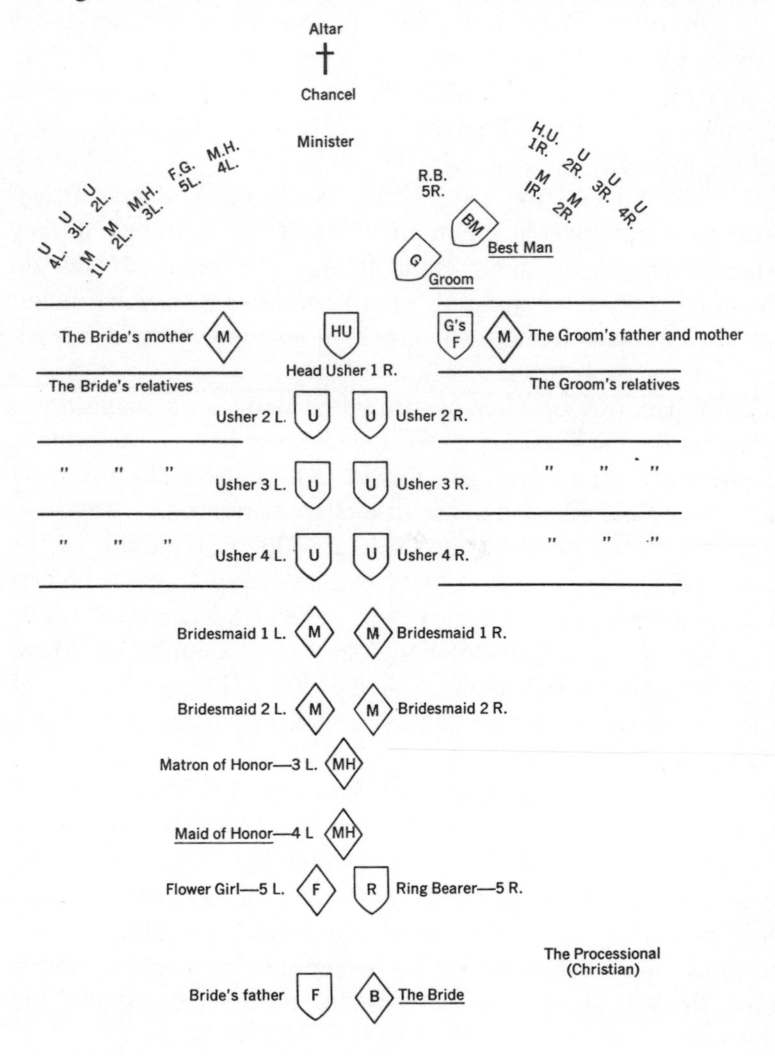

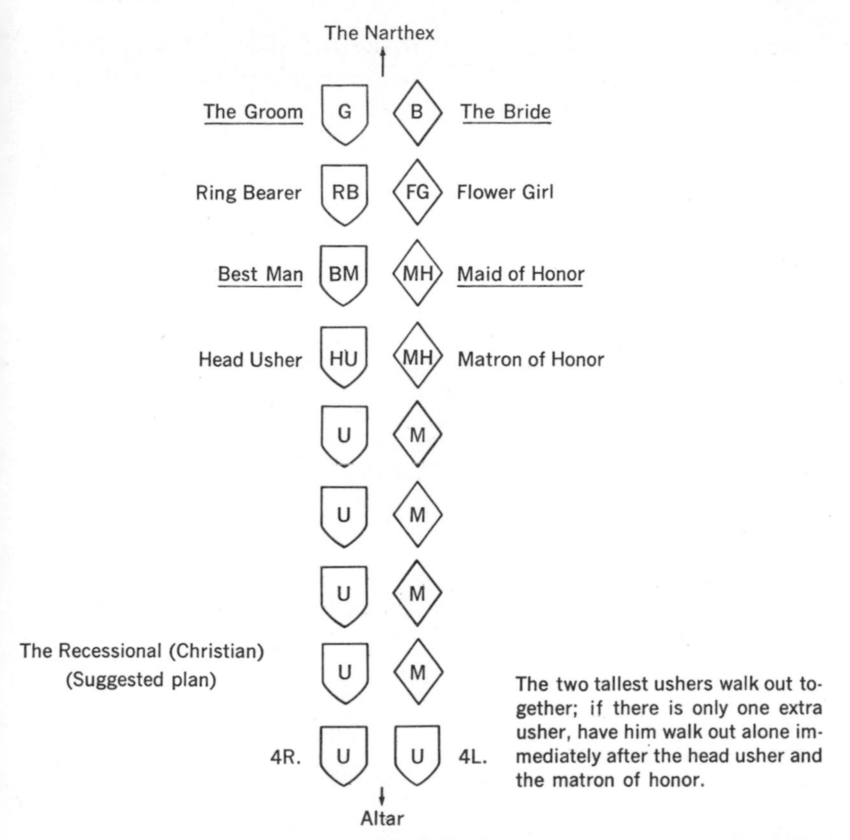

The Recessional (Christian)
(Suggested plan)

since it is less awkward in every way should an usher have to withdraw just before a wedding because of reasons of health or military obligations.

Although double weddings are rare, they are most impressive. The brides may be sisters, cousins, or very close friends. (For double weddings in some denominations the brides must be related.) Double weddings may be formal or informal. Each bride has separate attendants and, in the formal weddings, the attendants are dressed alike but in contrasting colors. The senior bride, on her father's arm, follows her attendants and the ushers and is followed in turn by the honor attendant or attendants of the younger bride. Then comes the younger bride herself, escorted, if she is a sister, by a brother, uncle, or godfather. (See also diagrams for processional and recessional.)

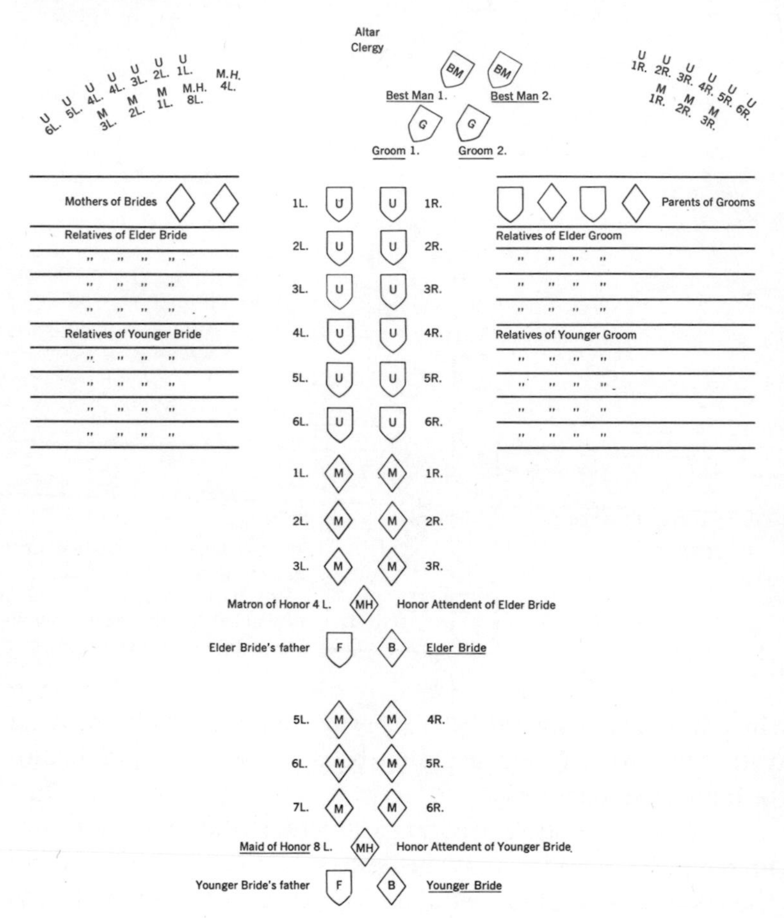

With respect to rehearsals and nuptial masses in Roman Catholic churches, there have been, and continue to be, so many changes in all procedures that we advise you to be guided entirely by the priest of your church for the latest details. The following diagram shows the seating plan for the

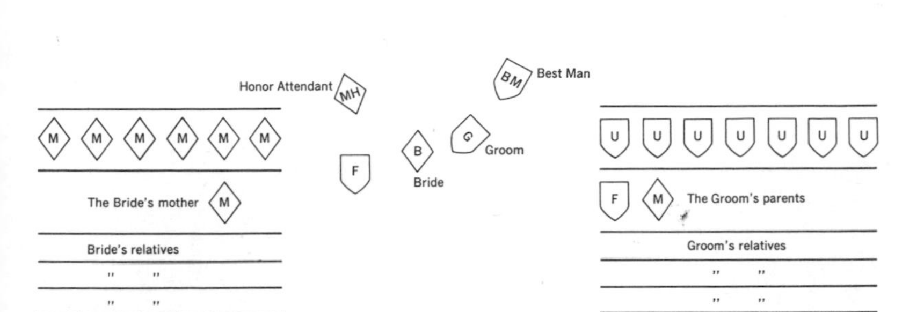

bridesmaids and ushers, the bride's parents and relatives, and the groom's parents and relatives in a Roman Catholic wedding.

As of this writing, the bride's father escorts her but does not give her away in a Roman Catholic marriage ceremony. He stops at his pew and the groom steps forward to meet her. Incidentally, the head usher or ushers who are to lead the processional in a Roman Catholic wedding should not begin their walk up the aisle until they see the priest or priests take their places in the sanctuary. Actually, this caveat is valid for any marriage ceremony, no matter what the denomination: no walking until the clergyman, the groom, and best man are in place—musical cue notwithstanding.

A Quaker wedding may take place in a private home as well as in the meetinghouse, but the notice of the couple's intention to wed must be made by them at a meeting one month in advance of their wedding date, and one of them must be a member of the Society of Friends. The notice of intention to wed is made by letter and, even if the couple is of age, it is customary for another letter from the parents, giving their

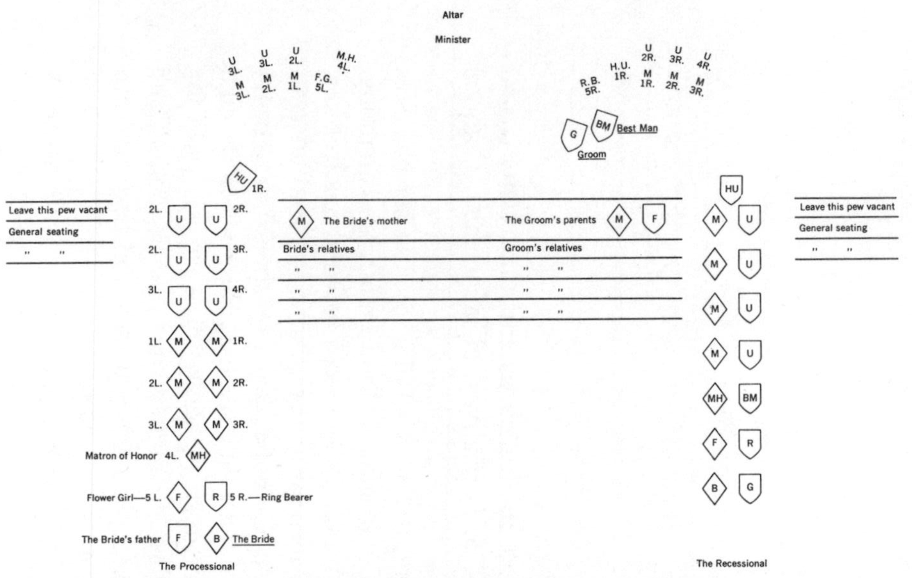

Altar
Minister
U 3L. M 3L. U 3L. M 2L. U 2L. M 1L. M.H. 4L. F.G. 5L.
R.B. 5R. H.U. 1R. U 2R. M 1R. U 3R. M 2R. U 4R. M 3R.
G Groom BM Best Man
HU 1R.
Leave this pew vacant
General seating
" "
2L. U U 2R.
2L. U U 3R.
3L. U U 4R.
1L. M M 1R.
2L. M M 2R.
3L. M M 3R.
Matron of Honor 4L. MH
Flower Girl—5 L. F R 5 R.—Ring Bearer
The Bride's father F B The Bride
The Processional
M The Bride's mother
Bride's relatives
" "
" "
" "
The Groom's parents M F
Groom's relatives
" "
" "
" "
HU
M U
M U
M U
M U
MH BM
F R
B G
The Recessional
Leave this pew vacant
General seating
" "

This shows a processional and recessional in a church with two main aisles. In this instance the two far left and right pews are left vacant because they are farther forward than the positions of the parents, who are seated on the left and right of the main seating section. Most churches with two main aisles have doors for each pew. No white ribbons and no white runners are used, but the last duty of the ushers before the processional signal is given is to go up each aisle and make sure that all the doors on each side are closed firmly. This must be done immediately before they line up for the processional. In this diagram, the head usher leads the processional and walks out alone as the last man in the recessional. Often the head usher is the bride's brother, or a younger brother of the groom—if an older brother or the groom's father is his best man.

Please note that in this kind of church the processional is up the left aisle and the recessional down the right.

permission, to be enclosed with it. The couple's letter is read at the meeting. Following the reading of the letter, a committee of two women and two men is appointed to discuss with each of the young people separately what is called the "clearness to proceed with marriage." These conferences are similar to those between a minister, priest, or rabbi and a couple who intend to be married. The committee reports on the conferences to a monthly meeting. The Committee of Oversight of the Society of Friends then appoints overseers to attend the wedding, whether at the meetinghouse or in a private home, and to advise the couple on the procedures.

On their wedding day the bride and groom walk in together (there may be the usual wedding processional) and take benches (chairs, if at home) that face the meeting. These are called "facing seats." The Quaker requirement of silence must be maintained (and this is very difficult at Quaker weddings in homes where the bride's family and friends may be members of denominations that are used to chatting happily before weddings). The couple rise when they are moved to do so. Usually the groom rises, then the bride, and they take each other's hands as the groom makes his vow: "In the presence of God I take thee——— to be my wedded wife promising with divine assistance to be unto thee a loving and faithful husband as long as we both shall live." The bride repeats the answering vow, and then they are seated again. Silence continues unless someone is moved to speak briefly. When it seems evident to all that no one else appears to be moved to speak, the ushers carry a table to the couple on which rests the Quaker marriage certificate. An overseer rises and reads it aloud to those assembled. The certificate is signed by the bride, the groom, and the overseers, and later registered officially. If this simple and quiet ceremony is being held in a meetinghouse, the regular Quaker meeting follows. If in a private home, the bride and groom walk out together into another room where the reception will be held.

As we have mentioned earlier, there is no marriage ceremony for members of the Church of Christ Scientist, because Christian Science readers are not ordained ministers of the church, but elected officers, and may not perform marriage ceremonies. Members may be married by any legally authorized ordained minister of the gospel or by a legal authority in a civil ceremony.

Among the Mormons (members of the Church of Jesus Christ of Latter-Day Saints) there are two distinctive kinds of marriage ceremonies. The first is that of the faithful who are considered worthy to be married in the temple of the church by a member of the Holy Priesthood, who concludes the ceremony by pronouncing that the couple are married "for time and for all eternity" instead of using the phrase "until death do you part." The issue of parents who have been married in a temple of the church by a member of the Holy Priesthood are considered by Mormons to belong to them throughout eternity. Members of the church, however, who are not considered worthy of being married as described may be married by bishops of the church or by any legally authorized person. They may be married later—if their daily lives become such as to comply with the requirements of their church—at a second ceremony at which they are declared to be wed "for time and for all eternity." While mixed marriages are permitted, they are not encouraged. Civil divorce is recognized by Mormons, but it is very rare between those who have been married in a temple of the church.

In the major cities of the United States there are many churches in the Eastern rite, including the Eastern Orthodox, the Greek Orthodox, the Russian Orthodox Greek Catholic, the Russian Orthodox Church Outside of Russia. At one of these, the Russian Orthodox Church of Christ the Savior at 51 East 121st Street in New York City, there are no pews, and the congregation stands or kneels throughout the long service. Chairs are provided only for the ill or infirm. Mass is not celebrated in connection with the marriage ceremony and only that vocal music provided by the choir is allowed. The double ring ceremony is always used, but the rings are placed on the right hands of the bride and groom.

The processional is the same as in other Christian churches, and the bride enters with her father to special wedding hymns sung by the choir. After her father has given her away, he moves back and stands beside his wife, and the ceremony begins, not at the altar, but in front of a table that is placed almost in the middle of the church and in line with the sanctuary. It is a long and deeply impressive ceremony in which the number three, signifying the Trinity, is emphasized with great reverence. The priest blesses the wedding rings three times at the altar before he places them first on the right hand of the bride and then on the right hand of the groom. The best man exchanges the rings three times on the couple's fingers, and, just before they take their final vows, the priest binds their hands together and leads them around the table three times. On the table is a cross, a chalice of wine, flowers and candles, and the church Bible, together with two gold crowns that the honor attendants hold over the couple's heads during most of the two-hour ceremony. The bride, instead of carrying a bouquet, holds a lighted candle, as does the groom. These candles are symbols of the light of God. After the final blessing, the choir bursts forth with a special chant known as "Many Years." This they sing three times—and then the recessional begins.

Civil divorce is not recognized in the Russian Orthodox church. Divorce must be granted by religious decree to be valid in the eyes of the church and is difficult to obtain. The remarriage of those who have a religious decree of divorce is allowed by the church.

We are always fascinated by both the contrasts and the similarities of the various kinds of marriage ceremonies with which we are familiar, but over the years we have discovered that they all have one phenomenon in common: This is the disappearance of tension for the bride, the groom, the attendants, parents, relatives—even the guests—once the marriage ceremony is concluded and the recessional begins. It never fails. It is as if everyone said to himself in a single voice, "The important event is over; now we can relax."

Chapter 14

The Reception

You've gotten through the ceremony without any real calamities befalling you. The nervous eye of the public is no longer upon you. The atmosphere has changed. Solemnity now gives way to celebration and happiness, and you are on home ground, even if that figurative piece of ground is only rented for the day.

In previous chapters we have mentioned several events that occur during the course of the reception. In our opinion a good reception, like any other party, flows effortlessly along to a climax. Then everyone goes home. It is still customary to receive guests near the entrance of any building housing a social event. Wedding receptions are no exception. The only difference is that there are more people doing the receiving. The bride's mother is always present as the hostess; the others are usually lined up as in the diagram on the next page.

Note that the maid of honor takes precedence over the matron of honor, which is why if a bride's *only* sister is married it is wise not to have *any* maid of honor, but just the *one* honor attendant. If the groom's sister is married, she may be called the matron of honor, but has no more duties than any other bridesmaid. The bridesmaids should be lined up accord-

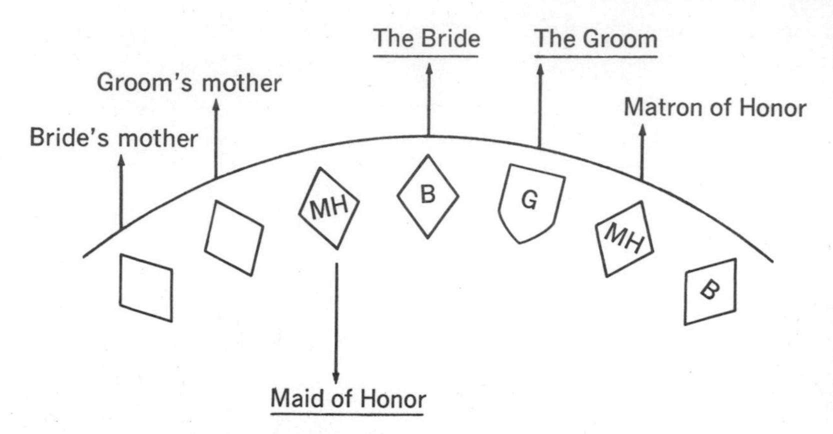

ing to the groom's height, if there is no matron of honor, either taller to shorter or vice versa.

In Jewish receptions there may be two or three maids or matrons of honor. There is never more than one best man, and he occasionally makes the lineup. Also, both sets of parents often appear, following the usual order, i.e., the father and mother of the bride, the father and mother of the groom, maid or maids of honor, the bride, and so forth.

Having the bride's father at the head of the line is the custom in certain parts of the United States. This is fine as long as he is also able to perform his host duties in the main area. The groom's father, we have often noticed, is the first to the bar, the first to find a quiet spot, but the one who is the last, when the photographer is looking for him, to get into the group picture. He is also often last for the "first dance."

Receiving lines are a hangover from a more formal era. In our opinion they should be either limited to the newlywed couple, or eliminated entirely. They take up an inordinate amount of time and generate vast boredom and general discomfort for both those who have to stand in line and those who have to pass by. We haven't yet found any spirits free enough to make their own tradition. Having no receiving line at all certainly seems sensible when the guest list comprises only close friends of both families. When the other situation obtains, both families, really working at it in a formal line, have collectively a hard time connecting the faces with the names of several hundred guests.

Having bridesmaids in the line when there are three hundred or more guests to receive is another time-consuming practice. What does one say to eight, nine, or ten pretty bridesmaids with sore feet? If your daughter has a large number of attendants, our suggestion to have them take turns in the line seems most sensible and is one which is being followed at more receptions every year.

Normally the whole bridal party has little time before the guests begin to swarm in. The bride and groom are greeted by the maître d' or the caterer in charge with champagne poured in their specially decorated glasses while the orchestra plays them in to the place where their reception is being held.

When the wedding party is ready, the line should be set up. If necessary, send ushers or the maître d' to start the guests coming in. Try, however, to have a breathing spell between the arrival of the bridal party and the formal receiving.

What is the order of events at a reception? While this may vary in different parts of the country, we have found it generally to be quite informal. The ushers should be the last to go through the line, and they should be told about this in advance. When they do this, the entire wedding party is together and submits to various and often too numerous individual, separate, and group photography at a place previously selected by the photographer. Next, the bride, if festivities are still awaiting her appearance and assuming there is dancing, has her first dance with the groom. Later on, she cuts the first token slice of the cake, and the groom cuts the second one or, with his hand over hers, they cut both slices together. Still later, before she and the groom leave to change into their going-away clothes, she throws her bouquet, and occasionally the groom then tosses her blue garter. Finally, the young couple, to suitable music from the orchestra, leave and are followed, hopefully, by the remaining guests.

The timing of these so-called events is important, but must be completely unobtrusive. Sneaky is a better word. This, in general, is what we work out with our brides: We begin by establishing the finish line, that is the time when the getaway of the couple, covered with rose petals and confusion, will finally take place. Ideally, this should be about three minutes before the contract with the musicians goes into overtime. For example, if the music is scheduled to end at 8:00 P.M., and allowing about forty-five minutes for the bride to change, and allowing also for the usual last-minute festivities, both planned and spontaneous, a bride should be ready to throw her flowers around 7:15. Since it often takes at least fifteen minutes to round up all the young unmarrieds, she should set in motion by 7:00 P.M. some kind of general agitation that she is thinking of leaving.

As soon as the bride and groom have gone to change, the maître d' or caterer should send chilled champagne and glasses to their rooms. This is done automatically in any club or hotel with an experienced staff. But often they will forget to send at the same time the bride's corsage which the florist has usually put in the refrigerator. Have a runner check up on the corsage, and at the same time remind the best man to take care of whatever liquid refreshments and accompanying glasses the newlyweds wish to have hidden in the getaway car.

There are a few magical moments when a good hostess can size up a party in terms of staying power, usually just before the bride and groom leave to change. If it looks like a real bash, she might as well find her daughter quickly and suggest that she delay throwing her flowers, tell the leader to go into overtime, and enjoy a longer reception. We have seldom had a bride demur at an extra hour. Even a seated and served luncheon reception, or evening dinner, or full buffet usually needs at least one hour of overtime "or any fraction thereof," as the standard union contract reads.

The time for cutting a wedding cake is more elastic. Let's assume that the receiving line is over by 5:15 and that the bride and groom have had their first dance somewhere around 5:45. The cake then could be cut between 6:15 and 6:30, but not any later.

On paper this sounds fine, and this is the way it strikes both the bride and her mother during a briefing session with us during the planning stage. However, we have never had a reception adhere exactly to any of the times planned in advance, except for getting the newlyweds into the getaway car just as the musicians were finishing "Good-bye, Tootsie, Good-bye." To achieve this alone takes a great amount of mother-henning from the background.

Timing is everything when it comes to making a reception move along effortlessly and graciously, as if there were no behind-the-scenes schedule in operation. Cutting the cake should be done while most of the guests are still there, and there should be more than a corporal's guard to see the bride and groom off. If the main body of the guests shows an inclination to leave early, particularly on prime dates when there are later events competing for their presence, it is better to move up the couple's departure by a half hour or so. Have the music end before you find the musicians playing for the staff and a few couples who simply don't know when to leave a party. If this adjustment in time is managed quietly, none of your guests need ever know you hadn't planned it that way. But whatever happens, unless you want your guests to stay on after the departure, make certain that the musicians are packing up as the getaway goes out of sight. That's real timing.

We have often encountered a bride who wanted to cut her cake without a musical fanfare. We have known others who elected to slip away, again without music. And then we have run into some who were having so much fun at their own receptions that they refused to leave. In this last case the members of the orchestra packed up with a flourish, but left behind a trio who hid in the kitchen tent. The caterer's crew dismantled all but a few tables and chairs so that it really looked as though the reception was over. After a decent interval and reports from scouts that the coast was clear, the bride and groom emerged to set in lively motion a postreception party for themselves and their close friends. To this day we don't know when that one finally broke up.

But it is the bride's day, and she doesn't have to go through with any of these ceremonies if she doesn't want to. There is no comparison between the ritual of the reception and that of the actual marriage. The ceremony could be all the formality she wants to endure for one day. If that is the case, let her visit around, dance when she feels like it, say good-bye to everyone, and just leave. This is what usually happens when there is no music. Almost the only formality, brief and with little fuss, would be if she ceremoniously cut her cake or threw her flowers from an upstairs window or the club steps. This procedure is not one we customarily suggest, but we have attended several such receptions, uniformly very pleasant and usually of short duration. They seemed, however, to lack the gaiety and air of celebration that music always engenders. They are more like high tea or an old-fashioned *fête champêtre*—without much *fête*.

We don't know from what the cake-cutting custom derives. The bride cuts a piece which she feeds the groom. This might well be a symbolic demonstration of her desire and ability to make a home for her new husband. The groom, for his part, cuts a second piece, which he in turn feeds the bride. We suppose that in effect he is saying that he accepts the homemaking arrangement. Or maybe he is suggesting that she had better sample her own cooking.

Very often the next step is for the bride to cut pieces for

her new mother- and father-in-law, but these she presents on plates and with forks. The groom then reciprocates in the same manner. This ceremony of cutting the cake is often performed to a little musical jingle, "The Bride Cuts the Cake," to the tune of "The Farmer in the Dell." The orchestra could also play college and fraternity songs applicable to the couple or their parents. But in this matter of songs, consider the bride. Does Daisybelle want "The Bride Cuts the Cake"? Many brides do indeed want this song, but others will have no part of it.

The cake ceremony is definitely one point when your photographer should be given center stage, if you want good candids. It is a matter of timing and background. He should never have to ask the bride to do it all over again just because he missed that spontaneous first act. The second shot never comes out right.

This is also an excellent and natural time for any toasts not previously given, or if all the toasting has been omitted at a previous gathering. The whole wedding party has been reassembled, and the guests who had drifted off to settle in small groups have also come together again to watch the ceremony. Also, if the best man or some member of the wedding party wishes to offer a toast, he now has the orchestra at hand. The leader, who normally will be standing by for the jingle, can signal the drummer that a long roll and fanfare is in order, and he can announce that so-and-so will now give a toast.

So often, after the actual cake-cutting ceremony is over and the staff has taken over the details of slicing and serving, the bride and groom are left suspended and aimless. If this ever happens, we usually have the orchestra play the music of their first dance. This gives the couple the cue to resume dancing or to dance across the floor to whatever table of guests they wish to visit. It also serves to start up the general festivities and to signal to the guests that they are free to resume dancing or visiting. The orchestra leader should always be provided with a brief schedule of events. The toasting, cake cutting, and so on are best handled by the leader working in close cooperation with the caterer or maître d', so include them in his schedule. If he is alerted by your runner a few minutes before the bride and groom are ready to cut the cake, he will play the opening bars of the jingle, or some other piece, which will induce the guests to gather around to see this ceremony. The jingle or music chosen will also notify the maître d' to have his cake-cutting expert on hand to move the table into position. Make certain that the leader knows he is to resume playing with his full orchestra as soon as the ceremony of the cake cutting is over. This will get the party swinging again.

The technique of gracefully cutting the first token slices of a three, four, or five tiered wedding cake does call for the expert coaching of a member of the catering staff standing by, but there need be no rehearsal. The trick is for each guest to get a piece that is not so small as to be a bare togen nor one that is slablike in proportions. Since almost all wedding cakes are made in tiers, it is often customary to cut from the bottom layer. This saves a nervous bride with strong wrists from slicing down through several tiers. Generally the top layer is removed intact, wrapped, and frozen for use on a future festive occasion.

Now, if a bride wants to be really formal, she should line up her bridesmaids on her left, groom on her right, next to him the best man, and then the ushers—all making a circle around the cake. Mighty fine protocol and high formality, but it would seem antediluvian if the orchestra had been playing modified rock all afternoon. However, in many sections of the country such a lineup is still quite normal.

Here we would like to point out that etiquette books and brides' magazines often go into how cakes are made, how to silce them, and how to achieve the formality of the cake-cutting ceremony. How dated or how current any of the publications are depends upon where you live and what your community is accustomed to doing. We have seen just about everything, including swords. We feel that the less ceremony the better these days.

Before we get into the "first dance" procedure, we would like to answer a question very often posed by the couple, sometimes anxiously, sometimes querulously, sometimes slightly antagonistically, but always apprehensively. "What are we supposed to do?" By the time some couples have been presented with all the ceremonial events of both wedding and reception, they feel as though they were having a dry run for a royal investiture. Whenever we are supervising a reception, we always say, "Have fun—we'll find you when you are needed."

Now, not having "us," or someone in our guise, you, mother of the bride, are going to have to act for us during this time. It means keeping one eye on your guests, one eye on your daughter, and one eye on your watch, all the time carrying on a vivacious conversation with whoever pins you down. If you have done all your prior planning, your caterer or maître d' will see to the needs of your guests while your bandleader keeps them moving according to some sort of casual, unobtrusive schedule. You are the supervisor, calling signals when you think something should happen. So you too can say to your daughter, "Have fun, circulate, see your pals, but don't get too far away." This is about the only way the couple is going to relax enough to enjoy their own reception. But to do this effortlessly while at the same time paying all due attention to your guests, you are going to need messenger service, someone to break through the crush to get to the orchestra or the maître d'. So, as already mentioned, arrange beforehand to have some responsible male member of your family, other than your husband, to tag around after you. Failing this, fall back on the best man or your new son-in-law's head usher to take care of this detail. Or the ushers can spell each other, just as long as you have that messenger service for the footwork.

In our minds the rite of the "first dance" occurs when the

new couple first step out on their own. Before this they have hurried out of the church supported by a bridal party. They have been seen in the middle of a line of people, but parental authority has still been ahead of them. That first dance really says, "We are now at last on our own, and alone at last." Sometimes the groom can't dance, less often the bride, but for once it doesn't make a bit of difference. This is one time when they somehow always make it.

Before we get into a suggested program designed to observe the courtesies due the entire wedding party, we want to enter a plea against one deep-seated tradition, and that is that no one else dances before the bridal couple has stepped out on the floor. So often there is a room or tent full of guests, a good orchestra playing, and the only activities for the guests for the first hour or more, while the receiving line is in action, are snaring passing canapés or visiting the bar. Doubtless both of these are worthwhile and time-fulfilling occupations, but our sense of New England frugality is offended by the waste of all that good music. A very special pox on that particular tradition, say we. Obviously this malediction doesn't apply in cases when there is only a background trio playing during the receiving line interval or when there is either no music at all or it is not laid on until later. In all fairness, we must also concede that in the event of a fast-moving line, particularly when only the five principals are in it and the entire proceedings take up less than an hour, the tradition we question above can still be observed.

A solution to this wasted music lies in having regular dancing begin as people start to congregate in the main banquet room or in the tent. This can be initiated by the host, aided by the ushers, who now have almost nothing else to do. Any who might protest could be told that when the bride is ready, all general dancing will be suspended. A nice touch is to have the bridesmaids and ushers lead the bride and groom out onto the floor and have them form a circle around the couple for that first dance. This is especially effective when the entire group proceeds from the area in which the group and family photography has just been completed. This way of handling the proceedings has an added attraction in that there is less general confusion during the photography, for almost everyone, unless he has something else to do, will kibitz on this activity. A large crowd converging on the scene distracts as well as interferes with the photographer. And some of the principals may be slightly gun-shy at being semiposed before the multitude. Strained expressions certainly show up in the proofs. The very essence of candid photography is naturalness. People are not as a rule themselves when being grouped together under the eyes of a couple of hundred spectators for what is supposed to be a family photograph.

If you decide on some such procedure, not only should the bandleader be apprised ahead of time, but some one should be appointed, when the procession is ready to escort the couple to the floor, to have the band stop the general dancing. This is usually done by having the band break off the melody it is playing and go into "Here Comes the Bride" (better here than for the processional in church). It should continue to play until the bride sets foot on the floor, and then it swings into the music she has chosen for the first dance.

The routine we use for the "first dance" is merely a card reminder system that indicates who dances with whom, and who cuts in on whom and when, to insure that all members of the bridal party and the parents of the bride and groom are on the dance floor. You may vary the order to suit your circumstances. We make out a master schedule from which we extrapolate separate cues for the groom, the fathers, the best man, and the ushers on three-by-five white cards, but you may well have your own system or your bandleader may have a routine that he has found to work. It really doesn't matter how you do it as long as the niceties are observed and no hurt feelings result from some oversight. Here is an illustration of the dance routine with samples of the reminder cards we mail to the groom for his use and that of his best man, his head usher—if any—and his father:

THE ORDER OF THE FIRST DANCE

The best man can give the orchestra leader the cue when the bride and groom are ready.

1. The bride and groom dance.
2. The bride's father cuts in on them.
3. The groom's father cuts in on the bride and her father.
4. The best man cuts in on the bride and her father-in-law.
5. The ushers and bridesmaids join in dancing.
6. General dancing.

We suggest to the bride and groom that they detail several of their male friends, not in the bridal party, to start cutting in on the bride as soon as she and the best man have danced for a few seconds or as soon as there has been enough time for the candid photographer to get some shots. This detail could be taken care of at the rehearsal dinner. Husbands or best beaux of bridesmaids—those fifth wheels—are the ones to ask to cut in. This gets general dancing started quickly so the wedding party does not keep on dancing around in the midst of a circle of happy friends—none of whom wants to be first to get out on the dance floor.

The procedure outlined above is followed where there is no seated bridal table and no meal to be served. If there is a bridal table, the first dance should be merely a token one, and the groom should cut back in on his bride after the best man dances with her. He then escorts her to their table, and they are followed *without fail* by every member of their wedding party. If a member of the clergy has been asked to say grace, they then wait at their places at the bridal table for him to do so, and then they are seated. The ushers will have an opportunity to dance with the bride between the courses of the meal, and every one of them should dance with her at some time during the reception, as well as with the honor attendant or attendants, and with the mother of the bride and the groom respectively.

We do the same for the bride's father; he receives an exact copy of what is sent to the groom. Knowing the general confusion that seems to be an inevitable part of wedding preparations, we make a duplicate set of reminder cards available to be given out at the reception immediately after the receiving line has finished when we have all the members of the wedding party and parents together for the group photographs. This is the time when many an anxious groom or father of the bride admits that he has misplaced the first reminder cards and asks to be told again how the first dance should be handled.

Here are sample reminder cards.

1.

REMINDER ABOUT THE FIRST DANCE

THE GROOM:
Dances with his bride
Dances with the bride's mother
Dances with his mother
Dances with the maid of honor
Dances with each of the bridesmaids before the reception is over

2.

REMINDER ABOUT THE FIRST DANCE

THE BRIDE'S FATHER:
Cuts in on the bride and groom
Cuts in on the groom's mother
Cuts in on his wife

3.

REMINDER ABOUT THE FIRST DANCE

THE GROOM'S FATHER:
Cuts in on the bride and her father
Cuts in on the bride's mother
Cuts in on his wife

4.

REMINDER ABOUT THE FIRST DANCE

THE BEST MAN:
Cuts in on the bride and her father-in-law
Dances with the maid of honor
Dances with both mothers and with each of the bridesmaids before the reception is over

Since you, mother of the bride, are going to be the second person on the floor, you are going to have a very hard time cueing in those who are to follow you. Don't try. Turn this job over to some responsible male of your family not in the immediate wedding party or make either the head usher or your son, even if he is an usher, stand on the sidelines and supervise the order. Quite a few orchestra leaders are adept at acting as emcee. If your leader has a routine, he can get things started and keep them moving smoothly. Whatever the arrangement, before you start things off, be certain all the participants are standing in the wings. This is another reason for having a runner at your side. Chances are he is going to have to chase down the father of the groom, the best man, and your own husband. These three can disappear awfully fast once the photographer turns them loose, especially the first two.

After the routine has been completed, general dancing should follow unless you have planned the first dance to be merely a token one just for the wedding party and the parents before a seated luncheon or dinner. If you are having just a token first dance, then the music must stop at a signal from the leader.

If there is to be general dancing immediately following the first dance, the best way to get it started quickly is to have several friends of the family not in the wedding party cut in on the bride and the mothers, etc. Otherwise, there is apt to be a time lag. This need not happen if one or two couples start by prearrangement. This is so much better for all concerned, particularly for the six-foot-two usher who has been going around and around with the junior bridesmaid. We have supervised only two receptions where people either sat on their hands or separated into several distinct groups staring at each other like leashed dogs meeting for the first time. It is going to take legwork and savvy on the part of both yourself and your husband to cure such situations.

Once you see the dance going as you wish, visit around like any other hostess. But remember that you are the egg timer, you have the watch, you are calling the signals, and you should still have a runner near you. But you must make allowance for traffic and, above all, the interruptions the bride will encounter when she tries to get from some remote corner to the cake table. She is going to stop and talk to all her friends along the way, and she is going to be stopped by others. We usually allow at least fifteen minutes after starting her on her way to the cake table or to where she is to throw her bouquet before we alert anyone else concerned.

So far we have been talking about an afternoon reception either under canvas or in a club or hotel. Now we would like to consider many variations on the usual moderate-sized afternoon reception for 150 guests and up.

First, let's take the package deal at the restaurant or hotel. Unless there is a seated and served dinner, the reception can follow the same general lines. The maître d', working with the band, will take over all the various bits of formality upon which you have previously decided. But do be sure of your maître d'. If he's a frustrated emcee or TV performer, you are in for trouble. All possible cues should be given as unobtrusively as possible; otherwise the reception will lose all spontaneity and be obviously overorganized. However, there has to be a time schedule. Have it as *invisible* as possible. In this connection you must keep in mind that there is a definite time when the rooms must be cleared. A good maître d' is a past master at this sort of timing. He knows how much time he will need to clear and prepare rooms for the new cast of characters who will shortly be panting at the door, awaiting their turn to go on. The more elaborate your reception, the closer the timing is, particularly if there is a seated and served meal. A good staff, however, will work so effortlessly that no guest should be aware he is, in fact, being tightly programmed so he will be on his way at a given minute.

A ceremony performed at the bride's house followed by a home reception, utilizing only the space provided by the house itself, is the simplest kind to have but requires, as we have already pointed out, the most careful planning. You also have to tailor your schedule to the space available, but you still might be able to have token dancing. Certainly there will be a place to cut the cake, as well as a place for the leave-taking ritual.

Basically, what you can do depends upon what you have to work with and how many guests are there. Thus, for a reception at home, whether or not the ceremony has been performed there, for seventy-five or less, we usually have only background music, even just a strolling accordionist, and several small reserved tables for the wedding party. We keep everything to a minimum—the more informal the better. A seated and served meal in a small area for just the immediate families and close friends will probably use up most of your available space. We always recommend, if it is at all possible, that in the event a meal is to be offered you adopt the buffet style to gain a bit of space. Also, any kind of abbreviated receiving line, and this means a receiving line of five, at the most, should be set up in a different room from the one in which the couple was married. This will give the caterer space to set up the necessary tables in the room where the ceremony was performed. As a matter of fact, the host and hostess can greet the guests as they arrive for the marriage service. Afterward, the bride and groom can either turn to face the guests or they can walk into another room where the receiving line may be formed.

A seated and served meal following a nuptial mass or an evening ceremony in a Protestant church has the same general pattern whether the meal is served at home or elsewhere. There seem to be few exceptions.

First, as the guests come in, someone must be on hand near the table on which table number cards have been arranged. (Many people use table number cards only and allow the guests to take whatever places at that table they wish; others use table number cards as well as place cards. This is entirely a matter of personal preference.) But in any large group there are going to be several couples who fail to pick up either table number cards or place cards, but who eventually find their places, usually with the help of the caterer or maître d', for there should be a master list showing the guests' names arranged alphabetically and followed by the appropriate table number.

After everyone has finally been seated, send the runner we mentioned earlier to gather up all the cards that remain unclaimed. A quick check of these will tell you who is absent. Their places may be filled by those few people who arrive unexpectedly or by any last-minute houseguests of your nearest and dearest friends who completely forgot to tell you about these people. Let the caterer or maître d' cope. Just give him the cards of those who have not arrived by the time you wish to have the meal served.

The order of the receiving line is the same, but the guests usually proceed into the space you have planned as the cocktail area. There they wait until the bride and groom appear, after the group photography, for their first dance. This dance should be an abbreviated one. Quite often it is confined to the members of the wedding party and the parents. In the case of a reception following a nuptial mass, the first dance may be a bit longer unless you have asked the priest, or another member of the clergy who is to say grace, to arrive at a certain time.

Whenever there is a seated and served meal, it is always difficult to get the guests to take their places. This can be accomplished with music, and there is one piece that just about everyone recognizes as the cue to be seated. The one piece most people will recognize, and the one with which all good musicians are familiar, is the March from *Norma*. If this is played emphatically and repeated several times, it seldom fails to get everyone headed for their respective seats. All the orchestra leaders know this is what they are to play when we say, "Let's have a little munching music."

During the course of the dinner the caterer or maître d' takes over the musical signals. As soon as he sees that the majority of the guests have finished the first course, which has been placed on the tables (usually during the cocktail hour), he signals the leader, whose band or part of it has been playing background dinner music, to swing into dance music. If the wedding party gets out on the floor, the rest will follow. This gives the staff a chance to prepare for the next course. Then, when this has been served, the bandleader signals the guests by ending his set and reverts to dinner music.

Cake cutting usually takes place when dessert is about to be served. Normally, if it is not already in place, the cake table is brought to the bridal table in front of the bride and groom. This, do not forget, is an ideal time for any toasts.

After this event the band should play for continuous dancing until such time as the bride leaves to dress. When the reception takes place in a hotel, the bride normally does not depart to music, but she does in a club or in your home.

For a seated and served evening reception after a Protestant ceremony we have modified proceedings so that the first course is already served prior to the bride and groom's first dance. Then the balance of the meal is buffet style. In this case, the caterer's staff informs all the guests that the buffet is ready. Also the band plays continuous music while the guests eat, rather than background music. This is a much more informal and relaxed way of doing things. It gives your guests more individual freedom to eat when they wish and allows you to hold the cake ceremony when you think it should take place.

The least formal way of feeding everyone is to have only the bridal table seated and served. Everyone else helps himself from the buffet tables; there is no first course. Here the caterers set up tables so that everyone has a place to sit, but there are no place cards or table number cards. But we suggest that certain tables be reserved, by using signs or white ribbons around all the chairs, for both families (including separate grandparents' tables if needed) and for those fifth wheels.

As far as tables reserved for juniors and the ankle-nipper set go, one of the caterer's staff should keep an eye on the former, while an appointed baby-sitter (aided by the caterer's staff) can see to the latter. However, it behooves you as the ultimate authority to glance in their direction occasionally and take action if necessary.

So much for the average reception. It can follow the pattern outlined above. But there are many weddings where everyone is invited to the ceremony but only a few invited to go on to some kind of postnuptial meal or gathering. This is usually confined to the immediate families and the bridal party. In many cases, especially among Roman Catholics, the bride and groom stand at the entrance of the church to be congratulated by the emerging congregation. Depending upon the size of the area there and just outside the church, they may have the maid of honor and often both sets of parents form a receiving line. Who is in the receiving line depends entirely upon the space and time available, and the weather. We have also on occasion helped with Protestant weddings when it was necessary to ask many to the ceremony, but when the house was far too small, without adequate grounds, and the clubs and hotels were already booked. One couple went right back to the house, another one received the congregation outside the church and then went on. In such situations, it is your choice; there is no universal rule as to what you should do provided you consider your guests. If you have friends who have come a great distance to attend the ceremony, you should, if at all possible, offer them some refreshment before they return home.

When you are holding the reception in church or parish assembly rooms where dancing is not allowed, you have only one real problem: when to cut the cake. You should allow everyone a decent interval, after the receiving line is completed, to sample whatever you may be serving, and then cut the cake. Consider this ceremony as the high point of the reception, especially if your church permits champagne. But only you can determine when this moment is at hand. It depends upon numbers, how substantial a repast you are offering, and the homogeneity of the assembly. It also depends on whether you are having background music. As we have already pointed out, any music present seems to act initially as an icebreaker and then later becomes an integral part of the reception. It makes an awful lot of difference. You can still use the musical signals we have been discussing. They are not dependent on dancing.

"Go eat your bread with gladness, and drink your wine with a joyous heart" (Eccles. 9:7). This sums up our idea of what a reception should be, no matter the faith or sect. There are many similarities between Jewish and Christian receptions, whether they are seated and served luncheons or dinners, are buffet style with places for all and a bridal table, or are afternoon "teas" or evening cocktail receptions at which there is a bridal table but the seating of guests is optional. But the meal following the ceremony at a Jewish reception is part of the fulfillment of the religious commandments of the ceremony. The meal itself is apt to be far more elaborate than most non-Jewish receptions, with less heed given to the potables other than champagne and wines.

A Jewish reception in which all are seated differs from Catholic and Protestant ones in two respects. Usually the tables for the closest relatives, in descending order on both sides, are set nearest the bridal table. The bridal attendants should also be placed as near as possible. Secondly, instead of the bridesmaids and the ushers, the parents and grandparents of the couple are seated, together with the rabbi and the cantor with their wives, at the bridal table. The bridal table setting may include the bride's Sabbath candlesticks and the groom's goblet. This seating is not liturgically determined in any way; it is merely a very popular custom.

The Jewish and Christian faiths have one delightful custom in common: the garden wedding and reception. Being married in the open air, especially under the stars, goes far back in history. Today, most weddings in Israel and almost all Hasidic weddings are out of doors. We have also used a variation on the theme of the usual reception, but we didn't know that by pure chance we had hit on a Canadian Jewish custom. It is quite a space saver, and economical as well.

Suppose that you have a large guest list and an area that will barely accommodate the crowd for a cocktail dance. In addition, you have a smaller group for whom you wish to provide dinner, either seated and served or buffet style. All those who are to have dinner are invited to the ceremony and to the dinner following. You would receive them in the usual manner as the hostess, but you have the maître d' direct them to find their places. The meal is to be served to continuous background music and without dancing between courses. If many guests are to arrive after dinner, the cake cutting is delayed. After dinner is over, all the tables are cleared away to provide more space. The full orchestra comes in, as do all the guests who were invited to attend the reception, but—due to space or other considerations—not to the wedding ceremony. At this point the normal routine of the receiving line, first dance, cake cutting and departure of the couple follows. This system requires only a bar and a light buffet supper for the later guests. And it has two advantages: you make the maximum use of a given area, and you don't have to feed everyone a consummate repast. However, you would have to send out two sets of invitations, one for the marriage ceremony and dinner, the other for the reception. The time of the reception should be three hours later than the ceremony, and you had better keep two separate boxes of lists, with a "rude" section in each!

On two occasions we have been called upon to arrange and supervise Jewish garden weddings and receptions. The physical arrangements of tables, chairs, and aisles are similar to those of the Protestant weddings we have done. In both these cases, the bride wanted to be married under a canopy, or *huppah,* which we had our flower arranger make, after due consultation with the rabbi.

The garden wedding and reception is equally popular with Protestants, especially the late afternoon or evening ones held in the South. This delightful custom has spread throughout the United States into all areas where the climate is sufficiently benign and predictable. In the greater New York area, we have often assisted at garden weddings, but we have always had to plan for absolute climatic disaster. It is much safer to plan on a small ceremony and a larger reception, whether you are using your house or a smaller tent for the ceremony. In either case, there is the normal recessional, and the bridal party moves to where the guests are to be received in the bigger tent. From here on, the schedule follows the normal course for any reception.

In one respect the arrangements for a Christian garden-type wedding and reception are less complicated than those for a Jewish one because the congregation stands throughout the ceremony. Therefore less space is needed. In both cases the area in which the ceremony takes place may later be used by the guests as an annex to the main tent. The table and chair setups then are placed along the side of the smaller tent, or even set up and stored under the main tent, and then moved back into the smaller tent, as the receiving line is completed.

Two questions are often asked of us concerning the reception. "When do we end it?" "How do we get them all to go home?" The latter is much easier to answer than the former. For example, let us take the situation in which the music is to end at 9:00 P.M., the bride and groom have finally pulled out of the front drive at 8:45, but you still have a considerable number of guests either milling around the front door or still in the marquee or club. If you are unwilling to have the party go on for another hour, you have your runner go back and tell the bars to close at 9:15 and you tell the band to pack up and go, even if there is still a little time running on your contract. Neither you nor your husband returns to the reception area. Stay put at the front door or out at the front gate.

There will be the inevitable two or three tables of guests either unwilling to call it a night or day, as the case may be, or too involved in conversation to notice that they are now alone. This is where a good caterer is worth his weight in platinum. His staff, after the bars have been closed, begin to clear tables, knock them down, and bag chairs, starting with the areas already vacated. They work up to and around the little islands of guests until it finally dawns on the latter that the party is over—no music, no booze, no food, no nobody. The staff never actually takes the chairs and tables out from under them, although we have heard that this has been done, but they may ask the guests to move to another table. However it is handled, the talkers finally wend their way out.

When to end the reception is a more difficult question. We have gone into the question of prolonging it into overtime when you have a real bash on your hands. But what about a fast-fading crowd of guests who leave much earlier than you had expected? Naturally, if there is no dance band, or just background music, you have absolutely no problem. Your daughter can leave as she had originally planned, regardless of how many there are to see her off. However, it is dismal for the newlyweds to depart with only a skeleton crew to send them off, although sometimes it happens.

We have always operated on the principle of ending any party, wedding receptions included, when it is at its peak, or near to it, rather than letting it drag out. But if you have an hour of regular music left and only a handful of guests to enjoy it, you would do better to pack up the music and treat the balance of the afternoon or evening as though there never had been any scheduled.

The situation requiring your very best guess is the one in which considerably more than a hard core of "never-go-homes" are still having a ball during that last hour. Madam, it's your gamble. Go on into overtime and have everyone begin to fade fast some twenty minutes into the overtime period, or end the party as scheduled, on a high note. We much prefer the latter. We always recommend this, if asked, during the course of a reception. But if you choose the former and the party suddenly thins out, or sags, don't feel that you have to use up the entire hour. If you see it fading, don't hesitate to wind it up immediately.

There is one final not so quaint and not a little barbarous rite that can easily ruin the entire day for the newlywed couple. We speak of, and with considerable feeling based on many, many experiences, the tricks ushers feel must be played on the bride and groom. We have had quite a number of brides who spent the entire reception worrying about, and even terrified of, the unknown plans of the ushers, and many of those worries and fears were more than justified.

If the ushers want to pi the groom's luggage, sew up his going-away clothes, or indulge in other such acts initiating him into benedicthood, that's fine, as is doing a complete decorating job on the getaway car, if they can find it. But painting the groom and, incidentally, the walls of the room in which he is dressing with gray deck paint, throwing him off a dock into shallow water with a rocky bottom at low tide, or massing to tip over the limousine just as the couple is getting into it is stark vandalism, not initiation. The two fathers should keep an eye on the groom if there is any real hint of brewing shenanigans. It is the host's responsibility, particularly, whether it is his own house, his club, or a hotel. We'll never forget an angry bride's mother who chased the entire clutch of wild Indians down the stairs of her home, brandishing a trimming axe. She had those ushers so frightened they never noticed in their haste that the axe was still in its leather case. At least she solved the last problem of her daughter's wedding day.

On quite a few occasions we have found the groom's parents wandering around the lower levels while everyone else—bridesmaids, ushers, photographer, bride's mother, and the family dog—was upstairs getting Suzy and her groom started on their way. Several wanderers have told us that they didn't think they were supposed to go up because this was the bride's last few moments in her house. We don't buy this at all. The groom's parents should go up if they want to and say good-bye. It is up to you to tell them this, and also where the groom is changing.

Just before the couple is ready to leave, send a bridesmaid down to see if the getaway car or other means of transportation is ready and waiting as planned. Then you come down, followed in a few minutes by the newlyweds. As soon as you are down near the door, send that runner you have to check on the bowls of rose petals that the caterer's staff should now have on hand near the exit. This is one thing you probably don't have to worry about. You should see handfuls of petals everywhere, but if you don't see any, then send word upstairs, or to wherever the bride and groom are waiting, to hold up for a few minutes. After you have taken care of this detail, send that bridesmaid up to start them on their way.

This, naturally, brings us to a discussion of how a bride and groom can leave, either with the least amount of trouble or in the most exotic way. We have used speedboats, a helicopter, antique cars, and, in New York, a hansom cab. All these were used to carry the couple to a more conventional form of transportation. We don't advise the chopper, however. The amount of red tape the bride's parents went through to get a permit to land the vehicle on their very extensive lawn was considerable. However, you may well be in an area where helicopter travel from one point to another is sufficiently normal so that there is little red tape to unsnarl. Probably one of the most unusual getaways was one pulled off a number of years ago in the northern snow country. The couple departed by dogsled drawn by a team of huskies. That was one vehicle no usher tried to follow.

In our opinion the best method for all concerned is to use a hired limousine, particularly if the couple is going into the city or, much more rarely, directly to the airport. This car can arrive at a given time, pull up to the front door on signal, and move out at once. Not only does no one have to worry about driving after drinking, but the driver and his car are so impersonal and professional that the ushers tend to respect his property. We have often used a limousine just to drive the newlyweds a few blocks to where their own car had been hidden. Switching cars is a favorite device. Very often some member of the family, or some responsible member of the wedding party, will start off with the couple in his car and then take them to their own.

Protecting a couple's departure is an excellent reason for having a uniformed policeman standing by at the exit of your house or club. So if you have any reason to suspect that matters will develop into a cross-country car chase, take it up with your police department. Not only will an officer prevent this from happening, but he can also see to it that those who shouldn't be driving a car don't.

Trying to wind things up and speed the lingering guests on their way may sound most inhospitable, but what we mean to suggest is that you tell your close friends to come on back to the house, or go inside, as the case may be, for a nightcap. During the reception planning stage, a great many clients have said, "They are all our nearest and dearest friends—all three hundred of them—and we certainly don't want any of them to hurry away," but those last four hours on top of the last four weeks can well prove to be the straw on the proverbial camel, as almost all these same clients have admitted to us afterward.

However, when you are having a postnuptial buffet in your home after a garden reception for those guests who have come from a distance, and scads of other guests not invited to this meal are still around, it's going to take tact on your part—and skill on the caterer's—to move them out gently without hurt feelings. Allow at least an hour from the end of the reception before you have the caterer place the food on the buffet. And—even then—we would be willing to bet that the loiterers turn out to be your nearest neighbors.

But finally everyone has taken his leave, and you and your husband are alone, comfortable, feet up, with something warm and soothing in your glasses, surrounded for the first time by wonderful, blissful silence.

Then you, O long-suffering and harried father of the bride, turn to your own bride and say, "Do you suppose we could slip away together for a few days?"

Epilogue

As we come to the end of this book, we would like to offer a semantic apology. All along we have been using the auxiliary verb *should*. What we really mean is not that you "ought" to do thus and so in the sense of obligation but that "it is going to be easier for you if . . ." It is suggestive, not authoritative.

In conclusion, we would like to point out that we have read numerous etiquette books, magazines, and other publications devoted to brides. In many we have found areas of agreement, but we have also found areas of total disagreement. We have tried to present in these pages some solutions to the problems of arranging weddings and receptions, solutions first evolved from our own experience and then modified to fit the needs of each of our clients. This is definitely a "doing it" and not a "telling it" book.

Appendix A
Heraldry

HERALDRY IS THE SCIENCE OF RECORDING GENEALOGIES and the precise classification and description, or "blazon," of hereditary emblems, which are called heraldic devices, coats of arms, or armorial bearings, and the rules that govern their use.

It is a very ancient and complex science on which lifetimes of research have been spent. We can touch on it only very briefly here, but it is interesting to note that in all ages and in all parts of the world emblems or symbols have been employed by tribes, nations, families, and individuals to establish identity. Homer uses the word *herald* to describe a trusted attendant or officer of a chieftain or king whose duty it was to perform certain confidential work of the highest trust and import, as well as to proclaim important announcements such as declarations of war or peace. These ancient officers took as their patron Hermes, the herald of the gods.

Heraldry, as we are concerned with it here, can be traced to the twelfth century, when it was revived in nearly every European country, including England, Wales, Scotland, and Ireland. This was due in large measure to advances in the development of plate armor, which so completely concealed a warrior that when he lowered the visor of his helmet to charge in battle, he could not be recognized by friend or foe. Leaders in the field, whether of a royal army or of a baron's men, quickly saw the military advantage of having shields and banners bearing devices that could be recognized clearly in the press of battle. Every warrior wanted his own armorial bearing, and these highly individual devices became their marks, or ID tags, as it were. The heralds' duty, among others, was to memorize and interpret these devices.

Warriors frequently had their helmets made in some special shape, and the crests of their devices—often the representation of a bird or beast—were forged to them. For more complete identification, their armorial bearings were sewn on the short sleeveless jackets they wore over their armor in the colors they had chosen for their own (not unlike the colors of a racing stable or the house flag of a boat), and thus they came to be called armor coats, or "coats of arms."

With the amazingly rapid adoption of coats of arms, the heralds became increasingly important. They were men of the highest character who had been especially recruited from among the leading families of the kingdom, and their very persons were inviolable. No one would attack a herald. It was they who issued and announced challenges, marshaled the combatants and identified those who fell in battle. Under their care were placed the arms of the kings, nobles, and knights, as well as the records of their genealogies.

In time, a corporation was instituted in England known as the Heralds College, or the College of Arms. It was dependent upon the crown and was led by three officers called kings of arms under the direction of the Earl Marshall of England, the heralds of Chester, Lancaster, Richmond, Somerset, Windsor, and York, together with four of their pursuivants, who were officers ranking below a herald. This college was, and is today, the official place of record for genealogies and the armorial bearings of persons with the right to bear them. The "right" was given in perpetuity to all direct male descendants of the original armiger who first bore them.

Later, in 1484, the Heralds College, or College of Arms, was chartered by Richard III of England. By the sixteenth century so many families who were not descended from armigers had "assumed" arms that it became necessary for the Heralds College to clarify matters. This was accomplished by means of official calls, or "visitations," on the old families in each of the shires and counties, who were *invited* to record their genealogies and arms—if this had not already been done. The research made during those early "visitations" formed the basis of the official records that are on file today in the College of Arms in London.

Coats of arms were in common use in America during the colonial period throughout the original thirteen colonies. The immigrants brought with them certain precious heirlooms, such as gold signet rings bearing the family heraldic device and silver and pieces of embroidery on which their arms appeared. Most of these first arrivals were the direct male descendants of the armigers of the twelfth century and, second sons or not, brought with them into the new world a taste for the distinctions of their homeland and their heritage.

During the period of the American Revolution, the use of heraldic devices fell out of favor for a time, only to be revived again with vigor in the nineteenth century, when many new and flagrant abuses were committed in their use. Much of this can be put down to ignorance of the science of heraldry at that time, but, in any case, something considerably more than pride of ancestry was abroad in the land as people right and left began to "assume" coats of arms. They apparently thought that because their names were Brown, Jones, Gildersleeve, Mason, Miller, Smith, Wheelwright, Lee, Rose, Dummer, Lemon, or whatever, they had the right to use the heraldic devices of families with the same name as their own. Nothing could have been more erroneous then—or now. A

Mrs. Brown who received an invitation from a Mrs. Smith bearing her husband's coat of arms would rush out with the speed of light to consult the pages of Burke's *General Heraldry*, where she would find one for Brown. Delighted, she would then locate an artist to make a sketch of it for her to take to the engraver where a dye could be made. And then she was in business. More than likely, Mrs. Smith or her husband had done the very same thing earlier.

Finally, the situation reached such proportions that in 1885 the New England Historic Genealogical Society appointed a Committee on Heraldry to take what appropriate steps it could to prevent people from "assuming" coats of arms to which they were not entitled. The society published all existing specimens of heraldic devices used in America prior to the Revolution. Following this, many armigerous families copyrighted their coats of arms. This served to produce the same results as had been accomplished by those official "visitations" of the College of Arms in the sixteenth century.

Just now we are in the midst of another revival of the use of armorial bearings, as people all over the country are busy tracking down their ancestors. The need for symbols of identity seems to be stronger than ever, so if you think that you have a claim to use a coat of arms, you may write to the New England Historic Genealogical Society at 101 Newbury Street, Boston, Massachusetts, and request its Committee on Heraldry to examine it. If your claim is found to be authentic, you will be issued a certificate to that effect. There is a small fee for this service. Please bear in mind that this service is one of *authentication* only, and that the society cannot be expected to establish your pedigree. This you must have done for you by a reliable, professional genealogist who, starting with the full name of your first ancestor to emigrate to this country and correct information regarding your descent from him, can prove out your line. This is done by finding the records of births, marriages, and deaths in each generation from your own to your ancestor's. In this way *his* connection to an armigerous British or continental family may be established and verified.

We have no legal governmental authority in this country that can issue a coat of arms or rule upon one's "right" to use one, but many other countries do have governmental heraldic authorities. If you are of English, Welsh, or Scottish descent, you may write to the College of Arms in London and request that it examine your pedigree and your claim to the right to use a coat of arms. Whether it finds your claim valid or invalid, there is a fee for the service. If your claim to a specific coat of arms cannot be established, you may request the grant of a new one. The cost of doing this can run into considerable expense, so do ask the College to give you an approximate estimate of the cost before you proceed.

If you know that your first ancestor to emigrate was a Scot, you may write to the Lord Lyon King of Arms, Edinburgh. And if you are of Irish descent, apply to the Genealogical Office, Dublin Castle, Dublin. Any of these authorities will verify your claim to armorial bearings for a fee or make a new grant of a coat of arms for a more considerable fee.

A coat of arms consists, usually, of the five elements as follows:

1. The Shield
2. The Crest (although not all heraldic devices have crests)
3. The Supporters
4. The Helmet and its Mantling or Lambrequin
5. The Motto

The shield proper is where the armorial bearings are displayed. It may be of any form with one exception: the lozenge, or diamond shape. This shape is reserved for women only, except for sovereign princesses such as Princess Margaret of England who is of the blood royal and is entitled to use the full coat of arms. An heiress or coheiress with sisters of an armigerous family has the right to her father's coat of arms in a diamond-shaped lozenge—provided she has no living brothers. If she marries a man who is also armigerous, she may "impale" her arms with those of her husband. This would be done by dividing the shield vertically, with his arms blazoned on the sinister, or left, side as you look at the shield and hers on the dexter, or right, side. Her children then "quarter" the arms of the parents. However, if an heiress marries a nonarmigerous husband, she and her children lose their armigerous standing, technically speaking, although the heiress may continue to use the lozenge on her personal stationery and silver if she wishes.

If a woman is not an heiress herself, she is not entitled to use her family's coat of arms after her marriage. And if a bride-to-be is the daughter of a man with the right to a heraldic device and is going to marry a man without one, she would be wise to forget about heraldry after her wedding invitations and the announcements are engraved. She may have a color reproduction made of her family coat of arms and hang it in her new home, or, better yet, use these arms as her personal *ex libris* or bookplate, or enjoy a gift of silver from her family marked with her father's crest and motto without the shield and helmet.

A coat of arms may be used either in its complete form or with the crest only, embossed without color, when the names of a girl's parents appear jointly on the wedding invitations or announcements.

If a bride's mother is a widow, she should not use her late husband's or her father's coat of arms, for "gentlemen's heraldic bearings" are never used by women. A widow may use her inherited crest or lozenge embossed without color.

If more detailed information is desired, see *The Elements*

of Heraldry by William H. Whitmore, first published in 1886. This book, prepared expressly for the American public, was published by Lee and Shepard of Boston, Massachusetts. It has been reissued by Charles E. Tuttle Company, Publishers, Rutland, Vermont.

If Mr. F. Clef Bass marries Miss G. Clef Treble and she is an armigerous heiress

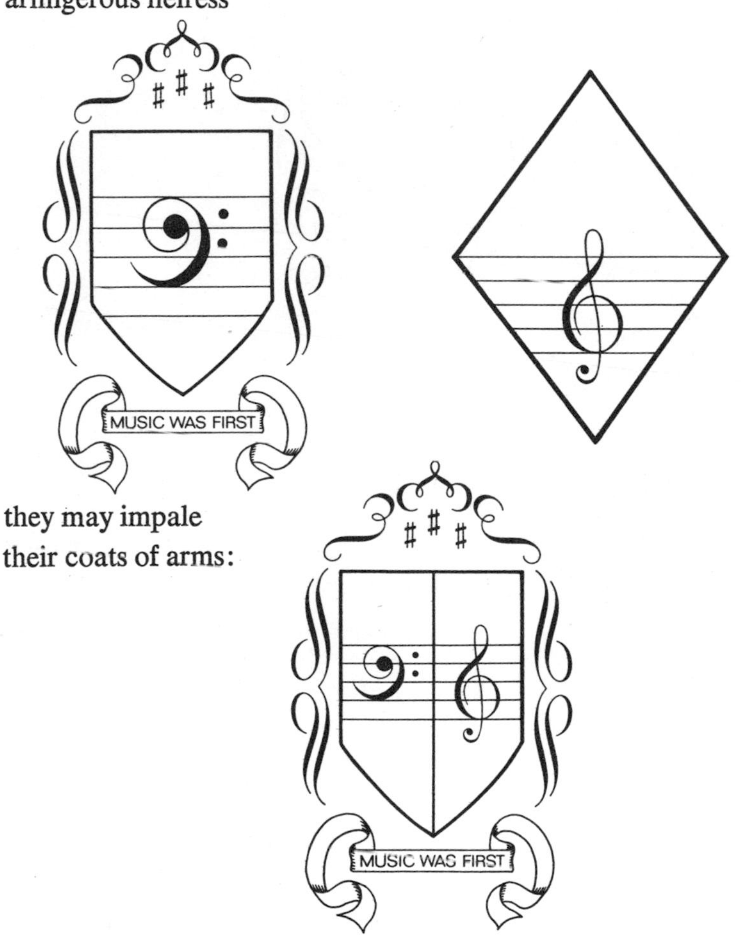

they may impale their coats of arms:

If they have a son and heir he would quarter the Bass and Treble arms, and he and his descendants would use them thus:

Appendix B

Sample Budget

DRAWING UP ANY WEDDING BUDGET, LET ALONE ONE that must be general enough to include not only the many religious sects but also the divergences found in all localities of the country, is not an easy job. We are offering only a suggested sample, one that may help you to keep track of where you are headed financially.

Bride's Expenses

Gifts to bridesmaids, maid/matron of honor
Bridal gown (family may pay)
Bridesmaids' luncheon
Groom's ring if double ring ceremony
Physical examination
Bridesmaids' dresses[1]

Groom's Expenses

Gifts to ushers and best man
Ring
License
Physical examination
Minister's fee

Minister's room and board
Bachelor dinner
Flowers for bride's bouquet
Flowers for both mothers[2]
Boutonnieres for ushers, best man, and both fathers

Bride's Family—Initial Expenses

Invitations, announcements, etc.
Formal portrait
Trousseau
Floater policy for gifts
Gift tables
Rehearsal dinner[3]
Board and lodging for ushers and best man

Bride's Family—Ceremony Expenses[4]

Fee to sexton or janitor
Fees to organist, choir, soloist, trumpeter
Contributions to church not your own
Canopy at church
Carpet and white runner
Decorations, candles, aisle ribbons, pew markers
Transportation to and from church
Traffic control, police, and parking
Bride's bouquet[2]
Bouquets for bridesmaids, matron/maid of honor[2]
Flowers for both mothers, grandmothers[2]

Bride's Family—The Reception Expenses[5]

In a club, hotel, or restaurant

Rental of rooms
Food per head
Champagne
Hard liquor

Rental of extra tables
Rental of extra chairs
Rental of special linen
Coat checking charges
Orchestra—contract price
Orchestra—overtime
Decoration of rooms
Decorations for tables
Tips and other gratuities
Cigarettes, if not included
Rose petals and monogrammed matches

At home, in church parlor, or in community house

Rental, if any
Catering totals
Canvas totals
Champagne
Hard liquor
Soft drinks and mixes not supplied by caterer
Ice, if not supplied
Ice tubs, if not supplied
Wiring and electrical charges, if at home
Orchestra—contract price
Orchestra—overtime
Flowers and decorations
Rental of special linen
Cake, if separate
Rose petals and monogrammed matches
Cigarettes, if separate
Traffic, police, and parking attendants
Parking system
House security/private guards
Extra grounds care
Extra house care

Guest insurance
Getaway limousine or transportation[6]

Both Families' Expenses

Board and lodging for relatives (optional)
Candid photography

[1] In many sections of the country it is customary for each bridesmaid and the maid/matron of honor to pay for their own. A matter for individual choice.

[2] Sometimes it is customary for the groom to bear these expenses, but again it is a decision determined by circumstances.

[3] The rehearsal dinner and other prenuptial festivities may be given by friends or relatives of the bride.

[4] The groom's family almost never has any expenses in connection with the ceremony.

[5] There is a possibility, particularly when the bride's family cannot afford the large reception that the groom's family wants, that the cost of the reception may be shared on several different bases.

[6] While the groom is responsible for the means of leaving the reception, the bride's father often makes a present to the newlyweds of the getaway transportation.

Appendix C

Chronological Checklist

IN CHAPTER 2, WE MADE REFERENCE TO A CHRONOLOGical checklist we have developed over the years for the convenience of our clients so that they may see at a glance what they should be doing and when. Here it is.

For those of you who are doing everything piecemeal and without the assistance of a caterer, club manager, or maître d', this list should be a very helpful guide if you adapt it to suit your own needs, time schedule, and situation. Your personal circumstances may cause you to alternate a sequence here and there. Keep it flexible, but, above all, do make provision in it for making three separate checks—a week apart during the last month—on all the essential elements of the ceremony and the reception, and on each and every firm you have engaged to carry out your plans for both. Please remember that it takes a minimum of five months—give yourself six—to arrange the details of a formal wedding and reception properly, that is, without having a bride and her family reach the date in a state of nervous, emotional, and physical exhaustion. Give yourselves time!

Decide upon and confirm with your priest, minister, or rabbi your choice of the date and the hour of the ceremony.

Decide upon the place where the reception is to be given and reserve it. You should have confirmation of the date and time in writing from your club, hotel, restaurant, or other place if you have decided not to have a home reception. With the exception of a private club, a deposit is usually requested.

The bride and her fiancé should make an appointment to see the clergyman.

Begin making up your guest list on three-by-five file cards. Have the groom and his family do the same so that you can set up the card file system. Remember, this is your control department for the wedding and reception. Only after this is in working order, and the total number of guests counted, can you order your invitations and announcements.

Decide upon the form, type of engraving, and number of wedding invitations and announcements, if any, and other wedding stationery needs, and order them. Remember to overorder by fifty both the invitations and announcements. Have the envelopes for the invitations sent to you immediately after placing your order so that the addressing may be done ahead of time. If you are using announcements, have them sent to you, together with their envelopes, at a later date, *after* the invitation envelopes have been addressed and stamped. Keep invitations and announcements completely separate so there will be no confusion.

Start shopping for the wedding dress, veil and accessories. Do the same for bridesmaids' dresses and accessories. Remember to take into consideration whether the colors of the latter are compatible with those of the place of the ceremony and the reception. Get color swatches as early as possible.

Engage a photographer for the engagement photographs. Take a tentative reservation on the photographer's time for formal wedding portraits and the candid coverage. Do not confirm or give a deposit until you have seen proofs of the engagement photograph. You may not be satisfied with the results.

Announce the engagement, unless you wish to hold this up until the last six weeks to a month before the wedding. If you live in a city, the longer you delay the announcement in the newspapers, the longer you will have the use of your telephone undisturbed by calls from solicitors of all kinds.

Engage the orchestra for the reception. It will confirm date and hours.

Engage your florist or flower arranger. Have confirmation sent to you.

If you are going to use one, and the wedding date is a prime one, *engage a limousine service.* Have them reserve two limousines and say you will let them know later if you need more.

The bride and groom should begin to plan for their new home.

Begin shopping for trousseau. Have your daughter choose silver, china, glassware, crystal, etc. Register the pattern with the bride's gift registry in the leading stores in your community.

If you are having a home reception and are using the services of a caterer and a canvas firm, you should have an initial meeting with both. If the reception is to be held in a place where the services of a caterer are needed, have a meeting on the spot with the caterer. Discuss menus and color scheme, linens, etc.

Remember to order wedding cake. If it is to be light or dark fruit cake, you must allow time for it to be made well in advance. Ask your caterer, club manager, or maître d' if he will supply it. Also inquire about matches with initials or names of bride and groom, the same for cocktail or other napkins, those little boxes with fruit cake, rose petals for end of reception.

Complete all arrangements at church, synagogue, or temple. Find out about cost of full choir, boys' choir, organist's fee, soloist, cantor, sexton, janitor. Who provides containers for flowers, additional candelabra, long-burning candles, white runner, carpet, aisle ribbons, canopy in case of rain? Who arranges for policeman for traffic control before, during, and after ceremony? Will the organist be at the rehearsal, and is this included in the fee? Will there be a *huppah*? Orthodox and Conservative Jewish ceremonies are always conducted under a *huppah* (canopy), while in Reform Judaism a canopy is not required. Its use depends upon the wishes of the bridal couple and on the consent of the rabbi, so be sure to check out this detail. Your florist should meet with you on the site of the ceremony.

Have a meeting with your florist at the site of the reception. If at home and you are using a marquee, select color of it and discuss with florist: size of marquee, number of center poles and sidewall poles, exits and entrances. The canvas firm will supply you with this information, or the florist can get it directly from them. The estimate you receive will have to reflect all these details, so be sure they are covered during your meeting with the florist.

Address envelopes for wedding invitations and stamp them.

The septic tank on your property should be cleaned before the wedding if you are using your grounds for a marquee.

If you need a piano tuner, make an appointment with him now.

Remind the groom to have forms giving necessary information about sizes sent to all male members of the wedding party.

The bride's mother should choose her dress and accessories and supply the groom's mother with a description of it, length of hem, color swatch if at all possible, type of headpiece, etc., so the latter may select her dress.

THE LAST MONTH:

Mail wedding invitations to arrive on a Friday or Saturday, give or take a day, ONE FULL MONTH IN ADVANCE.

Make reservations for out-of-town relatives, groom's family, ushers, and the bridesmaids if necessary. Get written confirmation of all reservations. If the wedding is on a prime date, you may be wise to make such reservations earlier.

Plan for a "goof-off" day the week of the wedding and tell your friends so that none of them will schedule parties on that day. The Thursday before a Saturday wedding is a good choice.

Check with bridal consultant on arrival date of bridal gown and veil, and set time for final fitting. Coordinate this date with your photographer and give him description of the bridal bouquet so he can provide a "pretend" one for the formal sitting.

Plan all details for rehearsal dinner if the groom's family is not giving it.

Arrange locations for the bridesmaids and ushers to dress. Try to avoid having them dress in your home or apartment.

Remind the groom to check out the clothes rental firm to be sure all his ushers have sent in their size slips and that arrangements have been completed for delivery or pickup of the suits and accessories and for the return of them after the wedding.

Gift tables should be set up and ready at least two weeks before the wedding.

Check with insurance agent to be sure the floater policy will be in effect by the time gifts begin to arrive.

The bride should have her gift book, stickers, and all stationery ready to start writing her thank-you notes.

Check out details of all showers, prenuptial parties, and the rehearsal dinner. If the wedding is large—three hundred plus—we suggest that you make out a master list showing where members of the wedding party, the groom's family, and out-of-town guests will be staying before the wedding. Note addresses, telephone numbers, dates and hours of brunches, luncheons, dinners, or parties along with information as to dress. Copies of this master list should be mailed to all concerned. If you live in a suburb or in the country, enclose directions for arrival by car, plane, or train and include information about nearest railroad, telephone numbers of station and local taxi service, airport, etc.

Take a check on number of regrets and acceptances to date.

Send press releases and glossies to newspapers three weeks in advance if the wedding is on a prime date.

Make appointment with your caterer, club manager, or maître d' and the florist to determine position of receiving line (if under canvas at home, you will have to wait until the marquee is up), seated bridal or reserved table, family table or tables, "fifth wheel" table, reserved table for small children, etc.

The bride should buy the groom's wedding ring if she is giving him one. Allow ten days to two weeks for it to be engraved.

If you are using table number cards, place cards, or both, buy enough cards for both purposes and start making up pie plates, or

Make out seating diagrams for bridal table with place cards, same for family table or tables and others so they will be ready to give your caterer, club manager, or maître d'.

Send out maps to out-of-town guests, orchestra leader, caterer's men, the candid photographer. Copies of master list of prenuptial events may be mailed with maps.

Make out pew lists, have copies made for ushers. Also copies of the reminders for the "first dance."

Mail pew cards two weeks before wedding date.

The bride should keep up to date on gift acknowledgment notes.

Make appointment for bride's physical examination. Remind the groom to make his own appointment.

Engage baby-sitters if needed.

Take a check on all firms and services involved. If you live in a suburb or in the country, call your local police station and tell them date, number of guests expected. Engage policeman for intersection and/or road in front of your property for traffic control. Engage policeman to be on duty in your home the night of rehearsal dinner if planned away from home.

If you are using a marquee and have an arrangement with a lawn mowing service, call them and remind them not to cut your lawn later than one full week before the wedding and to give it a crew cut after the wedding.

If your wedding is in the winter in snow country, be sure to have snow removal service you can depend on standing by for emergency ploughing. Check to see if your church, synagogue, or temple has similar arrangements.

Check with your septic tank service to be sure they will do cleaning job the week before the wedding.

Choose gifts for the bridesmaids.

Decide on where to have the luncheon for the bridesmaids, set date, and send invitations.

Complete all shopping for trousseau.

Keep up with those thank-you notes!

Address, stamp, stuff, and seal envelopes for wedding announcements. They should be put in a designated place ready for mailing AFTER the wedding.

Count regrets, acceptances, and peek into the rude box.

Have bride wear her wedding slippers around the house for several hours.

Make hair appointments for before the wedding early.

Get a blue garter if the bride is going to wear one.

If the bride is going to live in the same town, have her stop painting that apartment or house so her hands get back to normal for the wedding.

Make arrangements to transport the bride's personal effects, or to have them transported, to the new home. If she is going to live in the same town or nearby, begin to take the shower gifts to the new home.

If you can spare the time from other things, begin to separate duplicate wedding gifts and return them promptly for credit. You need exhibit only one, and the donors need never know the one they see is not the one *they* sent.

THE LAST WEEK:

The bride should begin packing for her wedding trip if there is to be one.

Take a final check with *all* the firms and services.

Remind the piano tuner if you are using one.

Call your orchestra leader and tell him what the bride wants him to play for her "first dance" and give him a list of her favorite pieces. Remind him of date, hours, and location.

Call the manager of your Western Union office.

Appoint that special runner, or pair of legs, and brief him.

Call the photographer and check out details with him.

The bride's mother should have her personal dress rehearsal complete with all accessories. Keep everything together.

If you are having a home reception, *call your garbage man* and remind him that you are counting on that special pickup on Sunday morning.

The bride should keep up as long as she can with her thank-you notes. *If she has ordered gift acknowledgment cards, start using them* on Wednesday before THE DAY.

Assemble the contents of the panic bag and have it ready for those two pals of yours who have agreed to be on hand an hour before the ceremony.

If the reception is at home, *remember to stock those bath-*

rooms the guests will use. Have everything ready to put in place on the wedding day.

The bride should give, or attend, her bridesmaids' luncheon and give them their presents then.

Check the limousine service. If the bride's parents are giving them a trip to the airport—a wonderful and very practical send-off—the bride could arrange for the chauffeur to pick up all her luggage and lock it in the trunk BEFORE he arrives at the club or other place where the reception is being given away from home. This means her luggage and the groom's also. At a club all the bride needs is one piece of hand luggage, which the best man can carry out before the couple make their getaway.

The bride should go with the groom and get the wedding license. It should then be taken directly to the church, synagogue, or temple and placed in the hands of a responsible person in the office. Failing this, get it to the priest, minister, or rabbi. Then there will be no worry about who has it just before the departure for the rehearsal.

If you are using a marquee, *go over the entire canvas setup* with your tent man, caterer, and florist AFTER the marquee has been erected. Before this meeting, try to have a final count for all concerned, especially the caterer. *Check out the rude box and take an educated guesstimate!*

Have a final on-the-site wrap-up with the club manager or maître d' and your florist. Give the club manager the final count. Alert him if you expect more.

Enjoy that "goof-off" day.

If you are having a reception away from home, *have the bride take all her going-away clothes to* the place where she will change on the night before the ceremony and have them locked up. *The groom should do the same.* The bride should take along a garment bag or box for her wedding gown so that her honor attendant and her mother will not have difficulty in packing her wedding clothes after the reception is over. If she receives a cake knife, this should be given to the club manager or maître d' along with any seating diagrams and place cards and/or pie plates and table number cards. All should be clearly marked and explained so that there can be no confusion. If you have followed the directions we have given you, there won't be any.

Be sure the groom has assigned his head usher, or two ushers, to escort the bride's mother and his own mother in and out. If the bride has two brothers in the wedding party, her mother may want one to escort her in and the other to escort her out. The groom should know her preferences on this and guide himself accordingly.

Take the pew lists to the rehearsal.

Remember to take the envelopes with the organist's, soloist's, or cantor's fees, and money for the sexton or janitor, and give them the money at the rehearsal. The bride's father usually does this. Remind him.

Take the reminder cards for the first dance at the reception and give them to the groom to distribute to his father, his best man, and ushers at the rehearsal dinner.

If you are having a ring bearer, take his white satin or lace-covered cushion with the "pretend" ring or rings attached to the rehearsal. This cushion may be left in the clergyman's study overnight. It's a good idea to have the "pretend" ring one that fits the bride's finger—just in case the real wedding ring has been forgotten. This *has* happened.

Take two ribbon bouquets for the bride and honor attendant to practice with during the rehearsal.

The bride and groom should be on time for the rehearsal whether their wedding party is or not.

Index